"Skip Heitzig's new book *Bloodline* follows the scarlet thread that runs through the lives of all believers in Jesus Christ. A friend, mentor, and Bible teacher of mine, the late Roy Gustafson, said of Skip that he was one of the most serious Bible students of my generation. I believe this is evident in the pages of this book. From Genesis to Revelation, Skip's insights about the precious blood shed for mankind will prick your mind and touch your heart."

Franklin Graham
President of Samaritan's Purse
Billy Graham Evangelistic Association

"This is Skip at his best, helping us understand the unity of the Bible and its central message. Many people find the Bible a confusing book. Here, its story line is clear and straight. And yes, it is the story of blood and redemption, of despair and hope, of hell and heaven. Thank you, Skip, for helping us grasp our Father's heart, as revealed in His Word."

Dr. Erwin W. Lutzer
Pastor Emeritus
The Moody Church, Chicago

"It is rare to find a book that both teaches good biblical theology and deeply touches the heart at the same time. This is one of those rare books. Skip Heitzig traces Christ's redemptive sacrifice chronologically from Genesis to Revelation, and he does so in a Christ-exalting, deeply devotional way. Highly recommended!"

Dr. Ron Rhodes
Author of *A Chronological Tour Through the Bible*
President, Reasoning from the Scriptures Ministries

D1120324

"Skip Heitzig is one of the premiere communicators of our generation, and *Bloodline* shows why. Here, he traces the thread of redemption woven through the narrative arc of the Bible, from Genesis to Revelation. At the same time, he plumbs the depths of Scripture and makes it accessible to everyone. This book is both easy to understand yet awash in fresh insights. An epic work!"

Ben Courson
Author of *Optimisfits*

"*Bloodline* will take you on an amazing journey through the pages of Scripture from Genesis to Revelation as you, along with Skip Heitzig, follow the scarlet thread of redemption. Pastor Skip masterfully brings the theme of salvation alive from each book of the Bible, and the message of God's redeeming love is beautifully revealed along the way. If you are looking for a next book to read, we suggest *Bloodline*, which will provide you with a devotional companion for every season of your life!"

Jim and Elizabeth George
Authors, *A Man After God's Own Heart* and
A Woman After God's Own Heart

BLOODLINE

Skip Heitzig

HARVEST HOUSE PUBLISHERS
EUGENE, OREGON

Cover by Kyler Dougherty

Cover photo © tigerstrawberry / Getty Images

Backcover author photo by Matt and Tish Photography

Published in association with William K. Jensen Literary Agency, 119 Bampton Court, Eugene, Oregon 97404.

Bloodline

Copyright © 2018 Skip Heitzig
Published by Harvest House Publishers
Eugene, Oregon 97408
www.harvesthousepublishers.com

ISBN 978-0-7369-7193-5 (pbk.)
ISBN 978-0-7369-7196-6 (eBook)

Library of Congress Cataloging-in-Publication Data
Names: Heitzig, Skip, author.
Title: Bloodline / Skip Heitzig.
Description: Eugene : Harvest House Publishers, 2018.
Identifiers: LCCN 2018028310 (print) | LCCN 2018034434 (ebook) | ISBN
    9780736971966 (ebook) | ISBN 9780736971935 (pbk.)
Subjects: LCSH: Bible--Devotional literature. | Bible--Introductions.
Classification: LCC BS491.5 (ebook) | LCC BS491.5 .H44 2018 (print) | DDC
    220.6--dc23
LC record available at https://lccn.loc.gov/2018028310

Printed in the United States of America

18 19 20 21 22 23 24 25 26 / VP-SK / 10 9 8 7 6 5 4 3 2 1

ACKNOWLEDGMENTS

I first want to acknowledge my parents for bringing me into this world. Though they have departed this world for the next, they passed on to me their own bloodline. My family was filled with lots of laughter and they set the tone. Even so, growing up with three older brothers reinforced the sinful nature of the human bloodline and the need for Christ.

My good friends and colleagues on our in-house publishing team have aided me greatly on this manuscript. Brian Nixon, Quentin Guy, and Lorin Bentley, you guys helped me with everything—capturing my voice and helping me to "say it better." So many of the witty section titles and subheads in this book have been their resourceful doing. Quent, you are a literary superstar! And Laney, thank you for gently cracking the whip to keep me writing.

A very special thanks goes to my wife Lenya. Her love for the God of our salvation and her compassion for people ever inspires me.

Thanks to my son, Nate, who helps me see the world through younger, fresher eyes and whose creative ideas for preaching and writing push me to new limits. This young Padawan has become a Jedi Knight!

I am again so thankful for the Christ-centered, Bible-believing, kingdom-minded staff at Harvest House. Thank you for not bending with the trends but being willing to turn up the volume of truth through publishing.

The greatest acknowledgment and thanksgiving must be to the Lord Jesus Christ. Without His willingness to shed His own perfect, precious blood, the world would be forever doomed and damned, without hope and always hopeless. I am humbly grateful that His blood covenant that affords total forgiveness included me.

CONTENTS

REDEMPTION'S SCARLET THREAD

istory hinges on a single pivotal event: the sacrificial death of Jesus Christ on the cross. There, God's great redemption of mankind was accomplished—a rescue mission that culminated at the end of Christ's three-and-a-half-year public ministry but began before the world was formed. This incredible tapestry is woven throughout the Scriptures in red. The great Bible teacher of yesteryear, William Evans, noted, "Cut the Bible anywhere and it bleeds." The blood of Jesus stains every page, every book, in both testaments. Evans observed that "the atonement is the scarlet cord running through every page in the entire Bible"; it "is red with redemption truth."[1]

Jesus Himself intimated this connectedness—this bloodline of redemption. After His atoning death and resurrection, He approached two unnamed disciples who were consumed with discouragement as they were walking to a town near Jerusalem. Disillusioned over Jesus's execution, they didn't recognize Him by face, nor did they expect what they were about to hear. They tried to explain to this "stranger" what had happened, even though they were unaware of what had *really* happened (Jesus was risen and standing right there!). He told them, "O foolish ones, and slow of heart to believe all that the prophets have spoken! Was it not necessary that the Christ should suffer these things and enter into his glory?" The author, Luke, then explained, "And beginning with Moses and all the Prophets, he interpreted to them in all the Scriptures the things concerning himself" (Luke 24:25-27 ESV).

I still groan with longing every time I read that passage, wishing that sermon from Jesus had been recorded. How I wish we could read Jesus's own interpretation of Old Testament prophetic scriptures! This first postresurrection message covered how Jesus was anticipated and predicted in the Old Testament. He must have pointed to highlights like Abraham's near sacrifice of his son on the very mountain where Jesus, the Son of God, would die centuries later. He probably told them how the exodus from Egypt prefigured our exodus from the slavery of sin, made possible by His death. I can almost hear Him describing the blood sacrifices of Leviticus, the servant prophecies of Isaiah predicting Christ, and so many psalms long considered to be messianic in nature.

Actual scarlet cords show up a few times in Scripture with some interesting overtones. For example, the garments of the high priest and the curtains of the tabernacle in the Old Testament included scarlets threads.[2] Many have seen these usages as prefiguring the atoning work of the future Lamb of God, Jesus Christ, through His shed blood.

When an advance team of Jewish spies scouted out Jericho and almost got caught, a faith-filled ex-prostitute named Rahab helped them to escape through her window via a scarlet cord. They promised her that when the day of Jericho's destruction came, she and her family could be identified for rescue by hanging that rope from her window on the wall of the city. The scarlet cord—the color of blood—was a sign of her faith that led to her salvation. The cord, for Rahab, worked much like the smeared blood on the lintels and doorposts of Jewish homes in Egypt on the night of the Passover decades before.

The main theme of the Bible is Christ. He's the hero of the story because His sacrifice on the cross provided salvation for mankind. The "scarlet thread" of redemption is interwoven through the entire story and can be seen in the many accounts of biblical *history* that tell *His story*.

It weaves together the hides of the animals slaughtered in the Garden of Eden to provide garments for Adam and Eve. It snares the ram provided in Isaac's place on Mount Moriah. It stains the doorposts in

Egypt and trickles down the altar in the tabernacle in the wilderness and the temple in Jerusalem. That blood-red cord binds the Old Testament to John the Baptist's introduction of Jesus as "the Lamb of God who takes away the sin of the world," and to the beams of a Roman cross at Golgotha, where Jesus declared, "It is finished!"

Though Jesus had an unusual and miraculous birth, though He performed many nature-defying signs and wonders, and though He taught the most sublime truths ever proclaimed, none of these provide salvation, and none are the focal point of His life and ministry. The epicenter of all history, especially redemptive history, is the cross. Bethlehem's baby was born to die! The Bible even refers to Jesus in its final book as "the Lamb slain from the foundation of the world" (Revelation 13:8). In other words, before God made the world, He made the plan to save the world. And why blood? Why is what most would consider so gruesome so important? Because "without the shedding of blood there is no forgiveness" (Hebrews 9:22 NIV). That's why the scarlet thread leads all the way to the cross.

We know the New Testament authors were keen to this by how much literary real estate they devoted to the details surrounding the crucifixion. In the four Gospels (Matthew, Mark, Luke, and John), there are only four chapters devoted to the first thirty years of Jesus's life. The same books provide eighty-five chapters about His last three-and-a-half years, the span of His earthly ministry. Of those eighty-five chapters, twenty-nine are dedicated to the final week of His life, and thirteen of those twenty-nine chapters focus solely on the last twenty-four hours! The events of Jesus's last day, leading up to and including the violent crucifixion, take up 579 verses.

All pre-New Testament history looked forward to that atonement act; all post-New Testament history looks back to it. The prophets anticipated it, and the people of God have continued to celebrate it. Jesus wanted to make sure that His followers never forgot it. "Do this in remembrance of Me," Jesus said as He distributed the familiar elements of the Passover meal and gave them new meaning.

In heaven, I believe you'll see Jesus bearing the wounds marking that event. When Jesus was in His resurrected body, He still bore those scars. He instructed his doubting friend, Thomas, to touch those lesions on His hands and side. Forty days later, Jesus ascended in that resurrected body into heaven itself. It's amazing to think that the only works of man that will be seen in heaven are the wounds inflicted on Jesus on the cross.

You'll notice that this volume is formatted according to overarching themes that tie redemptive history together in groups of biblical books. More than merely inform about God's astonishing rescue operation, I want you to be inspired to worship Him. My hope is that *Bloodline* will serve as a devotional companion for a season in your life, permitting you to focus on and be enriched by this grandest of biblical themes.

OUR RESCUE OPERATION BEGINS

GENESIS AND EXODUS

Every story worth reading has a beginning, middle, and end, and the greatest story ever told is no exception. The first two books of the Bible, Genesis and Exodus, are among its most famous, full of well-known characters and legendary events—from the beginnings of life on earth and humanity's sad fall to its worst impulses to the massive theme of deliverance and redemption, it all starts here. And God is here, too, the one who has no beginning and no end, the Lord and Creator of all, and the one who will pursue His stubborn children through thick and thin because of His unsurpassed love and mercy.

SUPERMAN IS ON HIS WAY

At some point before the creation of the world, one of God's best and brightest angelic beings turned from serving Him and rebelled. Lucifer's insurrection caused a momentous upset in the created order. Though he had been created in a perfect state, his swollen pride became his downfall. It seems that this dark prince, aka the devil, got cocky about his own beauty, intelligence, and position, and wanted the kind of recognition that only God deserves.[1] So God justly cast him out of heaven. Lucifer came directly to earth and showed up in the Garden of Eden sometime after God placed humans there.

Jesus, the Superman of God's redemption story, later said that He was there to watch it all happen: "I saw Satan fall like lightning from heaven" (Luke 10:18). The story of redemption began in the Garden of Eden when our Hero was first foretold. The plot thickened after the initial creation events, and redemption's scarlet thread was then woven from its starting point in Eden through the family line of four great patriarchs, the roots of the nation through whom this Messiah would come.

The Darkest Day

> *Now the serpent was more cunning than any beast of the field which the LORD God had made. And he said to the woman, "Has God indeed said, 'You shall not eat of every tree of the garden'?"* (Genesis 3:1)

All the misery in the world started with this simple question. Up to this point, God had given mankind only one negative command: not to eat fruit off a singular tree.[2] Everything else—all the good things in Eden—was theirs to do with as they pleased. However, the fact that God had to give such a command at all tells us something else: He gave us free will. From the start, we had the ability to choose our actions. And, as the saying goes, "No one likes to be told no."

Prohibition often becomes an invitation. Satan knew it and played off it. He questioned God, God's Word, and God's motives. Eve's first mistake was engagement. She couldn't have known any better, but once she started up a conversation, she was doomed. Satan is too intelligent, too devious, and utterly single-minded: He wants to destroy what God loves. God had established His creation and called it good, and now Satan was coming in to set up his MO of deception and destruction.

Where did this serpent come from? How did he end up in Eden, messing with God's beloved children? Like in school, the answer is in the back of the book: Revelation 12 identifies the enemy of Israel—of all mankind—as Satan. Formerly one of God's chief angels, Lucifer's pride drove him to seek God's throne.[3] He was fired, so to speak, from his high position, and the battle lines were drawn: Whatever God loves,

His adversary would hate, and whatever received God's blessing would become the target of Satan's attacks. When God made Adam and Eve as the pinnacle of His creation and called them good, Satan immediately moved to destroy the unblemished connection between the first two humans and their Maker. His ongoing war against God is a key factor in the story of redemption. His agenda is the serpentine evil that winds its way through history, a counteractive attempt to unravel God's good plans.

This was the darkest day in the history of the human race—where all our problems began. This is where "through one man sin entered the world, and death through sin, and thus death spread to all men, because all sinned" (Romans 5:12). By a single, simple act—a bite of a piece of fruit—the sin virus was introduced into the human bloodstream. Adam brought spiritual darkness that has permeated every generation since.

Thankfully, God wasn't content to leave it like that. When He made the world, the first thing He did was turn on the light. After the fall, He enacted His plan to send the ultimate Light, Jesus Christ, who said, "I have come as a light into the world, that whoever believes in Me should not abide in darkness" (John 12:46). As dark as that tragic day in Eden was, the light of Christ provides a path back to God's embrace. This is why confession of sin is so necessary. When you confess sin and invite God to reveal your flaws, you're letting Jesus bring recovery to your fall. That was God's plan, going all the way back to Eden.

The Cure for the Curse

> *I will put enmity between you and the woman, and between your seed and her Seed; He shall bruise your head, and you shall bruise His heel.* (Genesis 3:15)

When Satan entered Eden, he had one plan in mind: to bring about the corruption and consequent destruction of mankind. He went for the jugular, getting Adam and Eve to doubt that God was really in charge, that He really had their best interests at heart, and disguising their disobedience as a pathway to blessing.

When Adam and Eve fell, however, their decision brought a curse that affected them and every other person ever born. The curse brought sin and death into the world, marring God's creation.[4] Childbirth and work, for example—two things God intended to be blessings—became painful and toilsome. Adam and Eve's disobedience produced disaster. So right away God set a plan in motion to rescue fallen people everywhere. Genesis 3:15 is the first messianic prophecy, called by theologians the *protoevangelium,* or "first gospel," because it contains the first promise of redemption. God stated that the woman would have a Seed (the Messiah) who would eventually defeat Satan and end the curse of sin and death.

> Jesus is the only antidote for the disease of sin; He is the cure for our curse.

While Jesus is the promised Redeemer whose shed blood and resurrection made salvation possible for all people, Satan hasn't gone down quietly. His sole objective is to keep as many people as possible infected with the curse—and all he has to do to accomplish that is keep us in our default position as sinners in need of God's grace.

Jesus is the only antidote for the disease of sin; He is the cure for our curse.

The Beginning of the Rescue Mission

> *Now the LORD had said to Abram…I will make you a great nation; I will bless you and make your name great; and you shall be a blessing. I will bless those who bless you, and I will curse him who curses you; and in you all the families of the earth shall be blessed."* (Genesis 12:1-3)

God's promise to Abraham established the path of salvation for mankind—a nation that God would choose to bless and use to bless the entire world. This group of people would be the means of fulfilling the promise of Genesis 3:15. From them, the Seed would come, the one who would deliver Israel and all the nations of the world from sin's deadly grip—effectively crushing the head of the serpent.

In God's promise, we also see the dynamic of redemption: It's all one-sided. Mankind would not be able to save itself from its grave condition. No amount of good works or intentions, no religious commitment, no manmade institution or system would be able to release us from sin, death, and separation from our Creator. In the end, only God Himself, coming in the form of a mortal and subject to death, would be able to conquer sin's consequences.

Abraham received God's promise by faith,[5] another condition essential to receiving God's gift of salvation. God made him the father of the nation through whom the Messiah would come and blessed him with a multitude of descendants, both physical and spiritual. Although every person who has ever lived can trace his or her human heritage back to Adam and Eve, our spiritual inheritance in Jesus Christ began with Abraham.

Genesis, then, is a book about beginnings—not just the beginning of the universe, but the beginning of all the trouble in the world. It also presents the beginning of the nation of Israel, through whom the Messiah would come. Jesus would descend from the lineage of Israel's four major patriarchs, Abraham, Isaac, Jacob, and Joseph—a genetic line intertwined with a red thread that connects creation to the cross.

The fall was catastrophic, causing an insurmountable gap between God and us, and it would take a miracle to stitch up the wound. God knew this and immediately began preparations to send His Superman to the rescue. It would not be an easy journey, but God stamps His promises with *yes* and *amen*—they are as good as done.[6]

Foreshadowing Forgiveness

> *"You meant evil against me; but God meant it for good, in order to bring it about as it is this day, to save many people alive. Now therefore, do not be afraid; I will provide for you and your little ones." And he comforted them and spoke kindly to them.* (Genesis 50:20-21)

No one would set out God's plan for Joseph as an ideal pathway in life. For an offense no greater than being sheltered by his father as a favorite son, Joseph was roughed up by his brothers and sold to slave traders. Abruptly extricated from his family and his familiar life, Joseph marched in chains across the desert to Egypt, where instead of a father, he now had a master. Framed by the boss's cougar of a wife, Joseph ended up in prison, where he helped a pair of Pharaoh's servants and was promptly forgotten. But God gave Pharaoh nightmares and directed his attention to the young Hebrew languishing in his dungeon—and even though that was the turning point in Joseph's fortunes, the shedding of rags for riches, it was a tough row to hoe.

Faith in God fueled Joseph's hope, however, and furthered his perseverance. He understood that God's purposes were bigger than his individual life, but that they also included him as a crucial player. God never forgot Joseph, and He never forgot His promise to Abraham—or His pledge to crush the head of the serpent. Just as He orchestrated every moment that led to Joseph reconciling with his brothers and seeing his father again, He superintends every moment of every life, and all within the grander scheme of redemption.

All the knots we as humans have tied, and the ones that get snarled in our path, fall under God's sovereignty, and none of them prevent God's scarlet thread from reaching its milestones—the formation and preservation of a people chosen by God to be His special possession and bring forth His Messiah, and the ongoing work of the gospel in the hearts of hundreds of millions of people down through history and on until Jesus returns.

Joseph's story is the case study in God working everything together for good for those He loves, those He has called for His purposes. He orchestrated the moment bringing Joseph and his brothers together to reconcile, while at the same time preserving the future of His people and saving thousands in Egypt and Canaan from starvation. Each of the brothers knew this was a pivotal moment, a God-sponsored encounter that would change their lives forever. However, the contrast in outlooks between them and Joseph is noteworthy. The difference shows us what it is to live connected to God and His scarlet thread, as opposed to trying to unravel life on our own, which inevitably leads to knots and breaks in our path.

While Joseph's brothers were goaded by fear over the cost of their sin, Joseph himself was governed by faith. He lived by his theology, putting his beliefs into practice. He believed in God's sovereignty and providence, and determined that no matter what happened in his life, he was going to trust the Lord. Whatever anger and frustration he felt over his brothers' betrayal melted away in the warmth of God's loving mercy—something Joseph had seen firsthand. Joseph was a type of Christ, who extended mercy, liberation, and reconciliation to those who deserved it the least.

As with Joseph, the first and most crucial step in softening your attitude toward someone who has wronged you is expressing your gratitude to God. You will then learn to take on God's big-picture attitude—to "save many people alive"—and put your experiences in the proper perspective as part of God's bigger plan. Hint: Put your enemies on your prayer list and watch what happens—they won't stay your enemies for long.

During the journey of Genesis, God's redemptive plan went from a garden to a group. It included a family that became a nation. And that nation would grow strong on the foreign soil of Egypt, as God predicted to Abraham.[7] But eventually, this growing group became suffering slaves, and deliverance became necessary. What happened in Egypt became a template for what would happen at the cross.

DELIVERANCE!

The book of Exodus is one of the clearest pictures of redemption in or out of Scripture. The scarlet thread is unmistakable in this second book of the Bible. Though *exodus* means "an exit," the only way Israel could exit the bondage of Egypt was by acting in faith on the bloody sacrifice of an innocent lamb. God established His covenant with the Jewish nation based on this deliverance, which anticipated the new (and final) covenant through "the Lamb of God who takes away the sin of the world" (John 1:29).

From this point forward, Jews around the world would annually point back to and commemorate their ancestors' deliverance from Egyptian slavery. New Testament authors would also repeatedly use the vivid imagery found in Exodus to show its fulfillment in Christ. As the book opens, Prince Joseph had been dead for more than 300 years, and Israel's position had gone from favored status to vassal state to vanquished slaves. Egypt was faced with the need to deal with this burgeoning Jewish minority, and Pharaoh set oppressive measures in place. The messianic bloodline was prospering but oppressed; the need for rescue couldn't have been greater.

I Am God (and You're Not)

> *God said to Moses, "I AM WHO I AM." And He said, "Thus you shall say to the children of Israel, 'I AM has sent me to you.'"* (Exodus 3:14)

When God met Moses at the burning bush, He did something He hadn't done before: He told Moses His name. "I AM WHO I AM" seems straightforward in English, if a bit mysterious, but the truth is that no one is exactly sure how to pronounce it in the original Hebrew. Scholars' best guess is called the tetragrammaton, or YHWH, generally pronounced *Yahweh*—or in Greek, *Jehovah*. It has been translated as "The All-Becoming One," or "I Will Be That I Will Be"—indicating that God is God at all times, past, present, and future.

"I AM WHO I AM" speaks of God's self-sufficiency, self-containment, and omnipotence. He needs no one and nothing. Yet even though He is all-powerful, He chooses to engage with us in very personal ways. And His name suggests that whatever you need in your life, God will become that for you. When you need provision, He is *Yahweh-Yireh* (Genesis 22:14), "the Lord Our Provider." Because you need righteousness, He is *Yahweh-Tsidkenu* (Genesis 15:6), "the Lord Our Righteousness." Wherever you go, He is *Yahweh-Shammah*, "the Lord Who Is There" (Genesis 28:15).

Later, God reintroduced Himself to the world by another name—Jesus, who appropriated the name *I AM* for Himself with seven "I am" statements in John's Gospel, all pointing to His sufficiency to become what we desperately need—light and life and salvation. He told the Pharisees, "Before Abraham was, I AM" (John 8:58). He meant that

God's redemptive plan to eradicate our sin
through the blood of His Son was not an
afterthought. It was, as we saw in Genesis
3:15, the original plan in response to original sin. Jesus is the "Lamb slain from the
foundation of the world" (Revelation 13:8).

> Redemption is
> possible because
> God does the
> impossible.

When God introduced Himself to Moses, He told him he was
standing on holy ground. What made it holy? God did. The holiness
came from God's presence in that place of connection. The winding
path of redemption's scarlet thread is improbable; it only succeeded
(and succeeds today) because of who God is. *I AM* means that your
past is forgiven and your future is secure, and it also means that God is
ready to work in your life right now. Redemption is possible because
God does the impossible.

Passed Over

> *Now the blood shall be a sign for you on the houses where you
> are. And when I see the blood, I will pass over you; and the
> plague shall not be on you to destroy you when I strike the
> land of Egypt.* (Exodus 12:13)

Now the theme of deliverance through redemption is seen in bold
relief. The tenth plague God visited upon Egypt was different than the
first nine. Not only were its scope and intensity more powerful and
deeply personal—the death of the firstborn—but so was the way it
played out. For this final plague, God required His people's participa-
tion. As an act of faith, they were to take a lamb's blood and smear it on
their doorposts on the appointed night; in response, the plague would
pass over them, sparing their lives and setting the stage for their deliverance from bondage in Egypt.

Jewish families were to select their lamb and keep it for five days
until the Passover. They would see that cuddly little critter each day,
and the kids would no doubt grow attached to it. When it came time
to offer it up, there was a real feeling of sacrifice—an object lesson in
sin's offensiveness to a holy God and its ultimate cost.

It makes no human sense to do such a thing, but it makes God-sense. There's nothing intrinsically healing about lamb's blood on your doorposts, but in God's economy, the lifeblood of an innocent was required to atone for sin.[8] Every year since then, with rare exception, Jews the world over have celebrated the Passover—the emancipation God provided for those who took that step of faith. Nowhere else in the Old Testament is there such a clear prefiguring of the cross, of an innocent Lamb being sacrificed to pay sin's price once and for all.

Similarly, we should always be sensitive to what it cost God to send His truly good and perfect Son to die for us. A lamb changed the lives of Israel, and the Lamb of God changes lives today all over the globe, bringing fellowship with God in the only way possible—covering offenses with His life-giving blood—His death. No matter how long it's been since you made Jesus your Lamb—your Savior—it's good practice to regularly refresh the impact of what He did for you.

Remember that everyone needs that blood covering; it's the only way to avoid God's ultimate judgment. In Egypt, the penalty for not being in a blood-smeared house was the death of the firstborn. At Calvary, God sent His firstborn to die as the Lamb who could save anyone in any house ever (Hebrews 1:6). Be thankful for the price that bought you back to His love and be diligent to invite others to get covered by the blood of the Lamb, God's perfect Passover for all people.

Unlocking the Power of the Law

> *Now therefore, if you will indeed obey My voice and keep My covenant, then you shall be a special treasure to Me above all people; for all the earth is Mine.* (Exodus 19:5)

You are God's precious treasure, worth the best gift He had to offer, His Son. He gave the law because He is holy, but He understands that the problem with the law is the inability of the human heart to keep it. So when Israel said, in essence, "Sounds good; we'll do it all" (Exodus 19:8), God responded, "Oh, that they had such a heart in them" (Deuteronomy 5:29).

Because this was a conditional covenant—hinging on an *if-then* proposition—God knew the people would have a problem keeping their part of it: obeying His voice and upholding His covenant. And more often than not, the apple of His eye proved to be rotten to the core. That's sin's effect: We simply can't keep the law, but it serves as a tutor to lead us to Christ.[9] That's what the new covenant in Christ is all about. The Old Testament anticipates the New; in fact, the Old requires the New. "For the law was given through Moses, but grace and truth came through Jesus Christ" (John 1:17).

In the New Testament, the *if* is removed. God showed your value to Him in what Christ did for you. After all, the value of something is determined by what someone is willing to pay for it. Jesus shed all His prerogatives in heaven to come to earth and buy you back from sin.[10] You matter to Him. So the scarlet thread of redemption woven throughout Scripture thickens into a rope by the time the New Testament dawns.

That voice in your head telling you that you're good for nothing is stuck in the old covenant. It's only half the story. God's law shows you that you have a sin problem, but His grace in Jesus shows you the solution. Do you think of yourself the way God thinks of you? You are precious to Him—and He has a purpose for you. He told Moses, "You shall be to Me a kingdom of priests and a holy nation" (Exodus 19:6). Priests stand as mediators between God and men, but under the new covenant, our priesthood means serving as witnesses to what Christ has done to build a bridge that connects us with God.

The apostle Peter picked up on that when he called the church "a royal priesthood…His own special people, that you may proclaim the praises of Him who called you out of darkness into His marvelous light" (1 Peter 2:9). God's grace made a path through the perilous terrain of sin and pride—something the law illustrates repeatedly.

Camping with God

> *Whenever the cloud was taken up from above the tabernacle,*
> *the children of Israel would go onward in all their journeys.*
> *But if the cloud was not taken up, then they did not journey*
> *till the day that it was taken up.* (Exodus 40:36-37)

After a lot of ups and downs, Israel got serious about following God. The people all came together to finance and build the tabernacle according to the instructions God gave Moses. Once the tent of meeting was finished, the pillar of cloud that had guided Israel through the wilderness came down and "the glory of the LORD filled the tabernacle" (Exodus 40:35). For generations afterward, through the time of David, God not only led Israel by cloud and fire, He lived among them—and they let Him lead.

By the end of Exodus, Israel had become a theocentric nation, with God dwelling in their midst. The tabernacle was at the center of Israel's life geographically, spiritually, and culturally, with blood sacrifices punctuating community life. The cloud, which rabbis later called God's *Shekinah* glory, was proof of God's presence among them. God established a clear precedent: He wants to dwell in your heart, taking the place of highest importance, guiding, protecting, and providing for you. John referenced this when he wrote about Christ in John 1:14: "The Word became flesh and dwelt among us" (literally, "He *tabernacled* among us"). Jesus came as God's Son from heaven and camped out on earth for thirty-three years. When people saw Jesus, they were seeing God.[11]

That's the message of Exodus: God wants to deliver you from sin's slavery and take His rightful place at the center and as the substance of your life. Your heart is meant to be His tabernacle. As Paul later wrote, "Your body is the temple of the Holy Spirit who is in you, whom you have from God, and you are not your own" (1 Corinthians 6:19). When you're walking with God, anywhere you are is a holy place, any time is a holy moment because He is there with you. He redeemed you to live inside you. You are His tent now.

The two great themes of Exodus are redemption and revelation—key concepts that still apply today for each of us. If you haven't received God's redemption in Christ yet, consider this your revelation. If you have and are now engaged in that ongoing process of becoming more like Jesus, consider the state of your relationship with Him: What is He calling you to do, and are you willing to take the next step and do it?

The deliverance completed, the Israelites were now depending completely on God in their desert sanctuary. His glory could be seen over the tabernacle as they camped around the foot of Mount Sinai.[12] The next phase of redemptive history was the inauguration of a system of sacrifices to honor God and an education in what it takes to pay redemption's price—in blood.

THERE MUST BE BLOOD

THE LAW:
Leviticus, Numbers, and Deuteronomy

T he reason for the color of redemption's thread fills the pages
of the books of the law, Leviticus, Numbers, and Deuteronomy:
blood. Because death entered the world as the cost of sin, it makes
perfect sense that the physical representation of life would be required
to pay for it. As a central aspect of His law, God required that sin be
paid for in blood. Poured out on the altar to acquit the individual and
on the mercy seat of the Ark of the Covenant to absolve the nation, animal blood flowed freely in God's system of atoning sacrifices. But day
after day, year after year, it became readily apparent that there could
never be enough blood to completely cleanse the sin of the world.

A COSTLY CLEANSING

God knew this, of course. This insufficiency informed His master
plan to pay for sin once and for all—a redemption that in His perfection only He could accomplish. God the Father sent God the Son on
the ultimate rescue mission, and Jesus became our mercy seat, transforming the place of judgment into the place of mercy. The system

of sacrifices in Leviticus was never meant to be permanent, because they were sacrifices "which can never take away sins" (Hebrews 10:11). Everything that it was designed to accomplish—atonement, sanctification, and holiness—was made possible on a one-time, ongoing basis by the blood of the final sacrifice, Jesus Christ. Until He came, the law existed to remind God's people of their great need and of His great love in desiring to have a relationship with them.

A Spirit-Led Conscience

> *It shall be, when he is guilty in any of these matters, that he shall confess that he has sinned in that thing; and he shall bring his trespass offering to the LORD for his sin which he has committed.* (Leviticus 5:5-6)

Sin is an ugly word. Most people hate it, marginalizing its importance or simply denying its existence. But the plain truth is that sin impedes any relationship we as fallen creatures could have with God. Leviticus opens with seven chapters answering the question, How can I approach God? God wants a relationship with you, but His holiness makes it impossible for you to approach Him the way you would another person. Relativists say that all paths lead to God, but God's Word says that He is exclusive: Lifeblood is required to approach Him.

In the Old Testament, God's response was to have Israel come to Him through the blood of animal sacrifices. People couldn't just waltz in through the curtains of the Holy of Holies in the tabernacle and have a chat with God; they needed a blood sacrifice and a priest.

God established a series of offerings that made relationship with Him possible. The sin and trespass offerings were mandatory because sin requires payment,[1] and everyone sins.[2] We are sinners by nature *and* by choice.

Walk Away: A Tale of Two Goats

> *He shall take the two goats and present them before the LORD at the door of the tabernacle of meeting. Then Aaron shall cast lots for the two goats: one lot for the LORD and the other lot for*

> *the scapegoat. And Aaron shall bring the goat on which the*
> *Lord's lot fell, and offer it as a sin offering.* (Leviticus 16:7-9)

God instituted Yom Kippur, the annual Day of Atonement, for the Jews as a solemn observation of sin's cost and the need for forgiveness. Aaron, as the high priest, made an offering for himself and his family, and then brought out two goats. One had a good future, and the other, a bad one. One goat was let loose, and the other was killed—a perfect anticipation of New Testament atonement.

One goat was sacrificed because the wages of sin is death; the other went free, covered only by the priest's bloodied handprints and a confession on the people's behalf—given life, just as the apostle John later described: "If we confess our sins, He is faithful and just to forgive us our sins and to cleanse us from all unrighteousness" (1 John 1:9). That second goat was sent out of sight, and the people celebrated its disappearance—because, as David later said, "As far as the east is from the west, so far has He removed our transgressions from us" (Psalm 103:12).

Jesus's first words from the cross were, "Father, forgive them, for they do not know what they do" (Luke 23:34). It's noteworthy that, first and foremost, He addressed our greatest need: forgiveness. Centuries before, Yom Kippur made this clear. However, whereas in the Old Testament sins were never completely removed but only covered for a time, under the new covenant, Jesus took away the sin of the world[3] once and for all for those who receive Him.

Life Is in the Blood

> *The life of the flesh is in the blood, and I have given it to you*
> *upon the altar to make atonement for your souls; for it is the*
> *blood that makes atonement for the soul.* (Leviticus 17:11)

To please God, you must be sanctified—made holy. The law showed that sacrifice was required to become holy—more specifically, spilled blood was required. Blood coursing through our veins means life. To shed blood is to end life, and that's the cost of sin: death. Animal sacrifices were an acceptable substitute under the old covenant, and the key phrase in the law is right here in Leviticus, a book where blood is mentioned more than 400 times in 357 verses: "the life of the flesh is in the blood." Spiritually, the power of sacrificed blood shows the sanctity of life. It was the distinguishing factor for Israel as it became one nation under God.

God forbade the Jews from eating blood. The power of atonement was the main reason why—it took lifeblood to be made right with God, something that none of us could ever accomplish ourselves by giving or consuming blood. This was so ingrained in Jewish culture that Jesus shocked the Jews when He told them, "Whoever eats My flesh and drinks My blood has eternal life, and I will raise him up at the last day" (John 6:54). The startling metaphor came from an even more surprising truth: True life can come only by Jesus's death. His once-and-for-all sacrifice paid redemption's ultimate price.

> The key word embroidered on the new covenant isn't *do* but *done,* because Jesus completed and fulfilled all the requirements of the law.

Spiritual cleanness comes from belief in the blood of Jesus Christ to cleanse you from sin; it's not tied to what you eat. The key word embroidered on the new covenant isn't *do* but *done,* because Jesus completed and fulfilled all the requirements of the law. He blotted out "the handwriting of ordinances that was against us, which was contrary to us, and took it out of the way, nailing it to his cross" (Colossians 2:14 KJV).

Consider the tedious, endless nature of the old covenant system. There was always one more sacrifice, one more lamb, day after day, year after year: "According to the law almost all things are purified with blood, and without shedding of blood there is no remission [of sin]" (Hebrews 9:22). In the new covenant, remembrance replaced repetition. The next time you celebrate communion, breathe a sigh of relief and rejoice in the limitless atonement that transformed your relationship with your heavenly Father and brought you into His family. Grafting you onto the bloodline took a bloody cross, but the result is a saved and satisfied soul no longer bound to sin or its accompanying sacrifices.

Leviticus makes one fact abundantly clear: Redemption's cost must be paid in blood. The Levitical system, however, demonstrated that no amount of animal blood or human giving could permanently erase sin's debt. God's holiness requires that death must be overcome with life—a perfect, stainless life. And in His great love, He provided the one sacrifice that would fulfill His requirements: His Messiah, Jesus Christ.

EVERY NUMBER HAS A NAME

The book of Numbers gets its biblical title from a pair of censuses taken along the way—reminders of God's protection and provision of His people in a very inhospitable environment. The people multiplied under His care in the wilderness, but didn't progress in recognition of it—so they pretty much stayed put, turning an eleven-day journey to the Promised Land into a forty-year holding pattern.

Even though Israel's bad attitude kept the people from experiencing the abundant life God had for them in the Promised Land, He took care of them. But God's agenda went beyond their needs to the needs of the entire world. In preserving Israel, He sustained a genealogy within a nation that could present the Savior who would offer forgiveness for sin. The extent to which God was committed to fulfilling this need can be seen in His patience with the people of Israel.

Both Leviticus and Numbers have a wilderness setting. Their stage is the desert wasteland between Egypt and the promised land of Canaan. But whereas the central theological theme of Leviticus is atonement, Numbers focuses on the faithfulness of God to fulfill His promises to give the progeny of Abraham the land of Canaan. Thus, the nation that would bring forth the Messiah would have a homeland.[4]

God even organized Israel's camp in a way that foreshadowed redemption. With the tabernacle at the center, He set the twelve tribes around their meeting place with Him in such a way that, from the air, the camp was in the shape of a cross. The tribes placed east of the tabernacle were proportionally larger than the other three camps and required more space to extend in that direction. Is this significant? It most certainly is, because it points to God's ultimate purpose for all mankind: to know Him better as Lord and Savior.

Remember Your Deliverance

> *If anyone of you or your posterity is unclean because of a corpse,*
> *or is far away on a journey, he may still keep the LORD's*
> *Passover... They shall leave none of it until morning, nor*
> *break one of its bones. According to all the ordinances of the*
> *Passover they shall keep it.* (Numbers 9:10, 12)

On the first anniversary of the Passover, God told Moses to remind the people—in the midst of their busy lives—to stop and honor God for His deliverance of them from Egypt.[5] He specifically instituted the practice that none of the Passover lamb's bones should be broken in the process of sacrificing, preparing, or eating it. Seems like a harmless if peculiarly specific instruction—until we look at Jesus's crucifixion.

The anguished heaving and gasping of a crucified individual could last for days. For this reason it was a regular practice of the Roman soldiers to break their victims' legs after a while, preventing them from being able to brace their bodies to draw a breath, hastening the end. In Jesus's case, the Passover was fast approaching, and the Jewish leaders wanted to head home to observe it. So they asked Pilate to break the legs of all three men. But when the soldiers came to Jesus "and saw that He was already dead, they did not break His legs" (John 19:33).

John witnessed this, and later, as he wrote his Gospel, connected the dots to the practice of the Passover. He saw that it foretold Jesus as the ultimate Passover Lamb, bones unbroken and blood shed for the sins of mankind—not a victim, but the victor. John even pointed out that the fact the Roman soldiers had left Jesus's legs unbroken was a fulfillment of Old Testament prophecy.[6]

God's plan of salvation was not accidental but intentional. Jesus is the "Lamb slain from the foundation of the world" (Revelation 13:8). And just like at Passover, God wants His people to remember and celebrate His deliverance, which was a key part of His overarching plan to save us from sin and restore our relationship with Him.

Look Up to Live

> *The LORD said to Moses, "Make a fiery serpent, and set it on a*

*pole; and it shall be that everyone who is bitten, when he looks
at it, shall live." So Moses made a bronze serpent, and put it
on a pole; and so it was, if a serpent had bitten anyone, when
he looked at the bronze serpent, he lived.* (Numbers 21:8-9)

One chapter after Moses found out he would not be entering the
Promised Land, he modeled the Messiah's heart and interceded for
God's hardheaded people yet again. The harsh lesson God had taught
Moses when he struck the rock didn't go unheeded. Rather than let
bitterness take root, Moses submitted to God's punishment, trusting
God with the bigger picture rather than letting his own feelings gov-
ern his actions—"See? I told you how obnoxious these people are. Let
'em have it, Lord!"

And when it came to the episode of the bronze serpent, there was
definitely a bigger picture in God's mind. In the Old Testament, bronze
was often associated with judgment. The altar of sacrifice in the tabernacle's courtyard was made of bronze, and was regularly covered with
animal blood in payment for sin. So this snake on a pole represented
God's righteous judgment—but also His cure.

Jesus, in telling Nicodemus that a person must be born again to see
God's kingdom, compared being lifted up on the cross to Moses lifting up the serpent.[7] Now, there's nothing scientific about bronze or a
snake that either should heal a snakebite—just as there's nothing inher-
ently logical about a man's crucifixion saving mankind.

Both situations required faith. The snake was raised up to heal those
who had been bitten because of their sin, but they had to trust Moses's
instructions enough to look up at it. To do that, they first needed to
admit they had done wrong. Antivenin wouldn't heal those bites—
only confession, repentance, and trusting in God. Similarly, no religion
or self-help book or great works will solve a person's sinful state—only
looking up at the cross of Christ, an instrument of hopelessness made
hopeful by God's great love.

God's grace truly is amazing. Even though an entire generation
would die in the wilderness because of their failure to be faithful to
Him, He would try again with the next generation, bringing them up

to speed on all He had done to provide for His people, establish His standards, and preserve the line of the Messiah. Redemption's strands are coiled around this moment, reminders that with God there are no accidents, nothing unforeseen, and no one unaccounted for.

Seeking Asylum

> *You shall appoint cities to be cities of refuge for you, that the manslayer who kills any person accidentally may flee there.*
> (Numbers 35:11)

God's mercy and heart for justice often took physical form. He gave instructions that when the people of Israel eventually crossed the Jordan River into the Promised Land, they were to establish cities of refuge where those who killed someone by accident could seek asylum.[8] They could safely reside in those cities either until the community judged the case, or until the death of the high priest, at which time they were set free.

With God there are no accidents, nothing unforeseen, and no one unaccounted for.

What a striking image of Jesus Christ, our Great High Priest, whose death set us free from a just condemnation. The lowest of the low could find safety in a city of refuge, and we can do the same today in Christ, no matter what we've done, our wandering hearts redeemed because of His great love for us. In Christ, we're more than just the teeming millions of mankind; we're names that He wants written in His Book of Life.

THE ULTIMATE PROPHET

Jesus quoted the book of Deuteronomy ten times—and with impact. He summed up the Law of Moses by commanding that we love God with all we've got, and that we love our neighbors as ourselves.[9] He also used Deuteronomy to discuss the shortcomings of divorce[10] and to encourage the honest establishment of witnesses in disciplinary hearings.[11] Perhaps most impressively, Jesus wielded Deuteronomy like a shield as He deflected Satan's temptations during His forty days in the desert.[12]

It's fitting, then, that on the verge of entering the rest of the land of promise, the messages Moses gave to remind God's people of His deeds and His words provided a forecast of and touchstone for the greatest Prophet of them all, the Messiah, Jesus Christ. Redemption's scarlet threads are highly visible in the fabric of that chapter.

> Jesus would make possible for everyone the greatest journey of all—from sin's condemnation to redemption's forgiveness.

Jesus would make possible for everyone the greatest journey of all—from sin's condemnation to redemption's forgiveness, and the greatest rest of all—the peace and power of going through this life restored by His love and led by His Spirit.

The One

> *I will raise up for them a Prophet like you from among their brethren, and will put My words in His mouth, and He shall speak to them all that I command Him. And it shall be that whoever will not hear My words, which He speaks in My name, I will require it of him.* (Deuteronomy 18:18-19)

God sent many prophets to Israel over the years, revealing His word and will. All of them were training the ears of His people to hear His voice and obey in anticipation of the ultimate prophet: the Messiah. Here, through Moses, He made mention not of many prophets but of one. All of God's prophets spoke God's words, but this capital-P Prophet would be different. He would do that and more.

The Jews anticipated the arrival of this Prophet from this point on. That's why, thousands of years later, they asked John the Baptist if he was Elijah, who, along with Moses, was one of the most highly regarded prophets in Israel, and then if he was "the Prophet"—the Messiah (John 1:21). That was a direct reference to this prophecy. And when Stephen, the first martyr, testified before the Jewish leaders, he quoted this passage as being fulfilled in Jesus Christ.[13] Moses was telling the Jews to expect a coming Messiah. Even Jesus said as much: "If you believed Moses, you would believe Me; for he wrote about Me" (John 5:46).

The Messiah would be God's ultimate spokesman, His final Word, expressed in human form, on the most important issue people face: forgiveness for sin and restoration to relationship with their Maker. God's final word with regard to salvation is Jesus Christ. Jesus is the fulfillment of more than 350 prophecies about the Messiah, predictive promises given through multiple sources over thousands of years about God's plan to redeem mankind from sin's clutches. And one of His final statements was "It is finished," announcing that the transaction for salvation had been completed.

> When you're His, there's nothing you can't bring to Him, nothing you can't put in His hands and trust to His care.

God's perfect prophetic record is perfectly expressed in His Son. And just as God's perfect track record underscores His trustworthiness, Jesus Christ can be trusted with the most important matters in your life—salvation and sanctification (and everything else as well). When you're His, there's nothing you can't bring to Him, nothing you can't put in His hands and trust to His care.

Choose Life

> *I call heaven and earth as witnesses today against you, that I have set before you life and death, blessing and cursing; therefore choose life, that both you and your descendants may live.* (Deuteronomy 30:19)

God made it simple to follow Him. He gave Israel His law, and the command to study it and live it out. The people didn't need to have a mystical vision or make a far-off pilgrimage; they could draw close to God simply by choosing to obey Him. "The word is very near you, in your mouth and in your heart, that you may do it" (Deuteronomy 30:14). He allowed all people to have the power to choose Him or to turn away.

God's words are right there at your fingertips—and the choice that

Moses laid out is even closer, a matter of your own heart. Once you've heard with your ears, you must listen with the core of your being. God sets the choice before each of us: life or death, blessing or cursing, good or evil. Of course, He wants you to choose life because it's the best choice. It will bring blessings of a life filled with peace, joy, and fulfillment. Jesus said, "I am the good shepherd. The good shepherd gives His life for the sheep," and that those who choose Him "will go in and out and find pasture" (John 10:11, 9). Choosing Jesus as Savior is a one-time event, but choosing to submit to His lordship is a daily decision.

I read about a building in the Midwest with a pitched roof. If the rain falls on one side, it drains off and eventually ends up in the Great Lakes, and then the Atlantic Ocean. If it runs off the other side, it goes to the Ohio River, and then to the Gulf of Mexico. One breath of wind in either direction makes a huge difference in the end. Similarly, one choice can change your life and your eternal destiny. Redemption's tapestry is filled with such momentous decisions.

The way to God is still simple: Choose the life that Jesus Christ offers. Paul quoted this passage from Deuteronomy, concluding "that if you confess with your mouth the Lord Jesus and believe in your heart that God has raised Him from the dead, you will be saved" (Romans 10:9). If you haven't already made that choice, you can do so right now—and if you have, you've been connected to the bloodline of Christ. You are on the road to heaven, the path of God's blessing. And once you're on that journey, you can help others see the importance of that one simple decision. Israel would resolve to follow God and entered the Promised Land because of it—a foreshadowing of the rest anyone can have upon choosing Jesus Christ.

A STRONG CORD IN THIN FABRIC

BEFORE THE MONARCHY:
Joshua, Judges, and Ruth

A few centuries after the exodus from Egypt, Israel experienced a gradual leadership vacuum. Joshua, Moses's successor, maintained his predecessor's godly example and relied on God to lead Israel into the land of promise. But even then, the same impatience and lack of faith that threatened to undermine the people in the wilderness frayed the edges of redemption's tapestry.

When Joshua died, having warned Israel that each family must decide to follow God for themselves, no new leaders rose up. Israel fell into repetitive cycles of self-destructive and godless behavior, imitating the pagan cultures surrounding them, which ironically led to their subjugation to those same nations. Each cycle, however, God brought them a judge—a deliverer from among them—who acted as God's agent of liberation from their enemies.

Despite God's faithfulness in responding to the people's cries for help, Israel kept trying to emulate the habits and beliefs of their neighbors, seemingly desperate to shirk God's call to them to be holy—to be called out from among the flocks of mankind and be God's special, chosen people. The fabric of redemption's tapestry stretched almost to transparency during this era before the monarchy, but even in those dark days of everyone doing what seemed right to themselves, God kept His bloodline going, bringing in a pair of Gentile (non-Jewish) women who would play key roles in preserving the lineage of the Messiah.

THE GREAT DEFENDER

In Hebrew, the name Joshua is *Yeshua*, which is also Jesus's name. Joshua's parents named him Hoshea, meaning "deliverance," but Moses renamed him *Yeshua*, meaning "God delivers," or "God is a Savior." Moses couldn't bring Israel all the way into the land; only Joshua could. Moses saw the evidence of God's powerful work in Joshua's life, just as the apostle John saw it in Jesus. There was a difference, however, and John summarized it: "The law was given through Moses, but grace and truth came through Jesus Christ" (John 1:17).

The people of Israel repeatedly disqualified themselves from entering the land of promise, so here in Joshua, God simply gave it to them.[1] The law made it clear that no one could ever earn salvation, so God freely gave it to us, albeit at great cost, in Jesus Christ. And just as Moses brought the people to the edge of the land but Joshua brought them in, so Jesus brings us into the fullness of the Spirit, an empowering that we could never have without Him and one that the law could never accomplish.

Jesus sent His followers into the world to share the gospel, but He told them to first wait for the Holy Spirit to come upon them so they would be up to the task (Acts 1:8). The precursor to that is here in Joshua, founded on God's law and fueled by His promise: "Be strong and of good courage; do not be afraid, nor be dismayed, for the LORD your God is with you wherever you go" (Joshua 1:9). Joshua foreshadowed Jesus as the true defender of the faith, the one for whom following God was not an obligation or a pious show but the result of a heart committed to the glory of the only one who deserves it. In fact, as we'll see, it's even possible that Joshua *met* Jesus in this story.

A Matter of Cooperation

*As I was with Moses, so I will be with you. I will not leave
you nor forsake you. Be strong and of good courage, for to this
people you shall divide as an inheritance the land which I
swore to their fathers to give them.* (Joshua 1:5-6)

God appointed Joshua to replace Moses as the leader of His people, to take them into the Promised Land of Canaan. As is often the case with God, there was a higher spiritual meaning to crossing the Jordan River.[2] It wasn't, as some older hymns suggest, symbolic of crossing into heaven (there were still many battles ahead of them), but into the land of God's rest. So the land of rest isn't heaven, but your life as a believer now—rest, so to speak, from the forty years of wandering in the desert. Crossing over the Jordan under Joshua's leadership foreshadowed salvation by another *Yeshua* and then crossing into a new way of life—one under control of the Holy Spirit, as opposed to living under the control of your flesh. You rest from pursuing your own agenda and focus on God's instead.

The book of Joshua, then, can be seen as a template for victorious Christian living. I'll even suggest that as God brought the people of Israel through the Red Sea under Moses, delivering them from the Egyptian army, it was a baptism—a symbol, involving water, of their being raised from death into life and being joined to God. Crossing the Jordan was a second baptism, along the lines of what John the Baptist (who earned his nickname at the Jordan) said: "I indeed baptize you with water unto repentance, but He who is coming after me is mightier than I…He will baptize you with the Holy Spirit and fire" (Matthew 3:11).

That journey can begin at the least likely times and in the hearts of the least likely people. God is always on the lookout for people who see Him, recognize their need, and are willing to put their faith in Him. A pair of Israelite spies encountered just such a person.

Saving Faith

*As soon as we heard these things, our hearts melted; neither
did there remain any more courage in anyone because of you,*

*for the LORD your God, He is God in heaven above and on
earth beneath.* (Joshua 2:11)

God was sending His people into enemy territory—both in terms of
the pagan tribes that inhabited it and the spiritual forces arrayed around
them, the devil and his demons, who no doubt were drooling over the
thought of these hardheaded wanderers entering a situation that would
require both faith and more military firepower than Israel had.

However, when Joshua's spies met a local prostitute named Rahab
while they were scouting out Jericho, she gave them a startling report:
Everyone in Canaan was terrified of Israel because they had heard of
all the mighty works God had done as they left Egypt and crossed the
desert. That was a newsflash, since her account stood in contrast with
the report of the spies Moses had sent into Canaan some forty-five
years before. Of the twelve chosen to explore the land, ten freaked out
once they saw the giants who lived there. Only two, Joshua and Caleb,
believed that Canaan posed no threat.[3]

Caleb had said, "We are well able to overcome it" (Numbers 13:30)
because he knew that God was with them, bigger than any giant, mightier than any army. And Rahab confirmed that God's reputation alone
was enough to strike fear in the hearts of Isra-
el's enemies. She struck a deal with the spies:
She would help them in exchange for sparing
her family because there was no doubt in her
mind that Jericho was going down.[4]

> If you view
> God as small,
> obstacles
> become huge.
> If you see Him as
> big, any obstacle
> will become
> comparatively
> small.

The account shows that Rahab was now
an *ex*-prostitute, for she expressed a firm
belief in Israel's God. The agreement was
that she would tie a scarlet-colored rope to
the window of her house, by which these
two spies were let down the outside wall of
Jericho. When Israel invaded—however that
ended up happening—she would hang that blood-colored rope out
the same window. That crimson cord would be the outward sign of her
inward faith by which deliverance would come to her house.

Rahab had saving faith. It involved her mind as well as her emotions, and it involved her actions in response to her belief.[5] She saw that Israel's God couldn't be stopped and took steps to make sure she was on His side. From inside Jericho's walls, she understood something Joshua grasped from the outside: Difficulty must always be measured by the capacity of the agent doing the work. If you view God as small, obstacles become huge. If you see Him as big, any obstacle will become comparatively small. Redeeming the human race, for example, is a massive impediment, impossible for us, but God showed at Jericho that no challenge is too great for Him. He works on levels as intimate as a single heart and as grand a scale as the fall of mighty city walls.

The Ripple Effect

> *There is an accursed thing in your midst, O Israel; you cannot stand before your enemies until you take away the accursed thing from among you.* (Joshua 7:13)

After the monumental victory at Jericho, Joshua was left flummoxed when his troops were routed by the much smaller forces of Ai.[6] God quickly made it clear that the reason wasn't tactical but spiritual. The disobedience of one had introduced an infection into the camp. God had given Israel's enemies victory because someone had kept an "accursed thing" out of the spoils of Jericho. It wasn't about the object itself, but that the guilty person had put himself before God, to whom all the spoils of Jericho belonged.[7]

The things Achan (the guilty party) took became accursed because he took them for his own pleasure and prosperity, against God's expressed command. The result was that God withheld His favor from all of Israel in their military campaign against Ai. Achan's theft resulted in his execution, a brutal reminder that no one sins in isolation. We may think we're getting away with doing what we want, but we never do. God knows about it and eventually reveals it, and not only does sin separate us from God, but it creates division and destruction between us and other people. Until we deal with our sin, we won't be able to stand up to our enemies—to obstacles and obstructions that keep us from God's best.

Achan's action brought "an accursed thing" into the camp of Israel, and Achan would die for his own sin. Compare this to Jesus, who became the curse by dying on the cross for others' sins. "Christ has redeemed us from the curse of the law, having become a curse for us (for it is written, 'Cursed is everyone who hangs on a tree')" (Galatians 3:13, citing Deuteronomy 21:23). Achan lived selfishly; Jesus lived sacrificially. Achan brought a curse; Jesus removed the curse.

Despite the ups and downs that would come as Israel moved into Canaan, God was committed to His plan of calling a nation through Abraham and then preserving that nation that would bring forth the Messiah to be *Yeshua—God who is Savior*. The scarlet thread undergirds the words of Joshua's closing speech: "You have seen all that the LORD your God has done to all these nations *because of you*" (Joshua 23:3). God defended Israel because they were His chosen people, the nation through whom He would save the world—but they certainly didn't make it easy on Him.

RELEASE FROM THE VICIOUS CYCLE

No book of the Bible highlights mankind's need for redemption more starkly than Judges. Few places underscore so effectively the impact of the war that began in Eden—a conflict fought on both physical and spiritual planes. There's no direct mention of the Messiah here, but nowhere is the need for Him seen so clearly; nowhere does the demand for a scarlet rope as a lifeline arise more dramatically. Israel's imperfect judges were only local liberators. They were effective for God's purposes in delivering His people from the clutches of their own sin, but their efforts achieved temporary results at best.

Israel's judges pointed to the need for a better deliverance—one that didn't need to be continually repeated—building on the main issues with the Levitical system of sacrifices. No single offering, no amount of lifeblood, could pay sin's cost. A better deliverance, however, would require a better deliverer—something God had firmly in mind when He sent Jesus on His great rescue mission. Jesus was the ultimate Deliverer—the perfect Lamb offered once and for all for mankind's sin—and He will be the ultimate Judge, returning in glory to assess the living and the dead from every nation.

Filling the Vacuum—Carefully

> *Now after the death of Joshua it came to pass that the children of Israel asked the LORD, saying, "Who shall be first to go up for us against the Canaanites to fight against them?" And the LORD said, "Judah shall go up. Indeed I have delivered the land into his hand."* (Judges 1:1-2)

There is never a time when we don't need a deliverer. This fallen world can't spring back on its own. After Joshua's death, Israel experienced a leadership vacuum in which all sorts of problems occurred. Though they had some victories, there was an overall decline that centered on forgetfulness. God's own people forgot their history—more specifically, they forgot their God, who had delivered them and appointed strong human leadership for them as part of His general provision for them.

The book of Judges depicts a society that had forsaken its moral underpinnings and fallen prey to classic existentialism—everyone doing what was right in his own eyes.[8] The people blindly refused to acknowledge their great need and turned to a personalized form of moral relativism. Once they discarded the value system upon which God had built them, they were fair prey for their own worst natures. Obeying God was the ultimate moral value that united the nation under a common banner. When they held firmly to God, He gave them victory over their enemies.

God assigned the tribe of Judah to take the lead in battles against local menaces. Why is this noteworthy? Hundreds of years later, Jesus, "the Lion of the tribe of Judah" (Revelation 5:5), would rise from the grave to lead many to spiritual victory. But even so, we as Christians still battle the tendencies of our fallen nature,[9] and still wrangle with the enemy.[10] The fight exists on physical, psychological, and spiritual levels—but Jesus conquered them all at the cross. The deliverer mankind calls for is the Deliverer God provided.

A Short Memory Loses the Cultural Battle

*When all that generation had been gathered to their fathers,
another generation arose after them who did not know the
LORD nor the work which He had done for Israel. Then the
children of Israel did evil in the sight of the LORD, and served
the Baals.* (Judges 2:10-11)

Ronald Reagan once said, "Freedom is never more than one generation away from extinction."[11] And God's people are never more than
one generation away from apostasy. Every generation is a blank can-
vas, primed for God's artistic hand to shape—but the tendency is to
forget the previous generation's paintings! With each successive era,
the people of Israel forgot their redemptive past. They forgot about
the fall in Eden and the bloody sacrifices required to cover Adam and
Eve's shame; they forgot about the Passover lambs in Egypt and the
need for sprinkled blood on the mercy seat. During the period of the
judges, they forget their desperate need for God, and redemption's
thread faded from scarlet to a pale pink.

Every time God was with Israel, He gave them victory. They
were always outnumbered, outmanned, outgunned—the key factor wasn't their material power but their commitment to God. He
told His people to drive out the inhabitants of Canaan because He
knew that their pagan beliefs would water down Israel's commitment to follow Him. Sure enough, a pattern quickly developed. The
Israelites would leave a remnant of their foes in the land, either putting them under tribute or letting them live side by side with them.[12]
Maybe they were thinking, *These folks aren't so bad; surely we can all
just get along.*

Being neighborly with those who don't share your beliefs is
commendable, but in ancient times it could be fatal, and God had
instructed Israel to do otherwise. When they didn't, it came back to
haunt them. Israel didn't turn to atheism or agnosticism but *syncretism*:
They incorporated the attitudes and practices of the surrounding culture into their beliefs. They added ungodly practices to their worship of
God, diluting it so that they became ineffective. Eventually they forgot

about God and what He had done for them, and put themselves at the mercy of wrong practices and attitudes.

There's a tendency to do the same today. "Coexist" is one of the most popular bumper stickers in our country, urging Christians in particular to "lighten up" and realize all religions are essentially the same, and that we can learn things from other religious points of view. The problem, of course, is that none of these other belief systems can provide a true deliverance from sin—because none accept God's true Deliverer.

Having Jesus as your Savior means that you've been delivered from the ultimate condemnation of sin, but having Him as Lord means you bring Him into every part of your life, trusting that the Holy Spirit will alert you to issues you need to address in your life. The time you take to remember who God is and what He has done for you protects you from falling into the sin cycle.

Anticipating the Judge of All the Earth

> *They forsook the LORD and served Baal and the Ashtoreths...*
> *And they were greatly distressed. Nevertheless, the LORD raised*
> *up judges who delivered them out of the hand of those who*
> *plundered them.* (Judges 2:13, 15-16)

When God let His people reap the consequences of their spiritual infidelity, He had two purposes in mind. First, while they were under the thumb of their oppressors, they would eventually realize that serving God was much more satisfying. Whatever urges they had gratified by worshipping false gods faded, replaced by the shame and guilt of temporary pleasure. They realized that only by following God could they have internal peace. That peace, however, required them to take an outward stance against worldly practices and ways of thinking.

God's second purpose was that they "might be taught to know war" (Judges 3:2). The generations that kept falling into captivity hadn't been involved in the big military campaigns under Joshua. They hadn't seen God's hand at work for themselves, hadn't seen the Lord defeat their enemies in stunning and miraculous ways—and so they took Him for granted. For them, the Law of Moses was just a set of religious rules their ancestors had followed. It was old-fashioned, and all the Canaanite people around them seemed to be having much more fun in their religious experiences with their wild celebrations and sex rituals. But when the Israelites' disobedience led to their captivity, and their captivity led them to cry out for God's help, God raised up judges—deliverers who led them in battles for freedom from their enemies. This pattern happened again and again and again.

But even though God had definite purposes in His judgment, His judges were only temporary deliverers. As mighty as their deeds were, they couldn't change the people's hearts. That's why the cycle of sin kept being repeated during the few-hundred-year period of the judges. But all along, the very concept of a delivering judge served to point to the ultimate Deliverer and Judge, Jesus Christ.

One day, Jesus will return and judge everyone, living and dead.[13] He is the only one in the position to do so; after all, He accepted the judgment for all sin upon Himself at the cross. The only way for anyone to avoid condemnation in light of His holiness and righteous judgment is to receive His deliverance. Sin is real and God will judge it, yet Christ's mercy and power to deliver us from sin is also real. But unlike the temporary deliverance of Israel's judges, the deliverance that Jesus offers is permanent.

Breaking the Cycle

> *In those days there was no king in Israel; everyone did what was right in his own eyes.* (Judges 21:25)

Judges ends on the sourest of notes because of both individual and national failures to honor God. His intention was for Israel to represent Him well to the world. The whole role of these judges was to demonstrate that the Israelites had failed at that task—and also to bail them out of the trouble into which they'd gotten themselves. The sin cycle, however, kept repeating itself, indicating that these deliverances were temporary at best.

But even then, God's ultimate purposes won't be foiled; even in the harshest of circumstances, His loving mercy stretches out, looking for hungry hearts, ready to forgive and save. Because of Israel's infidelity, redemption's tapestry often threatened to unravel. But God, in His faithfulness, tightened it again each time.

That's why the sin cycle of the Old Testament isn't the final word. One day the leadership vacuum will be filled permanently. Instead of the misery of Judges 21:25, the reality will be "Jesus is King in Israel and everyone will do what is right in His eyes." He will return as "KING OF KINGS AND LORD OF LORDS" (Revelation 19:16). Clothed with a "robe dipped in blood," He will take His rightful place and reign (Revelation 19:13). After His return and quelling of the earthly uprising of Armageddon, His rule will end all wars as nations "beat their swords into plowshares, and their spears into pruning hooks" (Isaiah 2:4). Temporary conflicts and the need for local judges to bring deliverance will be over. Jesus, the Judge of all and the earth's everlasting King, will make sure everything is right in His eyes—both in the world and for each individual who trusts in Him.

> Providence means that God superintends the affairs of humanity and orchestrates them to suit His divine purposes.

A REDEEMER IN THE SHADOWS

Providence means that God superintends the affairs of humanity and orchestrates them to suit His divine purposes. No matter what happens or what choices people make, in the end, His will prevails. That's the overarching reality of all of history, especially redemptive history. God "works all things according to the counsel of His will" (Ephesians 1:11).

The book of Ruth is a short romance novel. It is also a story of choices made and how God, in His sovereignty, superintended them all. Elimelech chose to move his family from Bethlehem to Moab; his widow Naomi chose to stay there as her sons married local women. When her sons died, one of those daughters-in-law, Ruth, chose to stay with Naomi no matter what, and to follow Naomi's God. Ruth chose to go out and find work, no matter how menial, to support Naomi.

And Boaz chose to step into a hopeless situation and love Ruth and Naomi, seeking the best possible outcome for them.

God orchestrated all those options and decisions, putting the right people in the right place at the right time, both for the good of those who trusted in Him and to further His plan to send the Messiah. In the shadows of the story is a man of Bethlehem, Boaz, who foreshadowed another man from Bethlehem, the Lord Jesus Christ. Boaz is the hero of this story, playing the role of redeemer, saving a family from overwhelming debt and making a Gentile woman his bride. Sound familiar? It's a striking parallel to Christ's redemption, which made a largely Gentile church the "bride of Christ."[14] Furthermore, Boaz and Ruth's son preserved the royal bloodline from which descended both King David and the King of kings, Jesus Christ.

More than anything, the book of Ruth shows us how God chose us and paid the highest price to be able to call us His beloved children.

God Is into the Details

> *The LORD repay your work, and a full reward be given you by the LORD God of Israel, under whose wings you have come for refuge.* (Ruth 2:12)

After a series of family tragedies that included the loss of property, a stint as refugees in search of food, and the death of three husbands, Naomi and Ruth returned to Bethlehem. There, the brokenness that they had experienced began to take a turn. Hope loomed on the horizon for these two women. God was afoot and at work.

The name *Bethlehem* comes from two Hebrew words. *Beit* means "a house" or "a place"; *lechem* means "bread." Bethlehem, then, means "the House of Bread," or simply "Place of Bread"—likely named for the prolific grain industry in this area, enjoyed even in Ruth's time. For us, though, its enticing aroma points us to the other hero of the story, as the birthplace of the one who said, "I am the bread of life. He who comes to Me shall never hunger" (John 6:35). What seems to be an interesting but not particularly significant detail is in reality an important part of God's overarching design. A story of redemption happened in a place that fed Israel, and it pointed to the ultimate redemption achieved by Christ as He gave Himself to purchase eternal life for us. The scarlet thread is woven throughout that bigger picture; there's no escaping its reach, just as there is no detail that goes unnoticed by God.

> God loves you. And as in any great romance, love drives His pursuit of you.

During all life's busyness, the rollercoaster of the good, the bad, and the ugly, we often lose sight of the ride itself—that bigger picture that God always sees. And in the Christian life, it's easy to forget that, amid salvation and sanctification, there is a greater romance at work. God loves you. And as in any great romance, love drives His pursuit of you. Red is associated with love, a color of passion, fitting in Ruth's story because it demonstrates both God's desire for relationship with you and the careful way He has woven His redemptive thread into all the details of your life.

Love compelled God to give His very best for you in Jesus Christ, who in His pursuit of you left the glory of heaven for the pain and turmoil of earth. He will never leave you or forsake you, and He is always trustworthy. God cares about the details of your life and wants to provide for your needs; we see this love on display throughout the story of Ruth and Naomi. Ruth linked herself to the bloodline of the Messiah by faith, tapping into the resilience of hope that God offers.

Because she did so, Ruth's trials did not break her spirit. Following God wasn't something she did to get in good with her mother-in-law; it was a wholehearted pursuit. She knew she had everything to gain from it, so even in the things she didn't understand, she prioritized her relationship with God. The God of Israel in whom she chose to trust is the God who "so loved the world that He gave His only begotten Son" (John 3:16). Ruth chose the God who orchestrated redemptive history and placed her in the genealogy of Israel's Savior.[15]

Heroes of Redemption

> *Boaz took Ruth and she became his wife; and when he went in to her, the LORD gave her conception, and she bore a son.* (Ruth 4:13)

The book of Ruth is about two heroes, both men of Bethlehem. One is *in* the story, and the other is foreshadowed *by* the story. The first is Boaz, a businessman in Bethlehem around 1100 BC, who stepped up for Ruth and Naomi. The other, of course, is Jesus Christ, born in Bethlehem eleven centuries later, who stood up for the world. Boaz was a hero to two women; Jesus was a hero to humanity.

It was Ruth, however, who made a choice that changed history. Even though she was from Moab—a nation outside of God's covenant with Israel—her decision to stick with Naomi and Naomi's God set in motion the next step in the lineage of the Messiah. And Ruth embraced God wholeheartedly, trusting Him for all her needs.

When God brought Boaz into her life and he assumed the role of kinsman-redeemer to keep Ruth and Naomi from disaster, he pointed to the role that Jesus would play at the cross. Boaz put a significant portion of his resources and his reputation on the line to become Ruth's bridegroom, and Jesus set aside His heavenly glory for a season to buy your salvation with His blood. And there is coming a day when He will celebrate His union with His church at the marriage supper of the Lamb.[16]

The road to that future celebration continued through Ruth and Boaz. Their story ended happily, and the scarlet thread of Jesus moved forward through their children and grandchildren. Their first child, Obed, was the grandfather of David, the one whose throne God would establish both in history and for eternity.

You Are His Treasure

> *May he be to you a restorer of life and a nourisher of your old age; for your daughter-in-law, who loves you, who is better to you than seven sons, has borne him.* (Ruth 4:15)

God's redemption is an act of great love. Boaz, as a relative, met all the legal requirements needed to save Ruth and Naomi from destitution and to perpetuate their family's inheritance in Israel.[17] More than that, he was also willing to step in and save them. He was willing to buy the land and to marry a non-Jewish bride—not only out of duty, but because he genuinely loved Ruth. He didn't want the field he bought; he wanted her.

When Jesus came to save the world, He didn't want the world for its own sake. He made the world and everything in it, He holds it all together, and one day He will let it go and make a new one. Out of everything the world has to offer, He wanted only you. You are His treasure, the one He loves enough to give of Himself entirely.

In the parable of the hidden treasure,[18] Jesus gave everything He had so He could buy mankind back from sin's fatal grasp (though some interpret the parable's meaning in a different way). But Jesus had the heavenly mandate to do so from God the Father, and the legal right because He came from the human lineage of David, whose great grandfather was Boaz.[19]

In Revelation 5, the kinsmen-redeemer scenario portrayed in Ruth is played out in heaven with much higher stakes. John reported that God held a scroll in His right hand—indicating its authority—and an angel asked who had the authority to open it, but "no one in heaven or on the earth or under the earth was able to open the scroll, or to look at it" (v. 3). This scroll was nothing less than the title deed to the earth, handed over by God to Adam in Eden, who promptly handed it over to Satan through his disobedience and exile from the garden. In another letter, John confirmed that, for now, the devil oversees the world's ways, values, and systems,[20] and later, in exile on Patmos, he wept at the thought that it would always be so.

But an angel told John that the "Lion of the tribe of Judah, the Root of David" (v. 5) had prevailed and was able to open the scroll and claim its holdings. Like Boaz, Jesus was qualified by law and right to redeem. First, He was a near relative—accomplished when He became human, one of us, to save us. Second, He was able to pay the price for sin as the only perfect and innocent man ever. Third, Jesus was willing to pay. He chose the cross and said of His life, "No one takes it from Me, but I lay it down of Myself. I have power to lay it down, and I have power to take it again" (John 10:18). Adam lost the land, and Jesus, as the second Adam, was the only one worthy to take it back.[21]

What Boaz did was remarkable in its loving sacrifice and tenderness, but the true power and beauty of the book of Ruth is a human love story that points to the ultimate story of God's love for all people. There is a divine romance involved in our redemption!

THE KING IS COMING

THE MONARCHY:
1 and 2 Samuel, 1 and 2 Kings, 1 and 2 Chronicles

The Messiah's bloodline had traveled a long way as Israel moved from tribal leadership to a united monarchy. God's people cried out for a ruler, but even at the height of Israel's brief yet considerable glory and splendor under David and Solomon, the nation struggled to fully embrace their true King. The history of the kings is a powerful and often painful reminder of mankind's inability to solve its greatest problem—sin and its effects on the human heart.

Our basic issue always comes down to this: Who will reign over our hearts? Politics are a necessary institution in an imperfect society, but no system, party, or leader will ever be able to fix this sin-broken world. In the monarchies of Israel and Judah, however, God wove His scarlet thread of hope, promising that a King would one day come and set all to rights—first as a Lamb, and later as a Lion.

The kings of the Bible should remind us that no matter how powerful, influential, or wealthy a person may be, true leadership begins in the heart. The history of the monarchy of Israel was pretty straightforward. As long as God was reigning over a specific king's heart, that king was a good ruler. When God wasn't, the king wasn't either. No leader will ever be perfect, but any leader can seek the highest possible good of the ones he or she leads—something David touched on and Jesus demonstrated at the cross. We'll look at the progression and dissolution of Israel's monarchy in chronological order, moving freely through various books to get a sense of God's rescue operation as it unfolded.

Waiting on the King of Kings

> *The adversaries of the LORD shall be broken in pieces; from heaven He will thunder against them. The LORD will judge the ends of the earth. "He will give strength to His king, and exalt the horn of His anointed."* (1 Samuel 2:10)

What the prophet Samuel learned as he anointed David the next king—that God appraises the inner man over the outward appearance—we see in contrast with Saul's self-centeredness. Character always trumps countenance. In David's son Solomon, we see God's wisdom and mercy, but we also see the cost of self-indulgence. Integrity always trumps ingenuity. In all the kings that followed—so many more bad ones than good ones—we see God's faithfulness to fulfill His prophecy. Providence always trumps perniciousness. Nothing could thwart the coming of God's Messiah. Amazingly, of all these rulers over God's people, only David's heart was truly God's throne.

David was called a man after God's own heart[1]—not because he was perfect, but because whether he succeeded or failed, he always turned to God. He always came back to a place of worship and humility in his life because he was desperate for what God wants most with us: fellowship. Even though we should learn from David's mistakes—and they were big ones—we should always strive to follow his example in seeking God in the best and worst of times. Furthermore, David had the heart of a shepherd, developed during his days in the fields watching over his father's flocks. And Jesus called Himself the good shepherd,[2] the one whose voice His sheep know as He watches over them on His Father's behalf. David clearly heard and followed his Shepherd's voice, and his open heart was all too rare among Israel's leaders.

Given the poor leadership Israel experienced under so many of its kings, it makes sense to ask, "Did God really want Israel to have a king?" After all, when God told Samuel to appoint Israel a king in accordance with their requests, He said, "Heed the voice of the people…for they have not rejected you, but they have rejected Me, that I should not reign over them" (1 Samuel 8:7). It was the same pattern they had followed since they left Egypt, an inevitable pull toward idolatry. In this case, they insisted on putting a man on an earthly throne, a pale imitation of Almighty God ruling from His throne in heaven.

> When we give in to impatience and act out of fear rather than faith, we're likely to miss what God is doing.

Even when Samuel warned the people what having a king would mean—conscripting their sons for his armies and their daughters to work in his palace, taxing their crops and taking their firstfruits to feed his officers—they still wanted to be like all the other nations and have a king to tell them what to do.

The truth is that God had always planned to set a king over His people—it just wasn't the king they thought they wanted. Back in Genesis, Jacob's messianic prophecy included the promise that the "scepter shall not depart from Judah, nor a lawgiver from between his feet, until Shiloh comes" (Genesis 49:10). *Shiloh* means "the one to whom it belongs," a reference to Israel's true King, the Messiah.

Now, Saul came from the tribe of Benjamin, but the king God wanted for Israel, David, would come from the tribe of Judah—as would Israel's true King, Jesus Christ. We see that foretold in Hannah's prayer in 1 Samuel 2, where she praised God for defeating His enemies and strengthening His ultimate King—His "anointed," which in Hebrew is *mashiach*, or *Messiah*.

The gospel requires a certain patience—a trust that, however long it takes, God is working out all things for the benefit of His people and for His glory. When we give in to impatience and act out of fear rather than faith, we're likely to miss what God is doing, just as Israel did in demanding a human king. God would give them what they asked for, but all of Israel's kings were at best flawed and imperfect shadows of the great King to come. Nevertheless, God confirmed His plans for a Messiah who would be both David's creator and his descendant.

Play Your Part

> *Behold, a son shall be born to you, who shall be a man of*
> *rest; and I will give him rest from all his enemies all around.*
> (1 Chronicles 22:9)

David's great deeds mark many famous passages in the Old Testament. From protecting his flocks by killing lions and bears to slaying Goliath to his principled and skillful evasion of Saul's manhunt to his many military victories, he became the most beloved figure in the history of Israel's monarchy. The key to his accomplishments, which he freely acknowledged, was that in everything he did well, the Lord his God was with him.

That's why, when God informed David that he would not be building the temple because he was a man of violent deeds, David didn't sulk. More than anything else, he wanted God to be glorified, and that's why he rejoiced when God told him that his son Solomon would be the one to build the temple, and that Solomon would be a man of rest. The very name *Solomon* means "peace" or "rest," and it abundantly marked Solomon's wise reign. But it didn't stop there. After all the bad kings that came after Solomon, after all the conflicts that have scarred our planet since, peaceful rest will be the preeminent feature of the universal reign of the greater Son of David, Jesus. Isaiah even dubbed Him the "Prince of Peace" (Isaiah 9:6).

David's story also includes his failures—impatience in honoring God's ark, adultery, poor parenting decisions—but the central theme of his life was that he had spiritual priorities. He wanted what God wanted. That led to a lot of success, and it helped him overcome a lot of failure. David understood the bigger picture—that he was just playing his part in the greater story of God's interactions with mankind. He would have wholeheartedly embraced what his descendant, the Messiah, said about the work of serving the Lord: "One sows and another reaps" (John 4:37).

Paul put it this way: "I planted, Apollos watered, but God gave the increase. So then neither he who plants is anything, nor he who waters, but God who gives the increase" (1 Corinthians 3:6-7). David's example to us, then, is to keep our focus on God, the one who enables and ultimately accomplishes His work. That's key to how Christ builds His church—each of us submitting to Him as we play the part He has for us.

The Forever Throne

> *He shall build a house for My name, and I will establish the throne of his kingdom forever...And your house and your kingdom shall be established forever before you. Your throne shall be established forever.* (2 Samuel 7:13, 16)

Second Samuel 7 marks a pivotal point. The message of the Bible from here onward rests on the shoulders of God's covenant made with David. Whereas David envisioned building God a physical house— a temple—God told David He would build him a dynastic house—a lineage, a bloodline that would eventually birth His Messiah. We see in God's covenant seven *I will*'s—indicators that this promise is unconditional, centering on what God would do, not on anything David or anyone else would do.[3]

The covenant worked on two levels: First, God promised that David's son, Solomon, would build the temple and sit in peace on the throne God had given David. Second, God would establish that throne forever. In that sense, Solomon was a type of a greater Son of David, Jesus Christ (in the Bible, male descendants even in distant generations were called *sons*). And though David's dynasty would be interrupted by the Babylonian captivity, his throne will be restored when Jesus returns to set up His kingdom on earth.

Even though David wanted to honor God with a temple because of all that God had done for him and Israel, God reminded him that God's plans supersede man's plans. David learned here that you can't outgive God. The best way to honor God is to listen to Him and obey. If He tells you to take action, act in faith. If He tells you to sit still, wait in faith. If He tells you to give, give in faith, cheerfully and with expectation that God is going to do something greater than you can possibly imagine.

When David sought to build God a house, God told him, "That's fine, but actually, I'm going to build *you* a house." He promised David a lineage that worked on two levels: the near future, and the distant future. "I will be his Father, and he shall be My son; and I will not take My mercy away from him, as I took it from him who was before you. And I will establish him in My house and in My kingdom forever; and his throne shall be established forever" (1 Chronicles 17:13-14).

In the generations to come, David's descendants would occupy Israel's throne. In the long term, Jesus would come as Israel's true King and Deliverer, but would go unrecognized. He announced to Pilate, "My kingdom is not of this world" (John 18:36). But that was then. The plan all along was for Him to eventually return and set up an earthly kingdom as "King of kings and Lord of lords" (see Revelation 17:14; 19:16). And when Jesus does return, He will occupy David's throne in Jerusalem and rule from it for 1,000 years.

The angel Gabriel told Mary that her Son "will be great, and will be called the Son of the Highest; and the Lord God will give Him the throne of His father David. And He will reign over the house of Jacob forever, and of His kingdom there will be no end" (Luke 1:32-33). Based on the promise God made here in 1 Chronicles 17, the Jews understood that the one called the Son of David would be the Messiah. That's why Matthew was quick to establish the connection in his Gospel, beginning with these words: "The book of the genealogy of Jesus Christ, the Son of David..." (Matthew 1:1).

And David understood the prophetic length of God's promise. Peter later began his famous post-Pentecost sermon by establishing that David foresaw his descendant being the Messiah, the one who would provide hope of eternal life with God by His resurrection.[4] It's hard to fully grasp the prophetic picture that God has painted over thousands of years without comprehending this pivotal promise.

The throne that God established for David also reflected Christ's work on the cross—a covenant and future kingdom written in cleansing blood. David, as a man of war, would not build the temple, but his life's work made it possible for his son to do so. Solomon would reign in peace because of what God accomplished in and through David.

Pointing the Way to the One

> *You have shown great mercy to Your servant David my father, because he walked before You in truth, in righteousness, and in uprightness of heart with You.* (1 Kings 3:6)

Solomon's request to God to make him wise enough to rule His people showed a humble heart and mature faith. He had seen the faith of his father, David, and had seen God bless David and all of Israel because of it. "Solomon sat on the throne of his father David; and his kingdom was firmly established" (1 Kings 2:12). Solomon had inherited a kingdom at peace, secure within its walls and throughout its borders. His reign would be an unprecedented (and unrepeated) time in Israel's history, marked by prosperity and godly governance. The kingdom was strong and the people were safe. Rulers and dignitaries traveled from far and wide to visit Solomon's court, to see its splendor and hear his wisdom.

As amazing as all this was, it was just a taste of what Christ's reign will be like. The wisdom God gave Solomon helped save an infant, and all Israel "feared the king, for they saw that the wisdom of God was in him to administer justice" (1 Kings 3:28). Jesus was similarly respected for the authority with which He solved problems and taught God's Word. And during His coming millennial reign, every knee will bow at the mention of His name.[5] People from the surrounding nations will also flow into Messiah's capital seeking wisdom and justice.[6] The earth will be lush, verdant, holy, peaceful, and welcoming.[7]

However, when Solomon began to please himself rather than God, he lost the thread, and so lost his way and the loyalty of his subjects. By contrast, Jesus will rule eternally: "Blessing and honor and glory and power be to Him who sits on the throne, and to the Lamb, forever and ever!" (Revelation 5:13). Solomon's wisdom and kingdom were glorious, but they were merely a glimpse of the wonders and astonishment that will characterize the reign of Christ.

Your Heart, God's Temple

> *Now Solomon began to build the house of the LORD at*
> *Jerusalem on Mount Moriah, where the LORD had appeared*
> *to his father David, at the place that David had prepared on*
> *the threshing floor of Ornan the Jebusite.* (2 Chronicles 3:1)

David wanted to honor God by building Him a permanent house in Jerusalem. He acquired the resources and made the plans, but then God informed him that because he had been God's instrument of war to create peace for Israel, he wasn't fit to build a holy temple. Instead, God would give David a son who would fulfill his heart's desire, a man of peace in a time of peace to build a house of worship.

The beginning of construction on the temple was in keeping with God's promise, which established that the lineage of the Messiah would come through David. For a time, David's descendants, beginning with his son Solomon, would sit on Israel's throne. Ultimately, though, they would just be keeping it warm in their own imperfect ways for its greatest occupant, Jesus Christ. God's pledge helps us to make sense of a couple of details about Jesus's life. It helps us understand why Jesus was to be born in Bethlehem, David's birthplace and site of his coronation, because He was from the "lineage of David" (Luke 2:4). Second Chronicles 3:1 helps us to understand the crucifixion, for Jesus would die at Golgotha, the place of public execution that lay on the outcropping of Mount Moriah, not far from where the temple stood. It's no mere coincidence that this hill was where Abraham almost sacrificed his son and that it was also the place where God's temple would be built.

Building the temple of God was Solomon's greatest accomplishment. The splendor of his reign provided a fleeting example of what it will be like when Jesus returns and establishes His kingdom in Jerusalem. Jesus will one day have a physical throne on earth in Jerusalem, and in the new earth to come, He will be the temple and the source of light and life for everyone.[8]

In the meantime, however, Jesus's throne is in human hearts.[9] All who believe in Him as Lord are filled with His Spirit, effectively becoming His temple.[10] Though battles remain against the flesh and the devil, the war is over. Jesus won, and we can worship Him in spirit and truth from a place of victory.

The Invisible War

> *You shall surround the king on all sides, every man with his weapons in his hand; and whoever comes within range, let him be put to death. You are to be with the king as he goes out and as he comes in.* (2 Kings 11:8)

While the war is won, the battles remain—especially in the spiritual realm, where Satan refuses to go down quietly. If you're familiar with the Four Spiritual Laws (that simplified and effective version of sharing the good news of salvation), you'll recall that the first law says, "God loves you and has a wonderful plan for your life." Did you know the opposite is equally true? Satan hates you and has a miserable plan for your life! What is true personally is also true universally. God's good plan for humanity has always been met with Satan's bad one.

In naming Solomon as the son of David through whom the throne would be established forever, God also identified Solomon as the next in line to produce the crusher of Satan's head, thus painting a target on the back of the young king and all the rest of David's descendants.

Despite Solomon's good start, he forsook his God-given wisdom, forgetting that it was a gift that reflected not great intellect but a great heart for God. Second Kings is the sad story of how Israel reaped the consequences of their rejection of God's love—which opened the door for Satan's influence. Primarily through failures of leadership, on both political and spiritual levels, Satan worked relentlessly to terminate the messianic line of David. Because Israel was the nation at the center of God's promise to destroy him, Satan looked to snuff out the light at its earthly source.

It's an ongoing plotline in the Old Testament: From Cain and Abel to the flood, from Pharaoh's slaughter of Israel's firstborn to Haman's attempted genocide on Esther, the devil looked to disrupt God's plans. Here in 2 Kings, he worked through the evil Athaliah to slaughter the entire bloodline of the royal household. Only the baby king, Joash, was saved[11]—but that was enough to keep God's plan to redeem mankind going.

The wickedness of Israel and Judah's monarchies was rooted in the spiritual realm, in Satan's ongoing war to thwart God's plan to crush his dominion over the world. Ever since the promise given in Genesis 3:15, the devil has been on the counterattack, realizing that for God to fulfill His promise through a chosen people, that people had to survive to produce the Messiah. End that bloodline, and the promise comes to nothing. But God's plans aren't easily opposed. And so Cain killed Abel, but God gave Adam and Eve another son, Seth. Satan's influence created such havoc that God flooded the world, yet saved Noah and his family. Esau chose the way of the flesh, but God didn't let him kill Jacob, the father of the twelve tribes of Israel.

> God can provide you with purpose, a life full of meaning because of its connection to His sovereign power and merciful ways—that's the power of the bloodline.

Pharaoh couldn't kill all the baby boys in Goshen, so Moses returned to lead Israel out of slavery. Again and again, Satan's agents—Saul, Haman, Athaliah—attempted to cut off the Messiah's lineage, but through God's providence—seen in David, Esther, and Joash, among others—the bloodline remained unbroken.

Even in the most tumultuous of times, when the fate of the kingdom seemed to rest in evil hands, God still had His people on the job, some operating in the public eye, like the prophet Elisha, and many others working behind the scenes for His purposes. Whether it was Jehu carrying out the bloody political machinations needed to get rid of Ahab and his cronies or the priests and soldiers who secured the baby Joash until the throne could be stabilized, God's purposes were not thwarted. Once dubbed "the invisible war" by Donald Grey Barnhouse,[12] this spiritual conflict rages around God's plan of salvation for the world. Because the bloodline would become our lifeline, Satan perpetually tried to disrupt the redemptive landscape with fault lines. God keeps all His promises. He promised a Messiah, and all of hell's forces couldn't prevail against that royal lineage, though they hammered away at it for millennia. Nothing will prevent Jesus from returning, either, and establishing His kingdom on earth. Surely a God who can do such things against such odds can also watch out for you and your needs. Even better, He can provide you with purpose, a life full of meaning because of its connection to His sovereign power and merciful ways—that's the power of the bloodline. Many of Israel's and Judah's rulers lost the thread, forsaking God for religious and political expedience, and bringing ruin on their subjects.

The Battlefield of the Heart

He did evil, because he did not prepare his heart to seek the LORD. (2 Chronicles 12:14)

His heart took delight in the ways of the LORD. (2 Chronicles 17:6)

Contrasting these two verses sums up the spiritual battle for Israel's monarchy. Some chose to follow God and prospered; most chose not to, resulting in disaster. Satan's assault on the messianic bloodline continued throughout a long history of generally miserable kings—but a few chose to stick with God. Second Chronicles is, in that sense, a collection of narrow escapes.

When Solomon's son Rehoboam abandoned his pursuit of God, the kingdom split into two separate nations: Israel to the north, and Judah to the south. Since the messianic scepter would not depart from Judah's hand, Satan focused primarily on bringing down the southern kingdom. He used a tactic similar to the one that worked on Solomon: the influence of false religion. Solomon's ridiculous number of wives and concubines brought idolatry into his life and took his eyes off his God. This subtle, pervasive strategy upended many a king of Judah who started well, focusing on the Lord, but whose loyalty was to expedience and self-gratification.

To follow God wholeheartedly is to march to the beat of a different drummer. Jehoshaphat was that rare king who "sought the God of his father, and walked in His commandments" (v. 4)—like David and unlike most of the kings before him, who had led Israel to destruction through idolatry. It's not easy to swim against the cultural tide, to go against what everyone else is doing. It's tough to stand alone, but if you're standing for God, you're never truly by yourself. God blessed Jehoshaphat because he stood for God.

Notice the source of Jehoshaphat's faith: He "took delight" in God's ways. Like the future Savior who announced His own delight in God by saying, "I always do those things that please Him" (John 8:29), Jesus's ancestor, Jehoshaphat, was an exceptional king—that is, he was an exception to the general rule. Kings like Joash, Amaziah, and Uzziah started well and finished poorly. As long as they trusted God, He blessed them, prospering their subjects and delivering them from their enemies. But when they began to take God for granted, things fell apart.

The attitude that proved ruinous for so many of these kings lives on in the human heart. We are naturally rebellious against authority. We feel that God's ways will limit our freedom, and on some level we either resist connecting with His bloodline or we deliberately disconnect, choosing what seems right to us. And God's Word often checks us, reminding us that the way we're going about our business doesn't match up with God's desire. Rather than submit to God, we make excuses, justifying our behavior and resisting Him. Our basic problem isn't low self-esteem but pride; we think we know better than God. We love ourselves more than we love Him. We want people to think we're all that, even as we know somewhere inside that we're not. We rebel even as we know our rebellion is futile. That's what the devil counts on—and from a limited perspective, it works all too effectively.

Whether by subtle manipulation or direct rebellion, the kings of Israel and Judah moved their nations down the road to exile. For every step forward—the destruction of the high places of idol worship by Hezekiah or Josiah, there were two steps backward—Manasseh, Jehoahaz, Jehoiakim, and Jehoiachin each led the final charge away from God and into Babylon's hands. Satan, of course, took this as an ultimate victory; surely the messianic line would be disrupted, polluted in captivity beyond redemption.

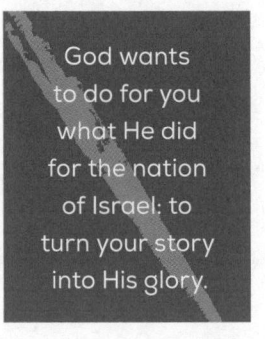

God wants to do for you what He did for the nation of Israel: to turn your story into His glory.

But God's redemptive tapestry covers a far greater span than any of us could ever imagine. While Satan's scheming carried real-world ramifications, it still fell short of ultimate success, and the kings of Israel and Judah rebelled in futility. Their failure to follow God with any level of consistency split the nation, which diminished from affluence and influence to poverty and paralysis. Despite their massive shortcomings, God never stopped pursuing His people, even into the exile their idolatry brought them to. Prophets like Elijah and Elisha brought warnings and worked miracles to "course-correct" God's people and to show them that they were still on His mind and in His heart.

In the scarlet thread that God was weaving throughout Israel's history, His faithfulness is unmistakable. Let it remind you that your value comes from Him. He made you, loves you, and wants good things for you—better than you want for yourself. Jesus dying on the cross is God saying, "I love you enough to give you My very best." To realize your need and receive His gift of freedom from sin is your first experience of delighting in His ways. To continue, you need to walk in the Spirit so that you won't walk after your flesh.[13] God wants to do for you what He did for the nation of Israel: to turn your story into His glory. The sad tale of Israel's monarchy demonstrates God's sovereign hand over all of history. It's His story, woven throughout with a unifying thread as red as blood.

BEYOND FATE AND NATURE

AFTER THE MONARCHY:
Ezra, Nehemiah, and Esther

Alexander Pope wrote, "A God without dominion, providence, and final causes, is nothing else but fate and nature."[1] Conversely, then, God can be identified when He displays all three—He gets the results He wants in the end, both by direct and indirect action. Israel's exile ended as God had promised it would,[2] and under the guise of the favor of the king of Persia, God arranged for the Jewish people to return and rebuild Jerusalem. Within the kingdom of Persia itself, God saved His people from genocide through Mordecai and Esther—two Jews who chose to rise to the occasion, praying, fasting, and putting their reputations and lives on the line. To the average observer, it all looked like fate and nature, but from God's perspective, it was all part of His plan to preserve the line of the Messiah and save the world from the fate occasioned by sin.

During Israel's captivity in Babylon, God's plan of redemption seemed to hang by a thread. But, as we've seen, this was no ordinary thread. The exile looked like a victory for Satan, but in fact it was the result of God's chastening hand, giving His people a good spanking for their disobedience and unfaithfulness but always planning to restore them to both their land and a good relationship with Him.

In the books of Ezra, Nehemiah, and Esther, we see God's sovereign hand overruling the dark plans of the enemy. Ezra wrote of God fulfilling His promise to restore Israel to the Promised Land and reforming her spiritual character, part of His ultimate plan to do both on a permanent basis in the millennial kingdom. Similarly, the book of Nehemiah focuses on a hopeful quest to rebuild Jerusalem's walls, population, and passion for God. Meanwhile, the story of Esther shows us that even when God doesn't seem to be present or at work in everyday circumstances, He is always behind the scenes, guiding and directing people's actions—whether they're aware of it or not—and moving the pieces on the board toward His ultimate goals, the salvation of individuals all over the world and the restoration of His chosen nation through His Messiah.

> God is always behind the scenes, guiding and directing people's actions... and moving the pieces on the board toward His ultimate goals.

THE GREAT REFORMER

Ezra was a Jewish scribe and a priest. His book provides proof that God keeps His promises. Through Jeremiah, He had promised that Israel would return from exile—that the people would not only return but would also call upon His name.[3] Under Ezra's spiritual leadership, we see them doing just that. And in so doing, God preserved the messianic line and revived the people's messianic hope. Just as Ezra worked to restore them spiritually, Jesus came to restore our hearts to God.

Regarding the scribes of His day, Jesus noted, "You search the Scriptures, for in them you think you have eternal life; and these are they which testify of Me" (John 5:39). As a scribe himself, Ezra would have nodded along with Jesus's follow-up statement: "But you are not willing to come to Me that you may have life" (v. 40). Like Jesus, Ezra was committed to a deeper application of God's truth as explained in His Word—the cutting of that sword that both lays the heart open and offers repair and healing.

Ezra's work in Israel's spiritual reformation reminds us that God's truly effective reformers weren't those who turned God's people to greater acts of holy-looking behavior, but those who turned the hearts of the people back to their Maker in both holy awe and grateful love. Ezra's example shows us what it means to draw close to our Lord and Savior, the greatest reformer of the human heart.

Moved by God's Spirit

> *The heads of the fathers' houses of Judah and Benjamin, and the priests and the Levites, with all whose spirits God had moved, arose to go up and build the house of the LORD which is in Jerusalem.* (Ezra 1:5)

Even though the book of Ezra isn't quoted in the New Testament, we can still find the bloodline of redemption here, coursing through the history of Israel's return after exile in Babylon. Ezra recorded the return of a relatively small group of about 50,000 Jews under the leadership of Zerubbabel, a descendant of David and ancestor of Jesus.[4] Also known as "Sheshbazzar the prince of Judah" (Ezra 1:8), Zerubbabel perhaps also represented the hope of restoring David's royal line in Jerusalem.

God also raised up a pair of prophets to encourage the people in their labors to rebuild Jerusalem's walls and temple, Haggai and Zechariah. And Zechariah had a word from God for Zerubbabel, reminding him that all the work he was doing would be impossible without God's help. But with God's help, it would be impossible for it to remain uncompleted! "This is the word of the LORD to Zerubbabel: 'Not by might nor by power, but by My Spirit,' says the LORD of hosts. 'Who are you, O great mountain? Before Zerubbabel you shall become a plain! And he shall bring forth the capstone with shouts of "Grace, grace to it!"'" (Zechariah 4:6-7).

While the rebuilt temple as a structure would not be as glorious as Solomon's temple, the odds against its completion were much greater. Zerubbabel and his builders faced opposition from the foreign locals and lacked the opulent materials that David had supplied to Solomon for building the first temple. This replacement temple could only have been built by the power and intervention of the Holy Spirit, which is no different than the odds Jesus faced in going to the cross and beating death and hell, thus making it possible for every Christian to be a temple of the Holy Spirit.[5] It also points to the temple that will be present in the millennial kingdom.

So far there have been three temples built in Jerusalem: Solomon's temple was the first; Zerubbabel's temple was the second, though reconstructed from the ruins of the first; and Herod the Great's temple, which we find in the New Testament, counts as the third. Most refer to Solomon's and Herod's structures as the first and second temples, both of which were destroyed. Two more temples are coming—one under the direction of the Antichrist, and the final one, the millennial temple, under the authority of Jesus Christ. Daniel and Revelation both speak of a temple present during a terrible time of tribulation,[6] and Paul chimed in, saying that the temple of those final seven years will be the staging area for Antichrist's blasphemous pogroms.[7]

A curious feature of the millennial kingdom (Christ's 1,000-year reign on a refurbished earth) is the presence of another temple, complete with some animal sacrifices. Ezekiel spent nine chapters giving the exact dimensions of a structure that has never been built historically. Many times more massive than any previous temple in Jerusalem, it will be a place for Jewish celebration in the kingdom age. The sheer number of details given to Ezekiel defies any allegorical interpretation. This will be a real future temple in the real city of Jerusalem.

But blood sacrifices? Whatever for? These offerings will not work to take away sin, for Jesus already did that once and for all. Rather, they will point in commemoration back to the cross and Jesus's finished work, much like the Lord's Supper is a memorial feast that looks back to the cross. Just as the sacrifices of Leviticus pointed forward to the cross, these sacrifices will be retrospective. Once the 1,000 years of restored earthly bliss are over, God will get rid of the old heaven and earth and replace them a new, eternal heaven and earth, complete with a capital city, New Jerusalem, with the Lamb (Jesus) as its light. Redemption's crimson cord will have threads extending even into the future!

Reconnecting the Scarlet Thread

> *Jeshua the son of Jozadak and his brethren the priests, and Zerubbabel the son of Shealtiel and his brethren, arose and built the altar of the God of Israel, to offer burnt offerings on it, as it is written in the Law of Moses the man of God.* (Ezra 3:2)

There are subtle but unmistakable references to Christ here. First, in the occupation and character of Ezra, who was a priest committed to ministering to God, and a scribe committed to studying God's Word. Second, in the head priest Jeshua—whose name is the same as Jesus's, *Yeshua*—we see a reflection of Jesus as our "great High Priest" (Hebrews 4:14), who both empathized with our need for redemption and provided the sacrificial means in Himself for it to be accomplished. For some this will seem only coincidental; for others, it's providential.

This also explains why getting the altar constructed was such a priority, along with rebuilding the temple. "From the first day of the seventh month they began to offer burnt offerings to the Lord, although the foundation of the temple of the Lord had not been laid" (Ezra 3:6). These were the first items on the agenda because they were at the center of old covenant worship.[8]

The blood of animal sacrifice provided temporary atonement for sin, anticipating the blood shed by God's sacrificial Lamb, Jesus Christ. His perfect life, symbolized in His perfect blood, provided the only true and complete payment for sin—the only way to buy mankind back from sin and death. Even though Ezra, Jeshua, and Zerubbabel likely wouldn't have grasped the full implications of the rites they were reestablishing, they knew enough about God's requirements in the law to make the resumption of sacrifices their number one priority.

A Heart for God

> *Ezra had prepared his heart to seek the Law of the LORD, and to do it, and to teach statutes and ordinances in Israel.* (Ezra 7:10)

While there's no direct mention of the Messiah in the book of Ezra, we see many of the traits of Jesus in Ezra himself. One of the first things we notice is that Ezra valued the Scriptures. As a scribe, he was committed to studying and preserving the Word of God—but more than that, he loved the God of the Word. He wasn't just a hearer of the Word but a doer, one who both taught the Bible and lived by its guidance because he loved the Guide. Similarly, Jesus loved the Scriptures, lived them, and taught them with authority, submitting fully to His Father.[9]

God used Ezra's passion for the Scriptures to teach the people His law, which would anchor them as they rebuilt Jerusalem and recommitted to following Him. Jesus also knew the law, but more importantly, He knew God's heart behind it. He called out the Jewish religious leaders for losing the plot, getting so caught up in legalistic details that they stopped looking for the one to whom the Scriptures pointed (John 5:39-40).

When the Jews returned from exile, their hearts were primed for revival, ready to receive God's Word and let it change them. Ezra modeled that commitment for them, pouring out his heart before the people in tears of confession and remorse over all the years lost to Israel's infidelity to God.[10] Jesus wept over Jerusalem for similar reasons—specifically, their hardhearted failure to recognize their Messiah.[11]

However, just as God had kept His promise to bring His people back from exile, He would keep His promise to bring His Messiah through the lineage of David, and Ezra records a crucial moment in Israel's historical preservation of redemption's scarlet thread.

GOD LOVES A GOOD RESTORATION PROJECT

The book of Nehemiah demonstrates that Jerusalem is at the center of redemption's map. The Bible always sets its cardinal directions relative to the city of David. It's also the setting for history's pivotal event, the crucifixion of Jesus Christ, and for the final capital, the seat of Christ's kingdom reign. All of that makes it the focal point of prophecy—the target of the enemy down through the ages and the future site of history's final battles.

So when Nehemiah set out to rebuild Jerusalem, he wasn't just taking on the challenge of reconstructing crumbled walls and infrastructure. He was going to the front lines of a spiritual engagement at the epicenter of God's redemptive plan. God wanted Jerusalem rebuilt so that Jesus could be crucified just outside its walls centuries later. Nehemiah's efforts demonstrate God's overriding ability to make a solid path out of broken stones, and His overarching desire to restore hearts and lives for His glory.

Availability Reveals God's Ability

> *They said to me, "The survivors who are left from the captivity*
> *in the province are there in great distress and reproach. The*
> *wall of Jerusalem is also broken down, and its gates are*
> *burned with fire." So it was, when I heard these words, that I*
> *sat down and wept, and mourned for many days; I was fasting*
> *and praying before the God of heaven.* (Nehemiah 1:3-4)

Nehemiah had an important job as the king of Persia's cupbearer—essentially his right-hand man—but when he heard the report of Jerusalem's fallen state, he felt an urgent calling to return and rebuild the city of God. Because he had a vision and a heart for God's people, he dared to ask a difficult question: *Lord, what do You want me to do?* Nehemiah cared. He had heard all his life about the siege and destruction of Jerusalem, but his heart wasn't hardened by the reports. He was willing to give up his position and move out of his comfort zone to answer the call God placed on him.

Nehemiah's sacrifice points to a similar move Jesus made when He chose to come to earth. He "made Himself of no reputation, taking the form of a bondservant, and coming in the likeness of men" (Philippians 2:7). Jesus left the glory of heaven, the face-to-face interaction with God the Father and the Holy Spirit, the perpetual praises of angels, to come live in the squalor of daily human life—the blood, sweat, and

> God tends to use the least likely people to accomplish the greatest of purposes.

tears of our existence. Like Nehemiah, God had given Him a mission, and He was dead-set on fulfilling it.

Furthermore, both Jesus and Nehemiah understood that with God, large doors swing on small hinges. God tends to use the least likely people to accomplish the greatest of purposes. A quick survey of Jesus's apostles underscores that—fishermen, tax collectors, zealots, none of them likely to play crucial roles in changing the world, but all of them willing to lay down their lives to do so.

Nehemiah understood that Jerusalem's broken walls meant no defense against outside attacks and no security for families inside. He reacted to the great need and took action, as did Jesus in view of mankind's inability to overcome the pervasive destruction of sin. Nehemiah let what breaks God's heart break his, foreshadowing the anguish Jesus would feel when He saw sin's effects and the rejection of God's salvation by His own people.

What Nehemiah modeled and Jesus accomplished should remind us that redemption's scarlet thread winds on, even today. With Christ as your Lord and Savior, you are connected to His bloodline, and part of His plan is to use to you help others get connected too. So your reaction to need is vital. It's what initially moves you to action. What makes you laugh or cry reveals a lot about your character.

God wants your heart to break over the things that break His, but He also wants you to remember that He has no limitations as to what He can do when you're willing to serve Him. God doesn't want forced laborers, but hearts willing to commit to His agenda. That's what connects you to God's great rescue mission—that combination of tenderheartedness, courage, and faith that will make you a productive agent for God's purposes.

The Anger of Love

I came to Jerusalem and discovered the evil that Eliashib had done for Tobiah, in preparing a room for him in the courts of

the house of God. And it grieved me bitterly; therefore I threw
all the household goods of Tobiah out of the room. Then I
commanded them to cleanse the rooms. (Nehemiah 13:7-9)

Nehemiah faced opposition from some of the pagan tribes who had settled in Jerusalem during the exile. One of his archenemies was Tobiah, who waited until Nehemiah journeyed back to see the king in Persia before setting up his own storehouse within the newly rebuilt temple. Under the poor leadership of the priest Eliashib, Israel's enemy had been allowed to set up shop right in the middle of the place of worship. Nehemiah returned and wasn't having it; he chucked all Tobiah's stuff out, right in front of everyone. Remind you of anyone?

Jesus cleansed the temple twice—once early in His ministry, and again closer to His crucifixion.[12] The same thing had happened in His day; weak priestly leadership had permitted merchants to set up their stalls in the temple courts and sell sacrificial animals at high prices. Jesus took a whip and drove them out of the temple—not in a fit of anger, but out of love. This wasn't the sappy sentimentality that people often associate with love, but a fierce response designed to redirect the people toward righteous behavior. The scarlet thread is a lifeline, but it is also something that binds you to God's will and demands that you surrender yours to Him.

Would you be willing to see your Christian life refined, honed, or purified—even if it meant discipline? Sometimes that's what it takes. Sometimes Jesus chased greedy people from the temple or called them hypocrites; others He reinstated, telling them to go and sin no more. His goal is always restoration, but His means never include blind tolerance of sin. We should share that consuming zeal for God's glory even as we share God's heart for eventual restoration.

STAGE-MANAGING SALVATION

From a scarlet-thread perspective, Esther's decision to go to the king and seek her people's preservation was a crucial moment. Facing the very real possibility of the king's disfavor, which would result in her death, Esther said, "I will go to the king, which is against the law; and if I perish, I perish!" (Esther 4:16). Her determined decision was likely fueled by her uncle Mordecai's challenge to ally herself with her people: "If you remain completely silent at this time, relief and deliverance will arise for the Jews from another place" (v. 14).

> God's promises are unbreakable, and as a result, so is His bloodline of salvation. God stage-manages all of history to get the final result He desires.

Mordecai understood that God's plans for His people couldn't be thwarted by a single person's decision, whether for good or bad. God would use Esther if she made herself available, but if not, He would use someone else. Meanwhile, Haman's diabolical plan was only Satan's latest attempt to destroy God's people—and even though it was a nail-biter, God was always going to win. His promises are unbreakable, and as a result, so is His bloodline of salvation. God stage-manages all of history to get the final result He desires.

History's Big Players Are Still God's Pawns

In those days when King Ahasuerus sat on the throne of his kingdom, which was in Shushan the citadel, that in the third year of his reign he made a feast for all his officials and servants. (Esther 1:2-3)

God isn't called on by name in the book of Esther, but it's a historical story covered with His providential fingerprints. As the book begins, we meet the Persian emperor Ahasuerus, who ruled over 127 provinces "from India to Ethiopia" (Esther 1:1), and is better known by the name given to him by his Greek foes, Xerxes. His son, Artaxerxes, would give the command for Nehemiah to go back to the land of Israel after seventy years of captivity. Persia had taken over the territory previously conquered by Babylon, and the book of Esther gives us a view of what life was like during Israel's exile. Israel was far from home, but never beyond God's sight or the reach of His hand.

Xerxes, like all conquerors, bore the burdens of his throne, and at the beginning of the book of Esther, he threw a six-month-long party for all his rich friends, hoping to generate support and funding for a war against the upstart to the west, King Philip II of Macedon. He could sense a power shift coming, and though it wouldn't happen till the days of Philip's son Alexander, Xerxes fretted over his reign. But the concerns of even the mightiest kings are just fodder for God's chessboard, and Persia would fall to Greece by His design.

Before the Greeks gave way in turn to Rome, they would build a system of roads (later improved by the Romans) throughout Alexander's empire (including all of Xerxes' 127 provinces), and make their language the common tongue from Europe to India. More than just fascinating ancient history, this was all part of setting up the arrival of the Messiah. "When the fullness of the time had come, God sent forth His Son, born of a woman, born under the law" (Galatians 4:4).

By Jesus's day, Greek would be common enough to be used to write the New Testament, and Roman roads would carry that good news to the broadest possible audience that history had yet seen. Here in Esther, God would work behind the scenes to preserve His people from Haman's evil plans as part of His bigger plan to send Jesus Christ to save all mankind.

More Than Just a Pretty Face

> *The king loved Esther more than all the other women, and she obtained grace and favor in his sight more than all the virgins; so he set the royal crown upon her head and made her queen instead of Vashti.* (Esther 2:17)

Esther won the first recorded beauty contest. In a sense, though, God rigged the result. He set up the circumstances that led to her candidacy, as Ahasuerus needed comfort after Persia's key military defeat at Thermopylae but found only a cold palace to greet his return, the result of his having "fired" his queen for standing up to him. God also protected this Jewish servant Esther, whose uncle Mordecai entered her in the contest, going against Jewish law, which forbade marriage to a pagan.

In captivity in Persia, the Jews remained in the backslidden state that had gotten them exiled, but God's will overruled Mordecai's risky endeavor. If Esther had lost, she would have become the king's concubine, but God gave her favor with Ahasuerus and she became queen.

In Esther, God picked a physically beautiful woman to get the king's attention, but it was her character that won his heart. There's nothing wrong with working on your appearance as long as it doesn't get in the way of developing your character. That's what matters most to God. Rather than overemphasizing your looks, win people over with "the hidden person of the heart, with the incorruptible beauty of a gentle and quiet spirit, which is very precious in the sight of God" (1 Peter 3:4).

Whereas physical beauty fades despite all our best efforts to put it off, spiritual beauty can continue to grow, and in Esther, we see true beauty that parallels the character and work of Jesus Christ. Esther could approach the throne of the king, something Jesus enables us to do. Jesus knew He would be heard as He approached God's throne on our behalf,[13] and His redemptive work on the cross made it possible for us to be heard too[14]—just as God used Esther's intervention with Ahasuerus to arrange the preservation of His people. Just as she came to Persia "for such a time as this" (Esther 4:14), Jesus came at God's appointed time "to redeem those who were under the law, that we might receive the adoption as sons" (Galatians 4:5).

Esther knew that death would be the result of the king's disfavor, but she chose to intercede for her people anyway. Jesus knew that sin's ultimate penalty was eternal spiritual death, and chose to intercede with His atoning execution because that was what it took to save mankind. And the king, out of love for Esther, took radical steps to save her people. Similarly, God the Father took the most radical step to save mankind, sending God the Son to sacrifice Himself and extend mercy to us.[15]

The Power of Providence

When Haman saw that Mordecai did not bow or pay him

homage, Haman was filled with wrath. But he disdained to lay hands on Mordecai alone, for they had told him of the people of Mordecai. Instead, Haman sought to destroy all the Jews who were throughout the whole kingdom of Ahasuerus— the people of Mordecai. (Esther 3:5-6)

While in exile, most of the Jews had gotten comfortable in Persia and weren't interested in following God. When Ezra and Nehemiah led the nation back home to rebuild Jerusalem, only about 50,000 went with them, while the vast majority didn't want to deal with the inconveniences of the journey. But even though the Jews were reaping the consequences of their hardheartedness and idolatry, God had not abandoned them. The beauty of Esther is that even though God's people continued to ignore Him, He had not forgotten them. The wonder of the scarlet thread is that even when we fail to see it, God is weaving it into the world around us, into the lives of individuals and groups and nations, whether they are aware of it or not.

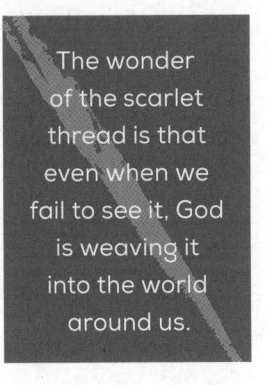

The wonder of the scarlet thread is that even when we fail to see it, God is weaving it into the world around us.

There is no doubt that God was working behind the scenes in Esther, using His typical methods to save His people from certain destruction. We call that subtle intervention *providence*—God stringing together ordinary events, places, and people so that they align perfectly with His will, His ultimate plan. God can always use a miracle to intervene, but most of the time, He works through providence. Here, He used Esther and Mordecai to preserve His people against Haman's satanic threat in a foreign land.

As Jesus said, "The kingdom of God does not come with observation…For indeed, the kingdom of God is within you" (Luke 17:20-21). In other words, God is building His kingdom now, here, in and around and through you. Even if you're opposed to Him, you're still playing your part in His master scheme. That's not to say that your free will is an illusion; we all make choices with real consequences every day. But God's ultimate plan can never be thwarted.

That plan involves saving anyone who will freely give their hearts to Jesus, His Messiah. He found leaders in Ezra, Zerubbabel, and Nehemiah who reflected qualities essential to Christ as they led His people back to the land of promise—hearts committed to His Word and service and connected to the royal line of David. Even as God put Esther in place to save His unrepentant people in exile, He did so with you in mind. He kept the lineage of the Messiah alive despite a scheme that could have wiped them all out. Even when we aren't actively thinking of or honoring Him, He is always actively loving us, working things together to bring us back to Him and glorify His great name.

6

HEART, MIND, BODY, AND SOUL

WISDOM LITERATURE:
Job, Psalms, Proverbs, Ecclesiastes,
Song of Solomon, and Lamentations

God's Word isn't just law and history; it's also a record wherein the full range of human emotions and experiences find a voice—especially in the poetry books. Biblical poetry followed Hebrew forms and conventions, but it also allotted space for the heart-cries of God's people—and even God's responses, in some cases. That tells us that in God's great redemptive plan there is room for our joy and sorrow, our triumph and heartbreak, our need and His provision.

This section of books in the Bible is often referred to as either the Books of Wisdom or the Books of Poetry. Here, wisdom and poetry go hand in hand, reminding us that God is concerned with our spiritual life and growth. These books are poetry in form only; they aren't human thoughts about God or life but accounts of human interaction with God, which happens on the level of the spiritual but affects (or should affect) our everyday lives.

Though they were written within a historical context, these books convey what it means to experience life with God—to go through ups

and downs while seeking the Lord, giving Him our anxieties, and praising Him for who He is and all He has done for us. The scarlet thread
marks the bigger picture of God overseeing people, events, and governments in order to maintain the lineage of His Messiah, but that
grand scenario also includes the thoughts and feelings of individuals
impacted by their encounters with God.

That's what we see in the books of poetry—the depth of the wonder and mystery of our relationship with God. The gamut of emotions
is represented: the hard questions about pain and suffering and God's
sovereignty in Job; the urgency, prophecy, and praise of Psalms; the virtue of praying for godly wisdom in Proverbs; the emptiness of earthly
pursuits in Ecclesiastes; the passion and blessings of unity in the Song
of Solomon; and the silver-lined despair of Lamentations.

One writer describes their place in the Bible as aspirational[1]—what
we're shooting for in our relationship with God. The law was foundational, laying the groundwork for Christ's lineage; the books of history
were preparational, establishing the staging ground for Christ's mission; and the poetry books are about people's need for Christ in their
hearts. "They aspired to a life fulfilled in Christ in both an explicit and
an implicit way, both consciously and unconsciously."[2]

YOUR REDEEMER LIVES

The book of Job deals with the hardship of pain and suffering, and
the questions that arise when they happen: *Is God really in charge—
and does He care about me? When I die, what could I possibly say to Him
to justify myself? What does it mean to live out my faith when bad things
happen?* God allowed Satan to wreck every aspect of Job's life that we
normally consider a sign of success and security, and even though He
was impressed with Job's righteous initial response, Job himself made it
clear that he needed someone to stand up for him with God—to bring
his pain before his Maker and request adjudication and even vindica-
tion. Job was desperate for deliverance and perplexed by his pain, and
yet he understood that death wasn't the end of life, and that God had
a redemptive plan underway.

The Accuser and the Advocate

> *Now there was a day when the sons of God came to present themselves before the LORD, and Satan also came among them. And the LORD said to Satan, "From where do you come?" So Satan answered the LORD and said, "From going to and fro on the earth, and from walking back and forth on it."* (Job 1:6-7)

One of the big questions that comes up when we consider God's redemptive work throughout history is, How much freedom does Satan have? If there's one thing we've seen so far, it's that the devil is always working to counteract God's plan, and we are often the collateral damage. If he is on a leash, why does that leash seem so long? We get some insight into the answers in the story of Job, a good man whom God allowed to suffer at Satan's hands.

True fact number one: You are being watched. Your enemy, Satan, is studying you, searching for weak spots, looking to exploit them and destroy you. He has access to both heaven and earth, and when he's not trying to wreck your life here, he's at God's throne, accusing you of all the things you've done wrong. That is why he is called "the accuser of our brethren" (Revelation 12:10). And he's not wrong about you, either. So in the invisible war the devil has waged to assault the Messiah—and all those who belong to Him—and avert his final destiny, you and I are caught in the crossfire.

True fact number two: God is watching you too. Satan is on a leash, operating within strict parameters—namely, God's permission. He is accountable to God. Because of that, God may allow the devil to bring hardship into your life—suffering, yes, but also sin and the guilt that comes with it. Satan's joy is to lead you astray, then whisper, "You call yourself a Christian? How can you even pray after doing that?" If you believe that his eyes are the only ones on you, you're in trouble. But if you remember that God is watching you too, and that Jesus is your advocate,[3] interceding on your behalf at God's throne right now,[4] then you can overcome your accuser.

To belong to Jesus is to invite persecution from the world and the devil. We're not guaranteed a comfortable life, but comfort in the troubles of life. We overcome our enemy by not holding onto what we think we want or deserve but by trusting God and following the example of the end-time martyrs: "They overcame him by the blood of the Lamb and by the word of their testimony, and they did not love their lives to the death" (Revelation 12:11).

Jesus's blood covers your sin in God's eyes; no accusation can stand against that. And then there's your testimony—your story of who God is and what He has done for you. Finally, there's your surrender: Do you consider spiritual loyalty more important than physical security? With those three strengths going for you, Satan can't touch you—not in any way that truly matters. God will pull the curtain down on his act one day; how you approach Satan's attacks now can be part of the glory God will receive.

Who Can Be Made Righteous?

How can a man be righteous before God? (Job 9:2)

The scarlet thread is unique in its ability to give us courage. It is hope in a world darkened by sin, pain, and despair. All the stitching surrounding it depicts the human predicament. Job summarized our situation well when he asked how anyone could stand on solid ground before God as equals. "For He is not a man, as I am, that I may answer Him, and that we should go to court together. Nor is there any mediator between us" (Job 9:32-33). Solomon later echoed his point, saying, "There is not a just man on earth who does good and does not sin" (Ecclesiastes 7:20). And we don't have what it takes to fix ourselves, either. Being good won't cut it, nor will being religious or sincere. But God didn't leave us grasping at straws, salvation forever just out of reach; He threw us a life preserver.

The Answer

Who is this who darkens counsel by words without knowledge?
Now prepare yourself like a man; I will question you, and you
shall answer Me. (Job 38:2-3)

Suffering stimulates searching. Pain prompts prying into some of life's biggest questions. Job suffered mightily, and he had questions—first of his friends, and then of God. *Why did God allow such affliction? Why can't I see God? What happens when we die? How can someone like me stand before God?* But he got no answers.

When God finally spoke, He said, "I'll do the questioning here." No answers, just a straightening out of perspective, at the end of which Job repented. It wasn't until Jesus came that we got answers to Job's questions. And the answers couldn't be clearer.

Jesus is God's answer. Regarding God's invisibility, Job lamented, "Oh, that I knew where I might find Him, that I might come to His seat!" (Job 23:3). And in Jesus, "the Word became flesh and dwelt among us, and we beheld His glory, the glory as of the only begotten of the Father, full of grace and truth" (John 1:14).

Knowing that he could never stand before God on his own merits, Job wondered, "How can a man be righteous before God?" (Job 9:2). Only in Christ: "Through one Man's righteous act the free gift came to all men, resulting in justification of life" (Romans 5:18).

Job, facing the very real prospect of his own demise, asked, "If a man dies, shall he live again?" (Job 14:14). Jesus said, "I am the resurrection and the life. He who believes in Me, though he may die, he shall live. And whoever lives and believes in Me shall never die" (John 11:25-26). All of Job's heart-cries, echoed down through the centuries, are answered in Jesus Christ. In fact, they can't be answered without Him.

Our pain can obscure the fact that God suffered so we would have hope. It's hard to imagine that our trials and hardships could have purpose, but the marvel of the scarlet thread is that it stitches your suffering into God's sovereign scenario, answering life's hardest questions by knitting your heart to Christ's.

Your Own Personal Redeemer

> *I know that my Redeemer lives, and He shall stand at last on the earth; and after my skin is destroyed, this I know, that in my flesh I shall see God, whom I shall see for myself, and my eyes shall behold, and not another. How my heart yearns within me!* (Job 19:25-27)

The idea that being a follower of Jesus doesn't exempt you from suffering is unnerving at first. Even when you understand that God uses pain for His purposes and your ultimate benefit, it's not easy. How amazing is it, then, that Job, who lived thousands of years before Jesus walked the earth, understood the power of resurrection? He grasped the same hope we have when everything else is going wrong—when the worst happens and we die, we'll instantly be face to face with Jesus. Eventually, everything will be all right.

> Even suffering and death can't weaken the redemptive threads that run through your life. That's an ongoing cause for eternal hope, peace, and rejoicing.

In that sense, Job preached the first Easter message. The word he used for "Redeemer" is the same used in the book of Ruth to describe the role Boaz played: *go'el*, the kinsman-redeemer, the one who was uniquely qualified to buy back a person or property that was lost. Our need for such a redeemer is at the heart of the gospel, and Jesus is that Redeemer. Jesus was related to us by flesh, willing to die for our sin, and able to accomplish the necessary sacrifice through His perfect blood.

Job lost his family, his possessions, and his health—and yet his trust in God was such that he anticipated that God would make things right, even if it took resurrection to do so. At his lowest point, Job had his greatest insight. So often, that's just how God works, coming to us in our darkest hour, offering comfort and peace when circumstances dictate the opposite. In such moments, the crimson cord glows in the darkness, showing us the way out. Job's hope was focused on a person, a Redeemer, who cared about him personally and perpetually. Because Jesus rose from the dead, if you have put your trust in Him, so will you. Even suffering and death can't weaken the redemptive threads that run through your life. That's an ongoing cause for eternal hope, peace, and rejoicing.

SONGS OF SALVATION

Psalms is a songbook, the hymnal of ancient Israel. It's also a remarkable collection of reflections on the human experience with God, God's worthiness to be worshipped, and His overarching plan to save mankind through His Messiah. From the lows of depression to the highs of praising God among His people, Psalms shows us repeatedly that nothing can stop God from accomplishing His plans and purposes. These are the heart-cries, the war songs, the victory chants of God and all who belong to Him heart and soul. They are an essential component of redemption's tapestry. A noteworthy tip-off to their significance lies in the fact that Jesus Himself pointed His audience to the Psalms more than to any other Old Testament book.

The World's Futile Resistance

> *Why do the nations rage, and the people plot a vain thing? The kings of the earth set themselves, and the rulers take counsel together, against the LORD and against His Anointed, saying, "Let us break Their bonds in pieces and cast away Their cords from us."* (Psalm 2:1-3)

There are about seventeen different messianic psalms; these psalms mention or focus on the suffering or victory of the Messiah.[5] They are recognized in the New Testament as pointing to Jesus, making Psalms the most-quoted Old Testament book in the New Testament. Psalm 2 is one of the most remarkable of these psalms, detailing experiences that its author, David, never went through himself, even allegorically. Scholars going back to ancient times agreed that it must refer to the future Messiah.[6]

The opening verses describe a global coalition in rebellion against God—and specifically, against Jesus Christ, "His Anointed" (the Hebrew word here is *mashiach*, or *Messiah*). It sounds a lot like the world today, where generic spirituality is on the rise, but to follow Jesus Christ and Him alone makes you a narrow-minded religious bigot. But these efforts to reject and break away from Jesus don't faze God in the slightest. In fact, "He who sits in the heavens shall laugh; the Lord shall hold them in derision" (Psalm 2:4), even as He seats Jesus on His rightful throne in Jerusalem, which will happen at the conclusion of the end times.

In Psalm 9, David wrote of the enduring throne of the Messiah, a common theme running the entire length of the scarlet thread, and His coming judgment: "He has prepared His throne for judgment. He shall judge the world in righteousness, and He shall administer judgment for the peoples in uprightness" (vv. 7-8). The Lamb who gave Himself for us is also our coming King, the greatest warrior ever, who fights for our good and His glory.

In these troubling times, we need to hold to our hope in Christ, following and encouraging our leaders to follow the advice given at the end of Psalm 2: "Now therefore, be wise, O kings; be instructed, you judges of the earth. Serve the LORD with fear, and rejoice with trembling. Kiss the Son, lest He be angry, and you perish in the way, when His wrath is kindled but a little. Blessed are all those who put their trust in Him" (vv. 10-12). Of course, to put trust in God's Messiah is to receive Jesus as Lord and Savior, to be grafted onto His bloodline and respond by honoring Him with all we are.

Assurance for the Weary

May He grant you according to your heart's desire, and fulfill all your purpose. We will rejoice in your salvation. (Psalm 20:4-5)

David frequently foresaw God's saving work, praising the Lord for the assurance of salvation and extolling His saving grace and hand: "Now I know that the LORD saves His anointed; He will answer him from His holy heaven with the saving strength of His right hand" (Psalm 20:6). David wrote of the "hill of the LORD,"[7] asking who was worthy to approach God, to seek His face, to be truly transformed by Him—and the answer is, "Whoever dwells in the shelter of the Most High will rest in the shadow of the Almighty" (Psalm 91:1 NIV). The shelter anticipated in the psalms was definitively provided by Jesus at the cross and by the empty tomb. He is the only one who can give us "clean hands and a pure heart" (Psalm 24:4).

The cost of doing this was staggering, and many psalms depict Jesus's suffering either through direct prophecy or indirectly through parallels with Israel's history. For example, David wrote in celebration of God's giving Israel victory over the Philistines, saying, "You have ascended on high, You have led captivity captive; You have received gifts from among men, even from the rebellious" (Psalm 68:18). Paul quoted him in Ephesians 4:8-10, using David's praise as prophesied proof that Jesus ascended only after descending to the depths of the grave to purchase us for Himself as "gifts."[8] I'm sure Paul would also echo David's praise when he sang, "Blessed be the Lord, who daily loads us with benefits, the God of our salvation!" (Psalm 68:19). Jesus didn't just bring us "up out of a horrible pit, out of the miry clay"; He also "set [our] feet upon a rock, and established [our] steps" (Psalm 40:2).

Jesus Himself found comfort in the psalms during His greatest trial. During His last Passover, He joined His disciples in the traditional singing of *Hallel,* or various commemorative psalms, including Psalm 116: "The pains of death surrounded me, and the pangs of Sheol laid hold of me; I found trouble and sorrow. Then I called upon the name of the Lord: 'O Lord, I implore You, deliver my soul!'" (vv. 3-4). He knew the full significance of the words; His impending crucifixion would make Him the final Passover Lamb—a trial He embraced only because He wanted the will of the Father to be done.

For the Joy of You

> *You, O Lord, do not be far from Me; O My Strength, hasten to help Me!... You have answered Me.* (Psalm 22:19, 21)

Psalm 22 is an anguished cry to God from a man in the process of being executed. While David went through many painful moments, none of the ones described in Scripture match the details of this poetic outpouring. However, in light of the New Testament, Psalm 22 does provide an accurate description of the crucifixion of Jesus Christ. In fact, it's almost like a firsthand account, similar to what we find in the Gospels—even though David wrote this psalm 1,000 years before Jesus was crucified.

The psalm opens, "My God, My God, why have You forsaken Me?"—words echoed from the cross in the darkness of Jesus's dying moments.[9] For the only time in His eternal existence, He was separated from the Trinity—and He felt it acutely. We see in Psalm 22 the torture a righteous man received, and in Christ, we see the reason: "Christ also suffered once for sins, the just for the unjust, that He might bring us to God, being put to death in the flesh but made alive by the Spirit" (1 Peter 3:18). Jesus came to die, something Psalm 22 predicted with vivid accuracy. When He uttered His final words—"It is finished!"—it marked not only the end of His life but the end of His mission.

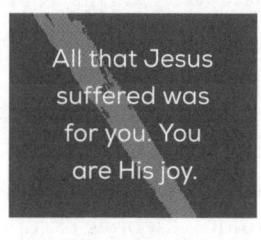

All that Jesus suffered was for you. You are His joy.

When we read in Psalm 22:21 that "You have answered Me," we might ask, "When did that happen? How did God answer?" We've all been through suffering, pain, and distress. Like Jesus, we've felt deserted by God and despised by men. But this psalm is His reply. God raised Him from the dead—reflected in victorious praise and a statement that foretells the endgame, salvation for mankind: "A posterity shall serve Him. It will be recounted of the Lord to the next generation, they will come and declare His righteousness to a people who will be born, that He has done this" (vv. 30-31). Amazing fulfillment!

All that Jesus suffered was for you. You are His joy. Because of that, you can confidently take your pain to Him, knowing not only that He identifies with you in it, but that He has redeemed it: Your pain will end one day, forever, and you will rejoice in the presence of your Savior. Because of that, it's clear that the scarlet thread is more than a symbol. It's your lifeline.

WISDOM PERSONIFIED

The main character in Proverbs is Wisdom, a personification of the concept that applying God's principles and commands to our lives will help us live the most satisfying way possible. As Solomon wrote, "The fear of the LORD is the beginning of wisdom, and the knowledge of the Holy One is understanding" (Proverbs 9:10). Wisdom itself isn't the goal; knowing God is. Jesus not only made that possible for us, He also modeled that ongoing pursuit of God, carving out time to pray and draw close to His Father.[10]

The Go-to Source to Get Wise

I neither learned wisdom nor have knowledge of the Holy One. Who has ascended into heaven, or descended? Who has gathered the wind in His fists? Who has bound the waters in a garment? Who has established all the ends of the earth? What is His name, and what is His Son's name, if you know?
(Proverbs 30:3-4)

Proverbs shows us Wisdom as standing in the streets of everyday life, calling out to us to seek her. "For wisdom is better than rubies, and all the things one may desire cannot be compared with her" (Proverbs 8:11). When Jesus created the earth, He used Wisdom to establish the laws of the natural world.[11] The path to gaining wisdom starts when we acknowledge, as Agur did in Proverbs 30:4, that we don't know everything, and that Jesus does.

Wisdom expresses the principles of God and His Word. It is personified here, as if it were speaking with us, telling us to spend time daily seeking it in the Scriptures. Then, we are to wait and watch with expectation. All the things that press you for time will come into clearer focus when you view them through God's lens. You'll see what needs to be done, and in what order, and what you can wait to do. You'll have the discretion to be able to give sound counsel when asked and have the courage to stand for your convictions.

Jesus is once again our perfect example of wisdom. The Bible records several times that He made time to pray—especially when He was busy. After He fed the crowd, "He went up on the mountain by Himself to pray" (Matthew 14:23). After a night of healing the sick and demon-possessed, He got up before sunrise and "went out and departed to a solitary place; and there He prayed" (Mark 1:35). Even though Jesus is "the power of God and the wisdom of God"

(1 Corinthians 1:24), He sought out the Father for comfort, counsel, and to provide an example for us. More than that, He generously gives us wisdom when we ask, and in Him we find all the answers we need. It's almost as though Jesus *was* the living, breathing book of Proverbs, for "in [Him] are hidden all the treasures of wisdom and knowledge" (Colossians 2:3). The wisdom Solomon pointed to in Proverbs took on flesh in Christ, the incarnation of all knowledge and the ability to use it well.

THE REASON FOR REDEMPTION

When Solomon wrote Ecclesiastes, he was searching for meaning, caught in a tangled web of observation, frustration, and desperation. God had given him the wisdom he requested, but he believed, as so many so often do, that there was more to life. We complicate what God makes simple. Solomon tried to find what it was—and instead, found out what it wasn't. Life's meaning wasn't in wisdom or wealth or women. It wasn't in philosophy or religion or good deeds. Solomon concluded that "there is nothing new under the sun" (Ecclesiastes 1:9), and that "all is vanity" (v. 2)—that life in and of itself is empty and ultimately futile. In all his worldly experiences, though Solomon was himself the son of David, he was actually searching desperately for a true, meaningful connection to God—one that only Jesus, the greater Son of David, could provide.

The Bottom Line

> Let us hear the conclusion of the whole matter: Fear God and keep His commandments, for this is man's all. For God will bring every work into judgment, including every secret thing, whether good or evil. (Ecclesiastes 12:13-14)

Although the Messiah isn't mentioned in the book of Ecclesiastes, the need for redemption is drawn in stark contrast. When Solomon, the wisest man who ever lived, wrestled with the big questions of life—*Why am I here? What's my purpose?*—it's a good idea to pay attention. After living a long life and pondering all its wonder and mystery and frustration, Solomon's initial conclusion was, "It's all a waste of time." His word of choice, *vanity*, means "emptiness," like a kid blowing soap bubbles. They're pretty but empty, glittering in the sun for a moment before popping in a wet burst.

> Through a relationship with Jesus, bewilderment becomes beauty, chaos settles into order, and procrastination becomes purpose.

If there was ever a book that anticipated the new covenant in Christ, this is it. Solomon looked everywhere under the sun for meaning. Work, wealth, power, wine, sex, possessions, academics—all of it, he concluded, is soap bubbles. But then he shifted his gaze from the horizontal to the vertical; he brought God into the equation. "I said in my heart, 'God shall judge the righteous and the wicked, for there is a time for every purpose and for every work'" (Ecclesiastes 3:17). As he brought God into his thinking more and more, his outlook shifted with his up-look.

Life under the sun may lose its shine, but life under the Son takes on a whole new meaning. It starts to make sense as you begin to see that, with God, life is not a series of random, meaningless events. Through a relationship with Jesus, bewilderment becomes beauty, chaos settles into order, and procrastination becomes purpose. Even when you don't understand life, you can rest in the knowledge that He brings meaning to the present and the hereafter.

Solomon's grave error was in thinking that God didn't want to be at the center of every part of his life—and so he separated his everyday life from his relationship with God. The scarlet thread is a perfect metaphor for the connection that God wants to have with us in Christ, and the danger of living life severed from it.

THE JOY OF UNION

We as humans typically set the sacred and the secular at odds with each other, particularly when it comes to matters of love, but the

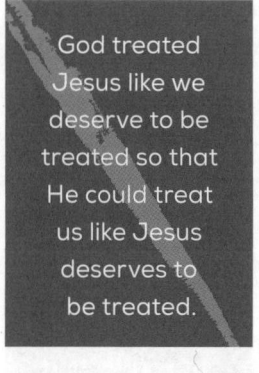

God treated Jesus like we deserve to be treated so that He could treat us like Jesus deserves to be treated.

Song of Solomon sends a different message. While there are certainly differences in the way Christians are to think and behave compared to non-Christians, we have to remember that God invented romance, marriage, and sex, and He wants us to enjoy them in their proper context—the one He established. Nowhere is this clearer than in the Song of Solomon, where emotional and physical desire are drawn together in a complete package that reflects the total intimacy God wants to have with His people—nothing hidden, nothing shameful, nothing separating godly purity and physical passion.

Under the Shadow of His Love

He brought me to the banqueting house, and his banner over me was love. (Song of Solomon 2:4)

The Song of Solomon details in poetry a relationship between a man and a woman from engagement to the wedding to married life. But there's a hint of divine love in it, a glimpse of the intimacy God desires with His people—something reflected in a godly relationship between husband and wife. We see that mystery portrayed in the New Testament with Jesus Christ depicted as the groom and the church as His bride.[12]

In the Song of Solomon, the bride-to-be describes her fiancé's love for her as a banner over her—like an identifying flag waving above her proclaiming his devotion. Part of her identity would become his love for her.

For Christians, of course, the banner of God's love over us is the cross. If you ever doubt God's love, just look back to the place where God gave His very best for you. As Paul wrote, "He made Him who knew no sin to be sin for us, that we might become the righteousness of God in Him" (2 Corinthians 5:21). God treated Jesus like we deserve to be treated so that He could treat us like Jesus deserves to be treated.

Jesus exemplified the kind of love God wants to see between a husband and wife. In the Song of Solomon, we see a reflection of that abiding love, faithful and true, and as one commentator put it, "it reminds us of a love that is purer than our own."[13]

In Praise of His Bride

> *Behold, you are fair, my love!... You are all fair, my love, and there is no spot in you.* (Song of Solomon 4:1, 7)

Though the Song is made up of verses that have no direct correlation to the scarlet thread, within the whole we can still find moments that reflect Jesus's desire and passion to be with us, His bride. When we read of Solomon praising his bride, we can see hints of what Jesus died to accomplish—to win His bride, the church, and to present her to God without blemish.[14]

Part of connecting to Christ's bloodline means realizing that God's original design for marriage and sex is good on both spiritual and physical levels. For example, it's not that praying is good and kissing is bad; in a Christian marriage, they're both good, and they should be intertwined in the sense that a good love life starts with a strong spiritual life. God never meant for us to separate the physical from the spiritual.

Jesus was a fully physical human being—a key part of His rescue mission that is too often overlooked. As John noted, the test for knowing whether the Holy Spirit is leading us is to confess "that Jesus Christ has come in the flesh" (1 John 4:2). And "every spirit that does not confess that Jesus Christ has come in the flesh is not of God" (v. 3).

We often have this mindset that anything related to "the flesh" is bad, but the Song joyously reminds us that our bodies matter to God. If Jesus wasn't fully God and fully man, He could not have fully paid sin's price. As one writer put it, human love, including sexual love, "always points beyond ourselves to the Love that undergirds all of reality and in whose Presence alone all longing can be satisfied."[15] God preserved the scarlet thread to connect us to the totality of His love, embodied in Christ and mirrored when there is complete unity in marriage and in the church. His plan of redemption includes buying back

His original intentions for our physical existence and making them good, as they were in Eden.

TEMPERED BY TENDERNESS

When Jerusalem fell to the Babylonians in the sixth century BC, the prophet Jeremiah wept. He knew it was coming—God had sent message after message through him, warning the people to turn back to Him, to no avail—but when it all came down, the exile broke his heart. Jerusalem is at the center of God's overarching plan and the place from which His Messiah is to reign one day. Jeremiah knew God would be faithful and would keep His promise to bring His people back at the appointed time, but he was not calloused to the pain and suffering Israel endured as a result of their hardheartedness.

Some consider tears to be a sign of weakness, but Jeremiah's foreshadowed those of Jesus, who also wept over Jerusalem when the people failed to recognize their long-awaited Messiah had come to them.[16] Jesus knew all that God had done to set up this pivotal moment in human history—everything we're looking at in this book—and to have it dismissed without a thought was unbearable. In the same way, Jeremiah suffered through his own version of one of Israel's darkest times, the exile.

A Ray of Light in a Dark Hour

> *Through the LORD's mercies we are not consumed, because His compassions fail not. They are new every morning; great is Your faithfulness.* (Lamentations 3:22-23)

Though Jeremiah's tears for Israel are at the forefront of Lamentations, again reflecting the compassion Christ feels for all His lost sheep, these verses—the single ray of light in this book—beautifully illuminate the heart of the gospel.

A big part of Jeremiah's prophetic ministry was predicting the downfall of Judah and the exile in Babylon that would result from the people's spiritual promiscuity. He didn't hold back in preaching God's call to turn back to Him, but tradition has it that not a single person repented because of Jeremiah's witness. Though he remained true to God's call on his life, bearing humiliation and even imprisonment, Jeremiah had little choice but to watch Judah's self-imposed darkness slowly descend and engulf his fellow Jews.

Lamentations is an outpouring of Jeremiah's breaking heart for his people—a series of funeral dirges mourning their spiritual demise and physical exile. So when Jeremiah, after all he had endured, still managed to seek God in the midst of heartache, it wasn't a rose-colored-glasses look at utter destruction. Rather, it was the desperate grasp of a drowning man who catches hold of a life preserver. Despite all the evil God's people had done and all they would suffer as they went into exile, Jeremiah didn't take a stance of "Well, I'm cool because I've obeyed God, but you guys are in hot water; serves you right!" His heart broke because he knew God's heart was breaking.

God faithfully offered Judah compassion each and every day. Even at the last, if the nation had truly confessed and repented, God would have likely delivered them from Babylon. Still, while they were in exile, He promised them a return, giving them hope even in their punishment. "You will seek Me and find Me, when you search for Me with all your heart. I will be found by you, says the LORD, and I will bring you back from your captivity" (Jeremiah 29:13-14).

The good news of Jesus Christ is that no matter how bad things get, or how low you've sunk in life, God offers hope through the scarlet thread—freedom from sin's fatal grasp and new mercies every day afterward.

NEAR AND FAR, DEEP AND WIDE

THE MAJOR PROPHETS, PART 1:
Isaiah

When we read the prophets, it's helpful to understand that there is often what we call a double witness—a more immediate, local fulfillment, and another one set further down the road. David did this in Psalm 22, speaking of his own suffering but then predicting the suffering of Christ on the cross in vivid detail, 1,000 years before it happened.

It's like looking at a mountain range. From a distance, the peaks look as if they are all in a row, like a postcard image. But as you draw closer, you begin to detect the depth of closer peaks and more distant ones, each separated by valleys. The prophets had the postcard view of the future, and because of Jesus and the wisdom of the Holy Spirit, we see a more three-dimensional view of fulfillments in the past and those yet to come, along with those that hold both a past and future fulfillment.

Prophecy is a layered tapestry, then, with each layer of warp and woof adding to the richness of the entire final image—but sometimes its scope is greater than we can take in at a single glance.

Isaiah took this view more than any other prophet, partly because God kept the gospel as a widespread message a secret until the church came into being.[1] Like other Old Testament prophets, Isaiah only saw the flat view of the future: Jesus's first and second comings side by side, the cross next to the kingdom, the Lamb alongside the Lion.

THE MESSIANIC PROPHET

Isaiah is known as the messianic prophet because of the number and potency of his predictions of God's Anointed One. His name means "Yahweh is salvation," which is fitting given that he pointed so often to the one who provides that salvation. In fact, Isaiah emphasized the Messiah as the servant of God—the one whom God sent to accomplish His great rescue mission. Four portions of Isaiah's book are called the Servant Songs because of this emphasis.

The second part of Isaiah focuses on salvation and restoration. It forms a parallel with the emphasis of the New Testament. The God who brought judgment on Israel for her disobedience and Israel's enemies for their cruelty (and who will bring judgment on the whole world in the end times) is the same God who sent His only begotten Son to die so that mankind could be brought into relationship with Him and Israel could be restored to Him. Isaiah addressed both the depths of sin and the heights of glory, intertwined in the life, death, and resurrection of God's perfect servant, Jesus Christ.

Branching Out (to the Future)

> *There shall come forth a Rod from the stem of Jesse, and a Branch shall grow out of his roots. The Spirit of the LORD shall rest upon Him, the Spirit of wisdom and understanding, the Spirit of counsel and might, the Spirit of knowledge and of the fear of the LORD.* (Isaiah 11:1-2)

Isaiah saw Judah's exile coming, and he also saw their return to the land of promise. But he also forecasted a time of peace and security, for that wasn't fulfilled after the people's return from exile in Babylon.

It can only be fulfilled by the Messiah—the Branch, the offshoot of David's line—when He establishes His reign on earth at Jerusalem. Jesus's return will be "beautiful and glorious; and the fruit of the earth shall be excellent and appealing for those of Israel who have escaped" (Isaiah 4:2). The prophet Jeremiah provided one example of corroboration for this, saying that "a righteous Branch" would spring from David's line to rule yet once again.[2] God's Spirit would rest on this Branch, and He will judge with righteousness and power. Jesse, as David's father, represents Israel and the continuation of the messianic line against all historical and spiritual odds.

Capitalized six times in the Old Testament, "Branch" refers to the Messiah and foreshadows the different perspectives of Jesus and His mission as shown in each of the Gospels. In Jeremiah 23:5-6 and 33:15-17, the Branch is a King, ruling over David's house and, prophetically, the world. That's the picture of Jesus reflected in Matthew. In Zechariah 3:8-9, the Branch is the "Servant" of God, matching Mark's depiction of Jesus, and in Zechariah 6:12-13, He is "the Man" who will build the Lord's temple and rule from His throne, serving as both Priest and King. That harmonizes with Luke's portrait of Jesus as the God-man. Finally, in Isaiah 4, the Branch is Christ as John shows Him, the Word of God made flesh, the mystery revealed: "In that day the Branch of the LORD shall be beautiful and glorious" (v. 2). It's a wonderful, hopeful picture: The beauty and glory of Jesus Christ, enthroned in Jerusalem as King of kings and Lord of lords, protecting His people and bringing peace to the world.

Pick a Miracle

> *Therefore the Lord Himself will give you a sign: Behold, the virgin shall conceive and bear a Son, and shall call His name Immanuel.* (Isaiah 7:14)

When enemies threatened to attack Jerusalem, Ahaz, one of four kings of Judah during Isaiah's prophetic ministry, received a generous offer from God: "Ask a sign for yourself from the LORD your God" (Isaiah 7:11)—no limitations! But Ahaz tried to be Mr. Spiritual and refused to test God. Isaiah responded by asking him if it was his intention to exhaust God's patience with his thinly veiled disobedience. Then Isaiah gave Ahaz a sign from God anyway—the famous Immanuel prophecy.

The Immanuel prophecy is a classic combination of both imminent and long-term fulfillments. In the near future, it would be fulfilled as Ahaz had a son by a woman who was still a virgin at the time of the prophecy. That son would still be young when Syria would break its pact with Israel and attack.[3] However, Isaiah 7:14 is also one of the best-known messianic prophecies, foretelling the virgin birth of Jesus. Matthew quoted Isaiah in his Gospel to explain why Mary was pregnant before she consummated her marriage with Joseph.[4]

A woman being a virgin before she has sex and gets pregnant isn't much of a sign from God; it happens all the time. But a virgin getting pregnant without having sex? That's a sign. The virgin birth of Jesus set Him apart as unique in the history of mankind. And His name, Immanuel, set Him apart in His unique mission on earth—to be "God with us" and save us from our sin.

A Broad-Shouldered Child

Unto us a Child is born, unto us a Son is given; and the government will be upon His shoulder. And His name will be called Wonderful, Counselor, Mighty God, Everlasting Father, Prince of Peace. Of the increase of His government and peace there will be no end, upon the throne of David and over His kingdom, to order it and establish it with judgment and justice from that time forward, even forever. The zeal of the LORD of hosts will perform this. (Isaiah 9:6-7)

Isaiah famously pointed beyond Christ's arrival as a baby to His second coming as ruler in one fell swoop. Israel, you see, was always in need of deliverance. The people had ongoing ups and downs, forsaking God, then repenting and being lifted up, then going through the whole cycle again. But Isaiah pointed them to a time when the changes God would make would be everlasting—a day when His

Messiah would rule with justice and compassion over not only Israel but the world.

The concept of the Messiah is central to Judaism—the hope of ultimate deliverance from sin, war, and death. Jewish prophets foretold the one who would make that happen, and the Jews were always on the lookout for Him, especially during the dark days of national suffering and oppression. In fact, when Jesus came the first time, Israel was under Roman domination, and messianic anticipation was at fever pitch.

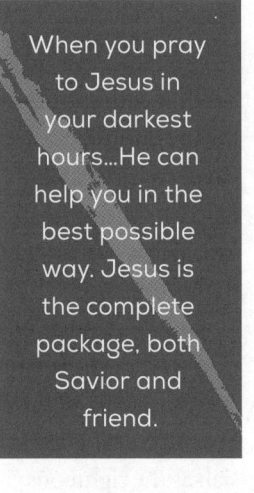

When you pray to Jesus in your darkest hours...He can help you in the best possible way. Jesus is the complete package, both Savior and friend.

But Israel expected the Messiah of Isaiah 9, not Isaiah 7. They were looking for the Lion who would throw off the Roman yoke and take over the government right then and there, not the Lamb who came to be with them and humbly give His life to save them. Jesus is, of course, both Lamb and Lion, and Isaiah 9 predicts His appearance as the latter, the one whose peace and governance will only increase and never end. Isaiah painted a picture of Jesus as both man and God—both everlasting God and also a child, the Son.

Why this combination? Why would Mighty God decide to wrap Himself in a package of skin and spend three decades walking the earth He had made? Well, He did it to save us, but also to identify with us. The very title *Immanuel* means "God with us." The New Testament reinforces this concept. "For we do not have a High Priest who cannot sympathize with our weaknesses, but was in all points tempted as we are, yet without sin" (Hebrews 4:15). Jesus endured pain, sorrow, fatigue, and frustration. He knew what it felt like to be rejected, betrayed, and abandoned. When you pray to Him in your darkest hours, He doesn't merely understand that you're enduring hardship; He knows what you feel like. He gets it, and He can help you in the best possible way. Jesus is the complete package, both Savior and friend.

THE SERVANT SONGS

*Indeed He says, "It is too small a thing that You should be
My Servant to raise up the tribes of Jacob, and to restore the
preserved ones of Israel; I will also give You as a light to the
Gentiles, that You should be My salvation to the ends of
the earth."* (Isaiah 49:6)

In a collection of messianic passages known as the Servant songs,
Isaiah contrasts a pair of servants, Israel and the Messiah. God intended
Israel to serve as His witness to the Gentile nations, a mission they
failed to accomplish—repeatedly. Then there is God's ultimate Servant, Jesus Christ, who after Israel's failure will one day restore it to its
full inheritance.

Isaiah 42 gives us the Servant as God's chosen one to bring salvation to the whole world, and Isaiah 49 speaks of His mission and its
success. Isaiah 50 shows the Messiah's obedience as the servant-minded
Son submitting to the will of the Father. Isaiah 52–53 depicts the Messiah as the righteous ruler, the one who will rule and reign forever from
Israel over the whole world, and then describes the painful price He
paid to bear our sin.

Song 1: The Elect One

*Behold! My Servant whom I uphold, My Elect One in whom
My soul delights! I have put My Spirit upon Him; He will
bring forth justice to the Gentiles.* (Isaiah 42:1)

The Messiah will accomplish what Israel never could because God's
Spirit uniquely rests upon Him and He will open up God's kingdom
to non-Jews—something that happened with the birth of the church
after Jesus ascended into heaven. And Isaiah's description of this Elect
One's behavior fits Jesus perfectly: "He will not cry out, nor raise His
voice, nor cause His voice to be heard in the street" (v. 2). Whereas the
Jews expected their Messiah to come as King, overthrow their oppressors, and establish His reign immediately, Jesus came the first time not
to conquer but to save.

When Jesus quoted Isaiah's words, saying, "A bruised reed He will not break, and smoking flax He will not quench" (v. 3),[5] we could read that as saying, "Jesus won't kick a person when he's down, and if there's even a spark of hope in his life, Jesus will fan it into flame." He brought a gentle message of peace. And though Jesus showed little tolerance for certain behaviors, particularly the hypocrisy of the Jewish religious leaders, He humbly stuck to His mission, to offer peace with God and rest from sin's burdens. He was a breath of fresh air after all the legalistic guilt heaped upon the people by the Pharisees. And, as Isaiah predicted, Jesus would do it with God's approval and authority: "I, the LORD, have called You in righteousness, and will hold Your hand; I will keep You and give You as a covenant to the people, as a light to the Gentiles" (v. 6).

Jesus is God's covenant of salvation, His promise to bring into relationship with Him anyone who comes to Christ in faith. Ideally, Israel would have fulfilled the function of spreading this good news, but Isaiah made it clear they had not been up to the task: "Who is blind but My servant, or deaf as My messenger whom I send?...Seeing many things, but you do not observe; opening the ears, but he does not hear" (vv. 19-20). God instead has used Jews and Gentiles alike to get His gospel out to the world, but in the end times, Jesus will restore Israel to the position He intended for them from the start, primary witnesses to His salvation.[6]

Song 2: The Mission That Saved the World

> *The LORD has called Me from the womb; from the matrix of My mother He has made mention of My name. And He has made My mouth like a sharp sword...And He said to me, "You are My servant, O Israel, in whom I will be glorified." Then I said, "I have labored in vain"...yet surely My just reward is with the LORD...Who formed Me from the womb to be His Servant, to bring Jacob back to Him, so that Israel is gathered to Him.* (Isaiah 49:1-5)

Here once again is the distinction between Israel the servant and Messiah the Servant, who spoke to Israel in this passage of His rescue mission to restore Israel, which God expanded to salvation for the world. Here the Messiah is intimately related to the nation He will one day rule. Addressing by the familiar names *Jacob* and *Israel*, the nation, the Messiah will restore her to the glory God originally intended. It's a loaded prediction: The one speaking here would be a Servant of God, rejected by Israel but a light to the Gentiles, His words would be like a sword, and other rulers would bow to Him in worship.[7] Jesus fulfilled all of it. What began on a cross in Jerusalem has become a light to the ends of the earth—and all of it was predicted.

That prophetic aspect is a key component of redemptive history. No one else can predict the future with the accuracy God demonstrates repeatedly in the Bible, and the combined might of every ruler and nation is not enough to accomplish any of the events God predicted. The same precision that foretold the downfall of Babylon and the rise of Persia in Isaiah's day, years before either happened, also forecasted the coming of the Messiah, the salvation He would accomplish, and His eventual reign on earth. So all of us, top to bottom, would do well to heed Isaiah's question: "Who among you fears the LORD? Who obeys the voice of His Servant? Who walks in darkness and has no light? Let him trust in the name of the LORD and rely upon his God" (Isaiah 50:10).

God's intention has always been to save as many as possible, and He let us know that—through Isaiah and others—hundreds of years before He made it happen. "Indeed He says, 'It is too small a thing that You should be My Servant to raise up the tribes of Jacob, and to restore the preserved ones of Israel; I will also give You as a light to the Gentiles, that You should be My salvation to the ends of the earth'" (Isaiah 49:6).

Song 3: The Good Son

> *The Lord GOD has given Me the tongue of the learned, that I should know how to speak a word in season to him who is weary... The Lord GOD has opened My ear; and I was not rebellious, nor did I turn away. I gave My back to those who struck Me, and My cheeks to those who plucked out the beard; I did not hide My face from shame and spitting.* (Isaiah 50:4-6)

Jesus often proved His complete submission to His Father's will, revealing a heart of mercy and love through words of encouragement and compassion, listening to the least-heard people in society, and enduring the sacrifice it would take to save us all. Isaiah foretold the scrutiny and scourging Jesus would endure—the spitting and name-calling and mocking, the beating and beard-plucking—and that He would face it all without complaint or doubt. More than that, as Isaiah foretold, He was flat-out determined to do the job: "The Lord God will help Me; therefore I will not be disgraced; therefore I have set My face like flint, and I know that I will not be ashamed" (v. 7).

Isaiah further identified the response of two groups to the Servant's sacrifice: those who fear the Lord, and those who don't.[8] Jesus also spoke of two options: the narrow gate and the wide gate, two paths to choose from in life. The former leads to life, and the latter, the more populated road, to destruction.[9] Jesus made it clear that He is the narrow path, the one way to favor with God.[10]

Song 4: The Suffering Savior

> *Surely He has borne our griefs and carried our sorrows...*
> *He was wounded for our transgressions, He was bruised for*
> *our iniquities; the chastisement for our peace was upon Him,*
> *and by His stripes we are healed.* (Isaiah 53:4-5)

God affirmed that no amount of money could pay sin's cost. He told Israel, "You have sold yourselves for nothing, and you shall be redeemed without money" (Isaiah 52:3). That led into the final servant song, which Isaiah began with a layered prediction: "Behold, My Servant shall deal prudently; He shall be exalted and extolled and be very high" (v. 13). This declaration could forecast either Jesus's resurrection, return, and worldwide exaltation, or His suffering—being lifted up on the cross with global ramifications: "So shall He sprinkle many nations" (v. 15). Or it could refer to both.

Isaiah spoke of the Messiah in what might be called the *prophetic past tense*—the verbs are past tense yet refer to a future time from Isaiah's perspective. This shows that God was so certain it *would* happen that He spoke as though it already *had* happened. Isaiah saw Messiah's torture and the power of His testimony as He endured it, a witness to God's glory that shamed Pilate and astonished a hardened Roman soldier.[11] It's as if Isaiah were there, at the foot of the cross, and yet, at the same time, he was also looking down the line to Jesus's resurrection and eventual reign. Paul quoted Isaiah in the context of bringing the gospel to everyone he could, saying, "To whom He was not announced, they shall see; and those who have not heard shall understand" (Romans 15:21).

> The wonder of God's redemptive plan is the enormous unlikelihood of it. Who would expect...the King of kings to allow Himself to be beaten and humiliated?

The wonder of God's redemptive plan is the enormous unlikelihood of it. Who would expect the Savior of mankind to come from such humble origins, or the King of kings to allow Himself to be beaten and humiliated? Who would expect the Messiah to grow up "as a root out of dry ground," or without "beauty that we should desire Him" (Isaiah 53:2)? Who would expect a God to be "despised and rejected by men, a Man of sorrows and acquainted with grief" (v. 3)? Most people looked at Jesus being flogged, carrying the instrument of His death through the streets, and "esteemed Him stricken, smitten by God, and afflicted" (v. 4). Some even looked at Jesus and thought, *He must have done something to deserve all that.*

But they had it backward. Everything that made Jesus unattractive that day started with us, our sin, our ugliness. It's astonishing, then, that even though He had "done no violence, nor was any deceit in His mouth" (v. 9), His death was what God wanted. "Yet it pleased the LORD to bruise Him; He has put Him to grief. When You make His soul an offering for sin, He shall see His seed, He shall prolong His days, and the pleasure of the LORD shall prosper in His hand" (v. 10).

Isaiah 53's detailed prophecies reveal some fascinating aspects of Christ's death. First, His death was voluntary. He chose the mission, knowing full well what it could cost Him. That's why He remained silent before Pilate's shortsighted questions, fulfilling Isaiah's prediction that when He was afflicted, "He opened not His mouth" (v. 7). Jesus had made His intentions clear to His detractors: "I lay down My life that I may take it up again. No one takes it from Me, but I lay it down of Myself. I have power to lay it down, and I have power to take it again. This command I have received from My Father" (John 10:17-18).

Jesus's death was also undeserved. Though the previous statement drew accusations of demon possession and cries for capital punishment, His enemies had no answer when He asked, "Many good works I have shown you from My Father. For which of these works do you stone Me?" (v. 32). They then accused Him of blasphemy, even though, as Isaiah had foretold, He had done no wrong.

In addition, Jesus's death was no mistake. Consider all the details in Isaiah's prophecy that came true at Christ's death: "They made His grave with the wicked…[and He was] numbered with the transgressors" (Isaiah 53:9,12)—fulfilled when Jesus was crucified between two thieves. His grave was made "with the rich at His death" (v. 9), a contrast provided when Joseph of Arimathea offered his tomb as a resting place for Jesus's body. From the cross, Jesus "made intercession for the transgressors" (v. 12), asking God to forgive His killers because they didn't know what they were doing. And with one word—the Greek *tetelestai*, "it is finished"—He confirmed Isaiah's prophecy that "He shall see the labor of His soul, and be satisfied" (v. 11).

Finally, Jesus's death pleased God. This sounds shocking, but it wasn't because it pleased the Father to see His Son suffer. No, God was overjoyed because of what that suffering accomplished—the possibility of relationship with anyone who would call on Jesus by name and receive the gracious gift of salvation by faith. God "laid on Him the iniquity of us all" (v. 6), and Jesus took on the burden to please His Father. Furthermore, God would honor Jesus above all because of His unique, heartfelt, and invaluable service: "Therefore I will divide Him a portion with the great, and He shall divide the spoil with the strong, because He poured out His soul unto death, and He was numbered with the transgressors, and He bore the sin of many, and made intercession for the transgressors" (v. 12).

The Servant songs in Isaiah are perhaps the most powerful portion of redemptive prophecy. Here, the scarlet cord is the bright red of the freshly drawn blood of Christ, vivid and immediate. No other portion of the Old Testament captures the urgency and poignancy of what God endured to accomplish a truly astonishing salvation for any of us who would embrace it.

ONE KING TO
RULE THEM ALL

THE MAJOR PROPHETS, PART 2:
Jeremiah, Ezekiel, and Daniel

The ups and downs of history can never derail God's determined plan. That testifies to His great love for the world generally and for you personally. Whereas Isaiah had prophesied in the midst of the divided kingdom and seen the fall of the northern kingdom of Israel in 722 BC, Jeremiah and Ezekiel were God's messengers near the fall of the southern kingdom of Judah in 586 BC. All three prophets saw the time coming when God would not only return His people to the land of promise but keep His hand firmly on them during the dark days of the end times, the great tribulation preceding Jesus's return to rule from Jerusalem.

Jeremiah and Ezekiel warned the people of Judah of their need to return to God, and the consequences of their failure to do so. The prophets also captured God's heart toward the people—that they be renewed and revitalized by an intimate relationship with God, which would be made possible through His Messiah.

Daniel's influential ministry happened during Judah's exile in Babylon, where God used him to provide interpretations of dreams and visions as well as prophecies of God's ultimate hand on His people, both in the near and distant future. Drawing on Jeremiah's prediction that Judah would be in exile for seventy years, Daniel foresaw not only the people's return to the land but the first and second comings of the Messiah, the one who would seal hearts in both Israel and the rest of the world to draw them into His kingdom.

THE UNQUENCHABLE FIRE BEHIND AN UNBREAKABLE PROMISE

Jeremiah, known as the weeping prophet, sent message after message from God to a nation that was swiftly spiraling down into exile. Few prophets capture the balance of God's holiness and love like he did, bringing news of impending judgment with a heavy heart while promising a bright hope and future because of a coming King and a new covenant. Jeremiah and Jesus shared a heart filled with compassion for God's people, brimming over with the hope of redemption, a new day when God would fill believers with His Spirit—something made possible by Christ's work on the cross.

The Righteous Branch

"Behold, the days are coming," says the LORD, *"that I will raise to David a Branch of righteousness; a King shall reign and prosper, and execute judgment and righteousness in the earth. In His days Judah will be saved, and Israel will dwell safely; now this is His name by which He will be called: THE LORD OUR RIGHTEOUSNESS." (*Jeremiah 23:5-6)

As we saw in Isaiah, the prophetic reference to "the Branch" signals Christ's second coming. Jeremiah saw this Branch as the coming King, ruling from Jerusalem in righteousness and wisdom. His name here, "THE LORD OUR RIGHTEOUSNESS," is *Yahweh Tsidkenu* in Hebrew. It stands in direct contrast to the names of the four unrighteous kings of Judah whom Jeremiah had been addressing before this pronouncement (Jehoahaz, Jehoiakim, Jeconiah, and Zedekiah). Clearly, it states that the Messiah is none other than God

Himself. The coming one will be the incarnate Lord. One day, Israel would no longer be plagued by poor leadership, but would "serve the LORD their God, and David their king, whom I will raise up for them" (Jeremiah 30:9). David's kingship pointed to Christ's, and his name is often used in prophecy to represent the Messiah.

Perhaps one of the most remarkable things about Jesus sitting on the throne as "David their king"—the greater Son of David promised by God in 2 Samuel 7:16—is the line of succession that put Him there. Of course, being God, Jesus could just come down and take over, and be justified and righteous in doing so. But God set up His royal lineage so that Christ would fulfill His promises of vast numbers of descendants to Abraham and the eternal establishment of David's throne, doing all of it according to the laws He established.

Nowhere is this more apparent than in the case of Jeconiah (also called Coniah). Even though he was David's descendant and therefore the legal option for carrying on the messianic line, Jeconiah was also the latest in a long line of kings who, with rare exceptions, rejected God and led the nation down the path of idolatry. God, fed up with the shameless idol worship of Judah's kings, cursed Jeconiah to go without an heir, saying, "Write this man down as childless...for none of his descendants shall prosper, sitting on the throne of David" (Jeremiah 22:30). Uh-oh—plot twist! God just cursed His own plan of a Messiah coming through the bloodline of King David. If David's line wouldn't continue, how would God keep His promise that one of David's descendants would sit on Jerusalem's throne? Even more importantly, how would God bring the Messiah through David's line, as promised?

When we get to the Gospels, we'll see how God worked around His own curse through the virgin birth of Jesus. It's an amazing solution! For now, it's worth mentioning that even though God reached His tolerance level with Israel and Judah's disobedient monarchs, that didn't stop Him from keeping His promise to bring His Messiah and bless the world through Him.

Even though God had cursed Jeconiah and seemingly ended the messianic line of David, He made it clear that He was still committed to keeping His promise to David. The covenant that would birth the

Messiah was unbreakable. Jeremiah called it both "everlasting" (Jeremiah 32:40) and "perpetual" (Jeremiah 50:5). God made it clear that to break His covenant with David and Israel would be like breaking the cycle of day and night—something that undermines His very position as the sovereign Creator: "If My covenant is not with day and night, and if I have not appointed the ordinances of heaven and earth, then I will cast away the descendants of Jacob and David My servant" (Jeremiah 33:25-26).

God is neither finished with Israel nor with any individual willing to put his or her faith in Jesus. God would somehow repair and restore this cursed bloodline that Messiah was to share. If anything, He was upping the difficulty level—as if the whole undertaking of redemption wasn't already up against astronomical odds!—just so it would be clear that only He could do it.

Again, we see the promise of the Branch, rooted in David's lineage—the Messiah who would save Judah and Jerusalem and set up His reign there—literally! "In those days and at that time I will cause to grow up to David a Branch of righteousness; He shall execute judgment and righteousness in the earth. In those days Judah will be saved, and Jerusalem will dwell safely. And this is the name by which she will be called: THE LORD OUR RIGHTEOUSNESS" (Jeremiah 33:15-16). The city itself will take on the name of its ruler, the one whose presence will make it holy, the one whose loving sacrifice shelters like the shade of a great tree all who rest in Him.

A Better Way

> This is the covenant that I will make with the house of Israel after those days, says the LORD: I will put My law in their minds, and write it on their hearts; and I will be their God, and they shall be My people. (Jeremiah 31:33)

The Law of Moses was God's covenant to bind His people to Himself through their obedience to His commands. He wanted them to make the law part of their everyday lives, as normal as getting dressed and eating breakfast in the morning, so He told Israel, "You shall lay up these words of mine in your heart and in your soul" (Deuteronomy 11:18).

But that heart connection proved elusive, just as the keeping of the law did. Their sin cost them everything—intimacy with God, the land of promise, and the messianic lineage of David. Restoration would take more than a reminder of the law or a promise that they meant when they made it but had no ability to keep. Even all the animal sacrifices they presented to temporarily atone for their numerous infractions couldn't fix the deeper problem.

> Everything we wouldn't and couldn't do, God has done; and everything we broke, He has fixed.

A better covenant was needed, and though it would come in Jesus Christ, Jeremiah predicted it six centuries before Jesus's birth—a covenant that God would write on the very hearts of His people. Jeremiah said, "Behold, the days are coming, says the LORD, when I will make a new covenant with the house of Israel and with the house of Judah—not according to the covenant that I made with their fathers in the day that I took them by the hand to lead them out of the land of Egypt, My covenant which they broke, though I was a husband to them, says the LORD" (Jeremiah 31:31-32). The new covenant in Jesus Christ wouldn't be based on their ability to keep the law, but on God's ability to save them from the root cause: sin.

This is the gospel—God's good news of salvation—and we see it here in the phrase "I will": God will do everything necessary to make it possible to save us. "This is the covenant that I will make…I will put My law in their minds, and write it on their hearts; and I will be their God…For I will forgive their iniquity, and their sin I will remember no more" (vv. 33-34). Everything we wouldn't and couldn't do, God has done; and everything we broke, He has fixed.

Furthermore, God's new order promises an inner transformation: "No more shall every man teach his neighbor, and every man his brother, saying, 'Know the LORD,' for they all shall know Me, from the least of them to the greatest of them, says the LORD" (v. 34). God's removal of sin through His Messiah makes it all possible. Under the old covenant, the law tried to control man's conduct. The new covenant promised a change in man's character.

Under the law, we are limited to reading the sheet music. In Christ,

God says, "I'm going to put My song in your heart. You'll just know it. You'll have a relationship with Me where you're not working off the notes anymore, but you will be able to hear My song in your heart. And in that day, you'll really sing."

THE REGENERATED GENERATION

The vivid symbolism of Ezekiel's prophetic ministry painted a tapestry of redemption's power. He depicted the mystery of God's audacious love in the power of the Messiah's priesthood, God's desire to cleanse His people of sin's stain, and the promise of a regenerated generation whose hearts would be purified and turned fully toward God—the very work of the gospel itself.

Change for the Better

> *Take off the crown; nothing shall remain the same. Exalt the humble, and humble the exalted. Overthrown, overthrown, I will make it overthrown! It shall be no longer, until He comes whose right it is, and I will give it to Him.* (Ezekiel 21:26-27)

The throne of David is empty. It has been since Zedekiah was captured and taken to Babylon, and it will remain so until Jesus returns and takes it for Himself. Ezekiel's prophecy is itself an echo of Jacob's prediction back in Genesis 49, when he foretold the future of his sons, the fathers of the twelve tribes of Israel. When he came to his fourth son, he said, "The scepter shall not depart from Judah, nor a lawgiver from between his feet, until Shiloh comes; and to Him shall be the obedience of the people" (v. 10).

The standard interpretation given by rabbis was that the tribe of Judah would hold the right to rule—to exercise the authority of the Law of Moses over Israel until the Messiah came—here called *Shiloh*, meaning "the one to whom it belongs." He is the one that Ezekiel said had the right to rule, of whom God said, "I will give it to Him." Even during the exile, under the rule of Babylon and Medo-Persia, the Jewish people had retained this national identity based on the law. After the exile, when Greece controlled Judah, the Jews were still able to maintain their authority over their own people.

That national identity would be disrupted by the Roman Empire, who occupied the land of Judah and took away Jewish authority and autonomy. That included forbidding the Jews to exercise capital punishment, a right God had given them way back in Genesis 9. This, in effect, meant the removal of the scepter from Judah's hand—and the Talmud records their response: "They covered their heads with ashes, and their bodies with sackcloth, exclaiming: 'Woe unto us for the scepter has departed from Judah and the Messiah has not come.'"[1] They thought God had broken His promise. But while they were having their little pity party in Jerusalem, over in Nazareth, a carpenter's son was about to lay down His tools and introduce Himself to His cousin John the Baptist at the Jordan River. Though the Jewish religious leaders would refuse to recognize Him, Shiloh had come, and He will come again.

The Servant Shepherd

> *I will establish one shepherd over them, and he shall feed them—My servant David. He shall feed them and be their shepherd. And I, the LORD, will be their God, and My servant David a prince among them; I, the LORD, have spoken.*
> (Ezekiel 34:23-24)

King David had been dead about 300 years when Ezekiel prophesied that God's "servant David" would come to rule over Israel. Some have said this means that God will resurrect David as coregent with Jesus in the millennial kingdom, but the context and Jewish commentaries of the day widely suggest that "David" here refers to the Messiah, a descendant of David. And even though the Jews have not recognized Jesus as that son of David, He will still come and set up His kingdom.

The ideal form of government is not a democracy of the people, for the people, by the people. That's probably as good as we can come up with on our own, but any manmade government is subject to human flaws and will ultimately fail. Even with God's law as their guide, the leaders of Israel had failed miserably, and the exile was the result: "They

were scattered because there was no shepherd…My flock was scattered over the whole face of the earth, and no one was seeking or searching for them" (Ezekiel 34:5-6).

The only form of government that will work and last is a theocracy—a benevolent dictatorship—overseen by a righteous, powerful, and caring King. Don't get this confused with the human form of theocracy like we see in certain countries in the Middle East, where authoritarian legalism has created an oppressive state. Instead, picture one run by God Himself. Jesus will rule a firm yet compassionate kingdom for 1,000 years: "I will make a covenant of peace with them…I will make them and the places all around My hill a blessing…And they shall no longer be a prey for the nations" (vv. 25-26, 28).

God's promise of redemption includes the promise of peace. Jesus will make peace possible among the people, with other nations, and with nature itself. Back in Eden, sin didn't just kill the human spirit, it broke God's creation, from animals and plants to climate and environment. Isaiah had a similar vision of the rule of the "Root of Jesse" (Isaiah 11:10), who would bring about a time of justice and righteousness, when the "wolf also shall dwell with the lamb…And the lion shall eat straw like the ox" (vv. 6-7). It will be a time for God's people both Jew and Gentile, when "the wilderness and the wasteland shall be glad for them, and the desert shall rejoice and blossom as the rose" (Isaiah 35:1).

Jesus will not only restore balance in creation, He will make possible blessings we haven't seen before. The blessings He promised in Deuteronomy 11 in return for Israel's obedience He will freely give in the kingdom—fruitful trees, plentiful rains, harmony with the animals, freedom, and safety—all under the hand of the Good Shepherd.

Ezekiel's Gospel

> *I will sprinkle clean water on you, and you shall be clean;*
> *I will cleanse you from all your filthiness and from all your*
> *idols. I will give you a new heart and put a new spirit within*
> *you; I will take the heart of stone out of your flesh and give*
> *you a heart of flesh. I will put My Spirit within you and cause*

you to walk in My statutes, and you will keep My judgments
and do them. (Ezekiel 36:25-27)

Ezekiel looked beyond the exile, beyond the return, and beyond the coming centuries of occupation and servitude to the time when God would establish His new covenant—not just with Israel but with the world. In a three-part promise, he detailed God's heart for mankind and what the Messiah would accomplish when He came. First, God would gather Israel in the land He promised them. Then He would transform their hearts, bringing them new spiritual life. Finally, He would establish His kingdom in the land and rule from Jerusalem. The first would happen after the exile, the second when Jesus came the first time, and the third upon His return. These glorious verses are sometimes called the gospel according to Ezekiel.

This reminds me of the rabbi who visited Jesus at night. Nicodemus knew of these promises that God had made to Israel. He knew that the first part, Ezekiel 36:24, had been fulfilled when Israel returned after the exile, and he was eagerly awaiting the third part—for God to set up His kingdom as foretold in Ezekiel 36:28. As Nicodemus stood eye to eye with the King of that future kingdom, Jesus made clear to him that he had neglected the all-important middle promise—the spiritual component of regeneration that Jesus called being born again.[2]

In fact, wise and learned as he was, Nicodemus couldn't wrap his head around the essential need for a better redemption than the law offered. He knew that Jeremiah had promised the return to the land,[3] and Ezekiel had promised that God would cleanse His people, "sprinkling" them with water and clearing out all the idols. But that was standard operating procedure for God. What was new—what was practically unthinkable—was the way that God would give His people "a new heart and put a new spirit within [them]" (v. 26).

The new sprinkling would not be water that a priest had drawn from a well, but the blood of God Himself, given to purify anyone who believed by faith. And when God said He would put His Spirit in their hearts, it was a new event, a new filling. The Holy Spirit wouldn't come upon people and strengthen them for God's purposes as He had in the past. Under the new covenant in Christ's blood, the Spirit would live in the hearts of those who received this new sacrifice—and He would do so on a permanent basis. That's how God would replace hearts of stone with hearts of flesh, making those hearts sensitive to Him, His will, and His ways.

When Jesus feigned surprise that Nicodemus didn't know these things as a teacher of Israel, He was in effect saying, "This new covenant has been there in writing for several centuries, since Ezekiel and Jeremiah wrote about it." Both prophets spoke of the need for inner transformation rather than restraining outward conduct. The former would enable the latter. Ezekiel made it clear that individual hearts would be revitalized and turned to God, and then, at the end of the age, God would establish those with new hearts in the Promised Land under His King, Jesus Christ.

One of Ezekiel's most famous prophecies pictured God reviving dried-out bones that filled a valley.[4] The bones represented the people of Israel, who had lost hope of ever being able to draw close to God. Similar to the new covenant described in Ezekiel 36, God promised both the regathering of Israel in the land and their spiritual regeneration, followed by the restoration of Israel as a nation under God. It's the promise of the gospel for all people, and also specifically for Israel, when they would be regathered back to their ancient homeland. It's a picture that may even have in mind the 144,000 Jewish people who, during the tribulation, will be sealed as witnesses for Christ.[5] The vision is packed with the imagery of rebirth and rejuvenation: "I will open your graves and cause you to come up from your graves, and bring you into the land of Israel. Then you shall know that I am the LORD...I will put My Spirit in you, and you shall live, and I will place you in your own land" (Ezekiel 37:12-14).

Ezekiel's prophecy here is a glorious promise made possible by the new covenant in Christ. "God, who is rich in mercy, because of His great love with which He loved us, even when we were dead in trespasses, made us alive together with Christ (by grace you have been saved)" (Ephesians 2:4-5). This millennia-old promise is for anyone, anywhere, who will receive it, and it's how we become connected to God's bloodline.

WRAPPING UP REDEMPTION

Daniel was a high-ranking government worker. His prophecies about what we consider the past—the rise and fall of many of the most powerful empires of the ancient world—came to such accurate fulfillment that many in our time have doubted that he could have written them. But Jesus settled the issue when He called him "Daniel the prophet" (Matthew 24:15). He verified that Daniel provided the very backbone of biblical prophecy.

Prophecy is God's flashlight into the future, authenticating Scripture through His knowledge of the beginning, the end, and everything in between. It's why the scarlet thread is worth tracing—because it's a done deal from beginning to end. The second half of the book of Daniel is a truly remarkable illumination of the progress of history toward the end times, particularly with regard to the return and reign of Jesus Christ. God gave Daniel a powerful gift of interpretation, which he used to inform Nebuchadnezzar, king of Babylon, of future events—from the downfall of Babylon itself to the eventual rise of a kingdom without end.

The Stumbling Block

> *You saw that the stone was cut out of the mountain without hands, and that it broke in pieces the iron, the bronze, the clay, the silver, and the gold—the great God has made known to the king what will come to pass after this. The dream is certain, and its interpretation is sure.* (Daniel 2:45)

One of the most amazing aspects of Daniel's prophetic record is the historical accuracy with which his interpretation of Nebuchadnezzar's dream was fulfilled (Daniel 2:31-45). The huge statue depicted a sequence of world-ruling kingdoms (Babylon, Persia, Greece, and Rome), all of which will be crushed by a single stone that represents the future and ultimate kingdom of Christ (v. 44). Other prophets identified a similar stone as the Messiah. God said, "Look! I am placing a foundation stone in Jerusalem, a firm and tested stone. It is a precious cornerstone that is safe to build on. Whoever believes need never be shaken" (Isaiah 28:16 NLT).

Jesus Himself spoke of the great stone that destroyed all the other mighty kingdoms: "'The stone which the builders rejected has become the chief cornerstone. This was the LORD's doing, and it is marvelous in our eyes'...And whoever falls on this stone will be broken; but on whomever it falls, it will grind him to powder" (Matthew 21:42, 44).

Christ's kingdom works on two levels in this sense: First, each of us must choose whether to "fall on this stone"—to surrender our lives to Him as Lord and Savior. Second, those who resist His saving grace are doomed, both to a self-centered and ultimately purposeless life, and then to hell, where they will spend eternity apart from their loving Maker.

Daniel's prophecy makes a couple things clear: One, resistance is futile. The day will come when Jesus will return and establish a physical kingdom on earth, and every knee will bow and every tongue will confess Christ's lordship (Isaiah 45:23, Philippians 2:10). Two, redemption is possible. Like Daniel, if you stick to your faith in these trying times, you will be able to celebrate the coming of His kingdom.

The Son of Man

> *I was watching in the night visions, and behold, One like the*
> *Son of Man, coming with the clouds of heaven! He came to*
> *the Ancient of Days, and they brought Him near before Him.*
> *Then to Him was given dominion and glory and a kingdom,*
> *that all peoples, nations, and languages should serve Him.*
> (Daniel 7:13-14)

Daniel's story is an account of how God is better than all the other gods people worship—better than the gods of Babylon, Persia, Greece, Rome, or any of our so-called modern deities—power, money, or fame. All the kingdoms Daniel saw in Nebuchadnezzar's visions underscored this fact, and when God gave Daniel his own visions of the end times, he saw the one he had served so faithfully all his life, the Ancient of Days.

In a vision of a final kingdom of men that will arise on earth, Daniel saw its ruler described as a "little" horn with a man's eyes and a big mouth spouting blasphemy against God (v. 8). In the Bible, a horn is a symbol of power, and this little horn is someone we know as the

Antichrist. In the grand prophetic scheme, his rule will come in the end times, and his defeat will happen when Jesus returns, a scene described in Revelation 19:17-21. The tribulation finished, God's wrath completely poured out, Jesus will come back and condemn the Antichrist and the false prophet to their permanent punishment in the lake of fire.

Daniel described the returning Messiah as "One like the Son of Man, coming with the clouds of heaven." In the Gospels, Jesus referred to Himself as the Son of Man nearly eighty times, more than any other designation. This means much more than just a male born of human parents, as God had referred to Ezekiel: "Son of man, stand on your feet, and I will speak to you" (Ezekiel 2:1). Rather, it's a direct messianic reference to the vision of Daniel 7, as Jesus linked Himself to the Son of Man who will be given an everlasting kingdom. And what a contrast to the images of the earthbound kingdoms before Him! Ravenous beasts, full of malice and violence—but none of their kingdoms lasted.

> Jesus will put the pieces of His creation back together with the help of those whose souls His work on the cross brought back from sin's grip.

The kingdom of the Son of Man, however, "is an everlasting dominion, which shall not pass away, and His kingdom the one which shall not be destroyed" (v. 14).

Daniel's vision points to one of Jesus's statements summarizing the end times—all the sealed judgments, the trumpet judgments, the bowl judgments, and His return:

> There will be signs in the sun, in the moon, and in the stars; and on the earth distress of nations, with perplexity, the sea and the waves roaring; men's hearts failing them from fear and the expectation of those things which are coming on the earth, for the powers of the heavens will be shaken. Then they will see the Son of Man coming in a cloud with power and great glory. Now when these things begin to happen, look up and lift up your heads, because your redemption draws near (Luke 21:25-28).

God's redemption is an ongoing work that will come to a head when Jesus returns—not as an impoverished baby in a feeding trough in some backwater of the Roman Empire, but as the all-conquering King of kings. He will make short work of the worst dictator earth has ever known and then set up shop in Jerusalem. Part of the work of the millennial kingdom will be the physical redemption of a world ravaged by centuries of misuse and absolutely rocked by the judgments of the tribulation. Jesus will put the pieces of His creation back together with the help of those whose souls His work on the cross bought back from sin's grip. It will be a glorious time.

The Timetable

> *Seventy weeks are determined for your people and for your holy city, to finish the transgression, to make an end of sins, to make reconciliation for iniquity, to bring in everlasting righteousness, to seal up vision and prophecy, and to anoint the Most Holy.* (Daniel 9:24)

The coming of the kingdom is scheduled. Daniel's most overwhelming and important vision established a timetable for the end times, specifically the persecution of Israel at the hands of the Antichrist. It's known as the seventy-weeks prophecy, a time marked out by God that demonstrates once again that He is involved in history in precise and deliberate ways. Here, at history's second most critical moment (after the cross), God planned "seventy weeks," or literally, "seventy sevens."

Seventy sevens could refer to weeks of days or weeks of years.[6] Here in Daniel 9, it must mean seventy weeks of years—seventy periods of seven years each. It was common practice for the Jews to calculate time by sevens, using heptads instead of decades. And because Daniel had been reading Jeremiah,[7] he was aware that the exile was to last seventy years because Israel had failed to keep God's prescribed Sabbath year for 490 years.[8] Daniel understood that the "week" of Israel's seventy-year exile in Babylon was coming to an end—and he would see that the exile was part of this vision he had received.

Six things are mentioned in Daniel's vision that must take place during that seventy-week period. Three have already been fulfilled. Three are yet to be fulfilled. Look at the list in verse 24:

- To finish the transgression: This probably refers to Israel's rebellion and their return to the land.

- To make an end of sins: This is why Jesus came the first time—to deal with the sin issue.

- To make reconciliation for iniquity: Through His atonement on the cross, Jesus paid sin's price.

Jesus dealt with these first three during His first coming. He will deal with the latter three when He comes back: to bring in everlasting righteousness, to seal up vision and prophecy, and to anoint the Most Holy.

The details of the rest of the prophecy are equally fascinating. We could spend a lot more time digging into them, but for the purpose of focusing on the scarlet thread, we'll limit ourselves to a few key details. The pinnacle is the prediction of the accomplishment of the Messiah's first mission, followed by Daniel's vision of the tribulation.

Daniel pointed to the end of the exile as the beginning of the countdown to the Messiah's arrival. "From the going forth of the command to restore and build Jerusalem until Messiah the Prince, there shall be seven weeks and sixty-two weeks" (Daniel 9:25). Those sixty-nine weeks of years add up to 483 years, at which point the Messiah would come. And after that second period of sixty-two weeks, He would "be cut off, but not for Himself" (v. 26). The question is this: When would that happen—what was the date of that starting point?

There has been a lot of debate over this subject, but Daniel's vision again holds the key: "The street shall be built again, and the wall, even in troublesome times" (v. 25). Initially, in Ezra 2, Cyrus gave the order for the Jews to go back to Jerusalem and rebuild the temple, an edict essentially repeated in Ezra 6. Ezra 7 records the recommencement of the temple sacrifices. But it's not until Nehemiah received permission to go back and build the city walls that we arrive at the green light for the seventy weeks. Artaxerxes Longimanus sent Nehemiah back to finish the job on March 14, 445 BC.[9] It took him forty-nine years—or seven sevens—to finish the city walls and gates, fulfilling the first part of Daniel's timetable.

Counting sixty-two weeks—434 years—after Nehemiah completed the walls, using a standard 360-day lunar calendar year, results in 173,880 days passing, which ended on the tenth of Nisan, AD 32. That was the time when the lambs were selected for the Passover, and it was the day when Jesus approached Jerusalem on a donkey's colt, pausing to weep outside the city gates because His own people hadn't known it was the time of His coming, even though the prophets had predicted it exactly for them.

Jesus further predicted the fall of the temple, which happened at Rome's hands in AD 70: "They will not leave in you one stone upon another, because you did not know the time of your visitation" (Luke 19:44). But Daniel could've told anyone willing to believe it that such would be the case: After Messiah was cut off, "the people of the prince who is to come shall destroy the city and the sanctuary" (Daniel 9:26). That "prince" was Titus Vespasian, emperor of Rome, whose army laid siege to Jerusalem before burning its walls, razing the city, and leveling the temple.

The historical accuracy of the timing here further cements Jesus's status as Messiah. The Messiah can't be someone who is going to come any day now for the first time. He had to have come before AD 70. According to Daniel's prophecy, there had to be a temple standing, and the temple then had to be destroyed, with the arrival and death of the Messiah in between. The final week of Daniel's vision is known as the seventieth week, or the seven years of the tribulation. Daniel said that the Antichrist would make and break a treaty with Israel when he predicted that, at some point after the fall of the temple, "the ruler will make a treaty with the people for a period of one set of seven, but after half this time, he will put an end to the sacrifices and offerings. And as a climax to all his terrible deeds, he will set up a sacrilegious object that causes desecration, until the fate decreed for this defiler is finally poured out on him" (Daniel 9:27 NLT).

This suggests that a new temple will be built before or during the tribulation, because the Antichrist will desecrate it. Jesus referred to the same event in Matthew 24 as a sure sign of the end times. The everlasting righteousness, the sealing of the vision and the prophecy, and the anointing of the Most Holy would follow upon Jesus's return, tied to the building of the temple during the millennium.[10]

God's redemptive work won't be completed until Jesus returns and reigns. The tribulation will be the ultimate proving ground of faith, for only those who trust in Jesus will have any hope at all. But as hard-won as that hope will be, it will prove trustworthy, comprised of the final threads of the scarlet cord pressurized to diamond-hard reliability by the prophesied promise of God's just judgment and the eventual restoration of creation and mankind to intimacy with Him.

9

GOING THE DISTANCE

THE MINOR PROPHETS
BEFORE THE EXILE:
Hosea, Amos, Jonah, Micah, Nahum,
Habakkuk, and Zephaniah

The minor prophets aren't minor in their importance; rather, the word *minor* has to do with the length of their books. Each of them is a little book with a big impact, and redemptive history runs through their pages. I've grouped the minor prophets according to the time of their ministries relative to the exile—either before or afterward. When it comes to the before group—the pre-exilic prophets—I see the power of God's promises for a group of people who were facing an uncertain future of their own making.

Whereas Israel and Judah had split as nations and were riding a rollercoaster of idolatry—which is pretty much cheating on God the way spouses might cheat on one another, a breaking of commitment, trust, and intimacy—God remained faithful to keep His promises to them. He didn't let them get off scot-free—that was the harsh lesson of the captivity in Babylon. But He never let them think He was abandoning them or giving up on what He had sworn to Abraham and David. In fact, there were no lengths He wouldn't go to ensure that they could one day be His special people again.

Faithful to the Faithless

> *The LORD said to me, "Go again, love a woman who is loved by a lover and is committing adultery, just like the love of the LORD for the children of Israel, who look to other gods and love the raisin cakes of the pagans."* (Hosea 3:1)

God transmitted messages through His prophets in a couple of ways. One was proclamation: God would tell the prophet, and the prophet would tell the people what God said. The other was demonstration: The prophet would follow God's instructions to represent or act out the point He wanted to make. Hosea definitely fell into the second category.

God told Hosea to marry a woman who would cheat on him. Their broken marriage was to be a demonstration of how God loved an unfaithful people, staying committed to them to the very end. Hosea's marriage exemplified a heartfelt message through a heartsick prophet from a heartbroken God. In an act of identification with God's pain, Hosea bore the scars of his torn relationship, speaking on behalf of a God who wanted reconciliation. He foreshadowed the ministry of Jesus Christ, "who was in all points tempted as we are, yet without sin" (Hebrews 4:15).

God loved us enough to become one of us, susceptible to the entire range of human emotions and experiences. Our sin has always pained Him, primarily because of the separation it causes between us and Him. And when He allows us to suffer the consequences of our sin, it's in the hope that we will turn back to Him, choosing Him and trusting that His ways are better than our ways.

The Burden-Bearer

> *"I will bring back the captives of My people Israel; they shall build the waste cities and inhabit them; they shall plant vineyards and drink wine from them; they shall also make gardens and eat fruit from them. I will plant them in their land, and no longer shall they be pulled up from the land I have given them," says the LORD your God.* (Amos 9:14-15)

Amos's name means "burden bearer," and he carried a hard message of God's impending judgment, both to Israel and her enemies. In a series of visions, Amos described devastation that proved shocking to Israel's leaders, who felt that they were beyond suffering any consequences for their sin.[1] It was a similar reception to the one Jesus received when He preached judgment against the hypocrisy of the Jewish leaders of His day.[2]

While these visions of judgment are correctly seen as punishment for sin, we shouldn't make the same mistakes King Amaziah (and later, the Pharisees) made in dismissing them—that God won't punish His chosen people simply because they're His chosen people. Amos foretold Israel's exile—the ramifications of their spiritual adultery over the years— but he also told of God's pledge to bring Israel back into the Promised Land. The frequency of this promise in the Old Testament underscores the necessity that the nation of Israel must exist for Messiah to come to it and then later rule from it. Regathering is required for redemption.

Israel has been back in the land in modern times for more than seventy years. And the growth of messianic believers in that land is unprecedented. These "dry bones" are coming to life spiritually as well as physically. Interwoven in the history and future of God's chosen people are thousands of stories of redemption—the renewed lives of those who laid down the burden of their sin at the foot of the cross, where Jesus carried the full penalty of sin for all mankind. Amos's vision of Israel's healing, as both a land and a nation, are a preview of coming attractions and a reminder that Jesus will return to avenge unrepentant evil and give all of His children an era of peace and blessing.

From Fish Guts to Good News

Now the LORD had prepared a great fish to swallow Jonah. And Jonah was in the belly of the fish three days and three nights. (Jonah 1:17)

Of all the prophets in the Old Testament, Jonah is the only one to whom Jesus compared Himself. When the scribes and Pharisees pressed Him for a sign of His power and authority, Jesus told them to expect only the sign of Jonah: "As Jonah was three days and three nights in the belly of the great fish, so will the Son of Man be three days and three nights in the heart of the earth" (Matthew 12:40).

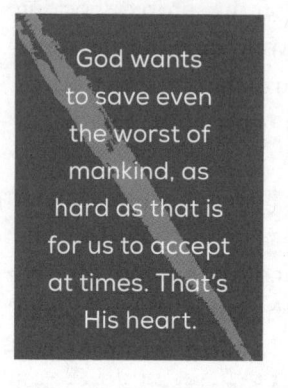

God wants to save even the worst of mankind, as hard as that is for us to accept at times. That's His heart.

Jonah's journey involved a spiritual resurrection as he eventually accepted God's will and repentance for Nineveh. Jesus's victory over death resulted in salvation for anyone who would believe in Him. But Jesus also noted an essential difference between Jonah's story and His. Unlike the people of Nineveh, the Pharisees and scribes would not repent—and in the end, they would be worse off than the Ninevites.[3] Imagine a nation comprised of the worst terrorists ever, cruel and murderous, without regard for age, gender, or belief. That was Nineveh, and they hated the Jews. Jonah ran away because he knew God would forgive them if they heard his message and repented. He wanted them to suffer God's justice.

But God didn't. He wants to save even the worst of mankind, as hard as that is for us to accept at times. That's His heart. Who is that person in your life whom you think is beyond saving? Will you pray for his or her salvation, hoping that he or she will buck the odds, that nothing is impossible for God? And what about that person you don't know but still hate—will you pray for that individual too? No one deserves God's mercy and forgiveness, but He went to great lengths to offer it freely. Who are we to hold back? It took Jonah three days engulfed in a fish's gut to come around; will it be sooner for you?

The Happiest Sheep Have the Best Shepherd

> *He shall stand and feed His flock in the strength of the LORD,*
> *in the majesty of the name of the LORD His God; and they*
> *shall abide, for now He shall be great to the ends of the earth;*
> *and this One shall be peace.* (Micah 5:4-5)

Micah's most famous messianic prophecy foretold Jesus's birth in

Bethlehem.[4] But the next few verses then point to His return, His second coming. We have in these verses a hint of the manner of the Messiah when He comes to reign on earth. And even though we are told in other places that He will rule with a rod of iron—a firm, unwavering hand of justice and righteousness—here Micah painted a picture of a loving shepherd nourishing His flock.

Immediately John 10 comes to mind, where Jesus said, "I am the good shepherd. The good shepherd gives His life for the sheep" (v. 11). We also understand that between His first coming at Bethlehem and His second coming to rule the world, there would be a monumental event: the cross. The Good Shepherd gave His life for His sheep, becoming the sacrificial Lamb who took away the sin of the world.

Micah drew a contrast between the earthly rulers of Judah, who had failed the people to the point of captivity in Babylon, and the promised Messiah, who will one day rule Israel like a caring shepherd, forever and ever. The quality of life in any flock is determined by the shepherd; when your shepherd is good, life is good, and if your shepherd is bad, life goes poorly. Why settle for anything less than God as your shepherd?

The scarlet thread binds God's people to His promises. Because of that, the hope of worldwide peace and liberating leadership in the kingdom age also exists here and now for the believer in Christ, the one who commits his or her life to the leadership of Jesus. Let Him lead you, meet your needs, and give you rest. He won't fail you, and one day, the whole world will recognize what a good shepherd you have.

A Complete Picture

> *God is jealous, and the LORD avenges; the LORD avenges and is furious. The LORD will take vengeance on His adversaries, and He reserves wrath for His enemies...The LORD is good, a stronghold in the day of trouble; and He knows those who trust in Him.* (Nahum 1:2, 7)

Some imagine God to be weak, sentimental, even sappy, but the ongoing tale of His bloodline refutes that. Here in Nahum (and in many other places in the Bible), we see that God is active and strong, and fierce with divine jealousy. This isn't the human vice that arises from selfishness but God's jealousy, which exists because He is unique, unequaled, and without rival. The idea behind the Hebrew word for jealousy is to be zealous for one's own possession—as if God is saying, "You are Mine. I have no rivals, and I want no false ones in your life." Why would anyone ever want to be God's enemy, resisting His desire to hold His rightful place in every heart? Fortunately, God wants to draw us in as beloved children, not overpowered minions.

> We must go through life with one premise firmly fixed in our minds: God is good.

Jesus said, "No longer do I call you servants...but I have called you friends" (John 15:15). It's a wonderful thing to be called a friend of God, and a futile endeavor to be His enemy. It's better to have God as your friend and all the world as your enemy than the other way around.

How can such a good God judge? It's because He is good that He brings destruction. If He didn't judge evil, he would be amoral and immoral. He would be neither good nor loving. Our good intentions and sincerity don't count; only His standard of good and evil does. God's judgment is part of His justice, and according to Jesus, God has entrusted all judgment to the Son.[5]

God's character is well-rounded. He will judge, avenging injustice, especially toward His people—and He is righteous, protecting those who have given themselves over to Him. We must go through life with one premise firmly fixed in our minds: God is good. He will avenge His children, and His desire is to save any who want to join the family.

The Fork in the Road

> *Behold the proud, his soul is not upright in him; but the just shall live by his faith.* (Habakkuk 2:4)

God set forth two paths here: faith and its counterpart, unbelief. Habakkuk's message forewarned Israel of the coming of Babylon as judgment for its sin. But exile would not be the end of the story. God would return His people to their land, and though Babylon had been His rod to punish Israel, the Babylonians would not go unpunished for their arrogance in conquering Israel.

Even if the Babylonians had the understanding to grasp that God was using them, they took it as an implicit approval of their own beliefs and behavior. They didn't respect the God who was using them, or how mighty His wrath could be if they didn't humble themselves before Him. And so God made it clear through Habakkuk that the tables would be turning on them. Instead of being instruments of God's justice, they would be recipients. Those who were just, however, would live by their faith, and this verse provides the key to unlocking the door of God's righteousness.

The great doctrinal books of the New Testament include this concept as a central tenet of their teaching: The just shall live by faith.[6] God's grace can't be earned; it's a gift. But once received, grace becomes the bylaw of the believer's life. Habakkuk contrasted the ways of the proud—those arrogant sorts who live outside of God's good ways—with the ways of the just. It's the difference between death and life. Pride leads to death, stopping the ears from hearing God's Word. Faith—trusting in God no matter the circumstances—leads to life, both abundant life before death, and eternal life afterward.

The Light of Justice

> *The Lord is righteous in her midst, He will do no unrighteousness. Every morning He brings His justice to light; He never fails, but the unjust knows no shame.* (Zephaniah 3:5)

Zephaniah prophesied against Judah's leadership, characterizing Jerusalem as a rebellious bride: "Woe to her who is rebellious and polluted, to the oppressing city!" (Zephaniah 3:1). He spoke God's words against her disobedience, faithlessness, insolence, and treachery. He used the strong language that some assume is confined to the Old Testament, where they see God as angry and vengeful, in contrast to His meek, loving ways in the New Testament.

That stance conveniently ignores much of New Testament Scripture, including several statements made by Jesus, who in Matthew 23 told the Pharisees multiple times, "Woe to you hypocrites!" He denounced the religious leaders of His day much the same way Zephaniah did here. It's the same God talking in both accounts—and anytime God uses the word *woe*, His audience better slow down—*whoa!*—and listen.

God spoke to Jerusalem here because of a scriptural principle: To whom much is given, much is required. Judgment is meted out according to the light a person receives. Someone who has received more of God's revelation is held to a higher level of accountability. At the same time, to honor what you know of God brings more blessing, more understanding, more peace.

People trip themselves up complaining about how a supposedly loving God could ever bring such terrible judgments to bear as the Bible describes. They fail to understand that God's love is pure, holy, and just. If He did nothing about evil, then He would be unjust and unloving. Even in the great tribulation, which will see an enormous outpouring of God's wrath, the saints will sing, "Just and true are Your ways, O King of the saints!" (Revelation 15:3). His love and justice are such that anyone can avoid His wrath by turning to Him in faith for salvation.

These minor prophets were major league hitters of truth. They demonstrated that whether Israel was dispersed or regathered, whether they were faithful or unfaithful, Israel's God was behind the scenes, weaving His scarlet thread into their history and preserving their race and land for redemption and restoration. The exile was a major bump in the road, but not one that God didn't anticipate.

10

MESSAGE SENT

THE MINOR PROPHETS POST-EXILE:
Joel, Obadiah, Haggai,
Zechariah, and Malachi

A common theme among the prophets after the exile is the Day of the Lord. More than a single twenty-four-hour period, the Day of the Lord is a season of God's judgment, particularly His coming wrath during the end times. Even if, as believers in Christ, we are saved from the worst of those times—the natural disasters, plagues, famine, wars, and widespread catastrophe unlike anything the world has ever known—the idea of God's wrath is a fearsome thought. We know that because of what Jesus did on the cross, we don't have to fear it, but the reach of the scarlet thread extends beyond our salvation and into the lives of others.

In fact, a key part of God's redemptive plan is that once you've been saved, you let others know how they can be saved. It's more than just fire insurance—accepting Christ so you won't go to hell—but that is the initial and lasting benefit. God's commitment to you goes way beyond the day of your salvation. It echoes forward from history, from the promise of the victorious Messiah in Genesis 3 to the glory of God living among the people in the tabernacle and the temple. It resonates through the kings, the psalms, and the prophets, growing in urgent expectation.

The message is simple and straightforward: God wants to bless you, to restore the purpose in your life, and to give you the authority to do everything He has set aside for you to do. Sin's exile may have ended, but God's glory will last forever, and He wants you to be part of it. The message was clearly sent centuries ago, but then, as now, each of us still must decide whether or not to receive it.

God's Reclamation Project

> *I will restore to you the years that the swarming locust has eaten, the crawling locust, the consuming locust, and the chewing locust, My great army which I sent among you.* (Joel 2:25)

Even when you receive Christ as Lord and Savior, and the work of God gloriously begins to change you, you see yourself differently. You discover that you have two natures—the old you, that person you used to be before Jesus, and the new you, rejuvenated and empowered by the Holy Spirit. Even though you have been saved from hell, your two natures battle each other continually. As you mature in your faith, you learn to sow to the Spirit to receive the life of the Spirit in you. And if you don't resist the urges to sow to the flesh—to give in to your old, sinful desires—you'll reap corruption.[1]

> God loves to take on tough projects, loves to fix those who have been ground down, broken, but want to cooperate with Him in rebuilding their lives.

You've switched allegiances from Satan to God, and the devil would love to sink his claws into your new life, decimating it, leaving hopelessness in his wake—a life chewed down to the ground as if a horde of locusts had been at it. In such a situation, you might think—mistakenly—*I can never return to the Lord; the Lord can never use me again.* But only if you truly believe that can the devil defeat you. Remember, Jesus said, "The thief comes only to steal and kill and destroy" (John 10:10 NIV). Turn back to Jesus, because God's response is this promise in Joel: *I will restore the years the locusts have stolen.*

Whatever stage you are at in your Christian life, walking but struggling or fallen away, God will still meet you right where you are. Even from captivity, God promises that if you seek Him with all your heart and soul, you will find Him.[2] God loves to take on tough projects, loves to fix those who have been ground down, broken, but want to cooperate with Him in rebuilding their lives. Whatever Satan has stolen from you, if from here you seek the Lord, God has so much in store for you. Get connected to Him, whether by confession or repentance or renewed dedication, and He will pour out His Spirit on you and restore your joy and peace.

A Great Benefits Package

> *Then saviors shall come to Mount Zion to judge the mountains of Esau, and the kingdom shall be the LORD's.* (Obadiah 21)

Obadiah's brief gut-punch prophecy to the nation of Edom detailed not only its inevitable judgment but God's eventual restoration of Edom's longtime foe, Israel. Judgment isn't a popular topic, and it's easy for those who oppose God to mock the idea that He will ever do anything about evil (even by ignoring Him as they do what they please without fear of repercussion). But judgment will come. That's the recurring theme in all the books of the so-called minor prophets: in His good time, God will judge justly and with righteousness. The question for many, then, is this: Which side of that judgment will you be on?

Obadiah made it clear that one of the side benefits of choosing Christ is working on His behalf. We get to do it during this life, and the work will continue upon His return. Another translation of "saviors" in this verse is "deliverers." Just as God at one time raised up judges in Israel to deliver Israel from its captors and to adjudicate issues for the people, so in the kingdom age, God will appoint similar leaders. And who will they be? The saints—followers of Jesus Christ. Paul wrote, "Do you not know that the saints will judge the world?" (1 Corinthians 6:2). We read of believers ruling the world, reigning with Christ for 1,000 years.[3]

God will raise up His government, and it will be the best the world has ever seen. That alone should move us past any hope in a political party or politician to lead the world out of the mess we've made. Only Jesus can do it, and one day He will—and those who belong to Him will help.

You Are Chosen

> *"In that day," says the LORD of hosts, "I will take you,*
> *Zerubbabel My servant, the son of Shealtiel," says the LORD,*
> *"and will make you like a signet ring; for I have chosen you,"*
> *says the LORD of hosts.* (Haggai 2:23)

Haggai brought a message from God to Zerubbabel to encourage him. After the return from exile, Zerubbabel had taken charge of rebuilding Jerusalem's walls and temple. Apparently he was feeling down, and it's easy to see why. Surrounded by massive empires who could rescind their permission and end his mission at any time, he had only a few thousand people who had returned to Jerusalem with him. They had a makeshift temple and struggled to sift through rubble and resist opposition while trying to rebuild the city walls.

God saw Zerubbabel's discouragement and sent him a personal note through Haggai: "I see you. I'm going to shake down all these surrounding kingdoms and enemies, and all that will be left is what's mine. You're a part of that, and as proof, I'm making you and your presence there like My personal seal of approval." A signet ring identified the bearer as an authority, and while God was looking to cheer up Zerubbabel in his current situation, He was also giving him a taste of the future.

Zerubbabel was from the tribe of Judah, and more specifically the house of David, listed in the genealogies of Matthew and Luke as an ancestor of Jesus Christ. God was telling him, "You're a part of My work here and now, but you're also part of My long-term plan to save mankind and bring about ultimate peace for Israel." Talk about significance! If there's a work you've been trying to do for the Lord and you've stopped, for whatever reason, let this scene encourage you too. You're also a part of God's plan in the present and in the future, and you have

His authority and stamp of approval in Christ to do what He has called you to do. "Delight yourself also in the LORD, and He shall give you the desires of your heart" (Psalm 37:4).

Dwelling Among Us, Living Within Us

> *"Sing and rejoice, O daughter of Zion! For behold, I am*
> *coming and I will dwell in your midst," says the LORD.*
> *"Many nations shall be joined to the LORD in that day, and*
> *they shall become My people. And I will dwell in your midst.*
> *Then you will know that the LORD of hosts has sent Me to you."*
> (Zechariah 2:10-11)

When I read of God's promise to dwell among His people, I go immediately to John's description of Jesus as the Word of God: "The Word became flesh and dwelt among us, and we beheld His glory, the glory as of the only begotten of the Father, full of grace and truth" (John 1:14). However, here in Zechariah, the word "dwell" in Hebrew is *shakan*, the same word from which we get *shekinah*, that Old Testament manifestation of God's glory in the temple. Zechariah was looking beyond the Messiah temporarily living among mankind, as Jesus did the first time He came, to His return, when He will dwell in glory among His people during the millennial kingdom.

The second coming is mentioned about 1,845 times in Scripture, eight times as often as the first coming. It's a theme that brings hope to every generation—hope that the world won't stay the way it is, that Jesus Christ will return, take over, claim Judah as His inheritance in the land of promise, and set up a just, righteous reign from Jerusalem. What we now call the Holy Land won't truly be a holy land until He does all this.

The Rock That Builds or Destroys

> *He answered and spoke to those who stood before Him, saying,*
> *"Take away the filthy garments from him." And to him He*
> *said, "See, I have removed your iniquity from you, and I will*
> *clothe you with rich robes." (Zechariah 3:4)*

Zechariah's prophetic ministry was loaded with messianic predictions about who the Messiah would be and what He would do. At one point, Zechariah saw a vision of Joshua, the high priest in his day. God cleaned up the filthy robes Joshua was wearing and gave him fresh, clean ones[4]—symbolic of how Jesus would cleanse the filth of sin from all who receive Him. God once again called His Messiah "the BRANCH" (v. 8), that reference to His connection to God's promises to David.

Furthermore, God described "'the stone that I have laid before Joshua: Upon the stone are seven eyes. Behold, I will engrave its inscription,' says the LORD of hosts, 'and I will remove the iniquity of that land in one day'" (Zechariah 3:9-10). Clearly, this is not a natural stone; it has eyes. Seven speaks of the fullness of knowledge, the omniscience of God, so this describes the Messiah. And when Jesus returns, He will deal with sin and set up His kingdom in a single day, bringing peace and prosperity to His people.

Later, Zechariah predicted that from the tribe of Judah would come the cornerstone—the foundation of the future of the nation of Israel.[5] Jesus is the cornerstone—the foundational building block—of the church.[6] He referred to Himself as the great stone upon which people would either be broken and saved, or crushed and condemned in their rejection of Him.[7]

In all of this, God was making a point: He didn't want empty religious observances. He wanted the hearts of His people to burn with desire for Him, to serve from gratitude and joy instead of duty. Christ either unites or divides people based on their willingness to give their hearts to God. In both the short and long term, God was committed to His people. Any commitment we make to Him we should make in full, letting ourselves be completely broken by His love so He can fully restore us. If we only wrap redemption's thread around our finger as a reminder to look holy instead of letting it pierce our hearts and renew us, we will ultimately be crushed by Christ's righteous judgment.

The View from a Donkey's Back

> *Rejoice greatly, O daughter of Zion! Shout, O daughter of Jerusalem! Behold, your King is coming to you; He is just*

and having salvation, lowly and riding on a donkey, a colt,
the foal of a donkey. I will cut off the chariot from Ephraim
and the horse from Jerusalem; the battle bow shall be cut off.
He shall speak peace to the nations; His dominion shall be
"from sea to sea, and from the River to the ends of the earth."
(Zechariah 9:9-10)

Zechariah gave us one of the last prophetic views of Christ's first and second comings, compressing the two into consecutive verses, not knowing when either would occur. In fact, there's at least a 2,000-year gap between verses 9 and 10, one of those valleys between mountain peaks that I mentioned a few chapters back. Zechariah saw the first peak pressed up against the second like in a flat postcard picture, and he couldn't make out the valley of the church age in between. That's because, as Paul noted, God had hidden the mystery of the church during the Old Testament, revealing it only in the New: "The word of God in its fullness—the mystery that has been kept hidden for ages and generations, but is now disclosed to the Lord's people. To them God has chosen to make known among the Gentiles the glorious riches of this mystery, which is Christ in you, the hope of glory" (Colossians 1:26-27 NIV).

Centuries later, however, there was no mystery behind Jesus's motives when He prepared to enter Jerusalem the week before His crucifixion. When He told His disciples to go into a village near the city gates, untie a donkey's colt, and bring it to Him,[8] He was making a deliberate statement: "I am the King who is coming, the one Zechariah told you about." Jesus had been keeping His ministry low key, telling people after healings, "Don't tell anyone about this." But this was His time, and He made His identity and intentions clear.

We look at this and marvel, but the proclamation went straight over everyone's heads. Between Zechariah 9 and Daniel 9 the timetable of Jesus's arrival was laid out, but even though there was an upsurge of messianic fervor and anticipation, no one could believe that God's Messiah was actually among them. That's why Jesus wept as He looked over Jerusalem, predicting with a heavy heart its downfall at Roman hands, because the people didn't recognize the time when their Messiah visited them.[9] That's the first part of Zechariah's prophecy.

The second part takes us to the second coming, when Jesus will end all wars, both within Jerusalem and around the world, setting up a peaceful reign. It will take the blood-filled battle of Armageddon to accomplish that, but that conflict will be earth's last war for 1,000 years. "God will save them in that day, as the flock of His people. For they shall be like the jewels of a crown, lifted like a banner over His land—for how great its goodness and how great its beauty! Grain shall make the young men thrive, and new wine the young women" (Zechariah 9:16-17). It's a joyful picture of redeemed people living in a world made new by their Creator and Savior.

It's All About the Message

> *"Behold, I send My messenger, and he will prepare the way*
> *before Me. And the Lord, whom you seek, will suddenly come*
> *to His temple, even the Messenger of the covenant, in whom*
> *you delight. Behold, He is coming," says the* LORD *of hosts.*
> *"But who can endure the day of His coming? And who can*
> *stand when He appears?"* (Malachi 3:1-2)

Malachi's unique prophecy worked on several levels, and all of them focused on God's message and messengers. First, Malachi's name means "messenger." We don't know much about him, but that serves to illustrate the truth that the messenger isn't as important as the message. Fittingly, Malachi predicted the messenger from God who would announce the coming of the Messiah, whom we know to be John the Baptist.[10] John, of course, observed that he wasn't fit to untie Jesus's sandals,[11] reinforcing the importance of the main Messenger. Then, foreshadowing the same humble spirit of John's proclamation, Malachi predicted the arrival of the Messenger Himself, bearing the new covenant of grace.

There is some debate over whether the first the part of this prophecy refers to Jesus's first coming or His second. In His first coming, He did appear suddenly on the scene, turning over the moneylenders' tables in the temple courts. However, Jesus will also come suddenly to His temple upon His return in power and glory.[12] This indicates a temple must be standing when Jesus returns. Though it will be superintended by Antichrist at that time, Jesus will return in power from heaven: "In that day His feet will stand on the Mount of Olives, which faces Jerusalem on the east. And the Mount of Olives shall be split in two, from east to west" (Zechariah 14:4). Jesus will burn away the pretensions of those who thought they didn't need Him and overpower those who thought they could stand against Him. His judgment will be swift for those who failed to heed the message He brought the first time.

It's fitting, then, that the final chapter of the Old Testament focuses on God's overarching theme, His most important message to the world, embroidered in red throughout the Scriptures: Help is desperately needed, but cheer up! Superman is on the way. God thinks we are worth saving—even though the first generation of mankind ushered sin and death into paradise, and each one since has disappointed in seeking holiness, justice, and righteousness. God knew that no human prophet, priest, or king could makes things right, so He took on the task Himself. The scarlet thread up to this point has stitched a giant arrow pointing in one direction—to Christ alone.

When Jesus came the first time, He came as Savior, to deal with the impact of sin; the second time, He will come to judge sin. He will judge the world for unrepentant sin, for its rejection of Him as Messiah, and He will purge the earth through the tribulation period. Both then and now, the message—the gospel—remains the same: We need saving, and God has provided the way in His greatest message to mankind: Jesus Christ.

RESCUE OPERATION: COMPLETE

NEW TESTAMENT HISTORY:
Matthew, Mark, Luke, John, and Acts

As I've mentioned, one of my favorite quotes is by Bible teacher William Evans, who said, "Cut the Bible anywhere and it bleeds."[1] This scarlet thread of redemption runs throughout the Scriptures, from Genesis to Revelation. No matter where you jump in, as we've seen, you will find predicted or displayed the sacrifice of Jesus Christ. But nowhere else will you find that sacrifice so clearly manifest than in Matthew, Mark, Luke, and John. These Gospel accounts are the epicenter of salvation history. By telling the story of the life, death, and resurrection of Jesus Christ, the very acts that dyed redemption's thread scarlet, the drama of the bloodline reaches its narrative climax.

In this chapter, we'll look at some of the key moments and words in the life of Jesus in the Gospels, then we'll move into the earliest years of the church in the book of Acts, following the birth and growth of this new community of people whom God had purchased with His own blood.

REDEMPTION'S EPICENTER

Taken together, the Gospels provide a complete, dynamic look at the life of the God-man Jesus Christ and His redemptive work on the earth. Matthew paints Jesus as the Messiah-King, the Sovereign predicted and promised in the Old Testament. The Gospel of Mark portrays Jesus as the obedient servant of the Lord, showing in rapid succession all that Jesus accomplished as He lived out the will of the Father. Luke, on the other hand, established Jesus as the Son of Man by focusing on His humanity. And John zeroed in on the incarnation— that God became flesh and blood so that His flesh could be broken and His blood poured out for us. It's in the Gospels that the scarlet thread shines most prominently in the tapestry of redemption, signaling the greatest news of all: Jesus died for you and for me. God's words that "the life...is in the blood" (Leviticus 17:11) get their fullest meaning in the Gospels: *Our* life is in *His* blood.

Fixing the Broken Bloodline

> *Jesus Himself began His ministry at about thirty years of age,*
> *being (as was supposed) the son of Joseph.* (Luke 3:23)

There have been a number of unusual births throughout history. According to the Guinness World Records, the largest baby ever born weighed twenty-two pounds and eight ounces.[2] That's more like a toddler than a newborn! The Old Testament has its own repertoire of unusual births, but none of them are truly unique. In the history of humanity, only one person has ever been born to a virgin, and that singular birth started a singular life that rocked the world to its sin-stained core.

Besides fulfilling prophecy,[3] part of the reason for Jesus's unusual birth begins in His family tree. Both Matthew and Luke provided a genealogy of Jesus, showing that He had the right pedigree to be the Messiah, coming from the tribe of Judah and the lineage of King David. The difference is that Matthew showed Jesus's legal right to rule as the son of David through His legal father Joseph, and Luke recorded Jesus's connection to the biological bloodline of David through Mary.

Sound dry? Well, sometimes the driest orchards yield the richest fruit. Taken together, these two genealogies solve for us the biggest problem in the Old Testament: The bloodline of King David had been cursed through his descendant Coniah (or Jeconiah), thus none of

Coniah's descendants would sit on the throne to rule.[4] So how would the Messiah, the son of David, be able to rule and reign?

Matthew's genealogy follows the bloodline of Jesus back to David through the royal line of King Solomon, including Coniah, on whom the blood curse was pronounced. This meant that Jesus had the legal right to the throne, the dynastic right of succession via David's royal line. That supplies Joseph's direct line of ancestry. But because that bloodline was cursed, Luke, in his genealogy, went back to David through another son of David named Nathan, an ancestor of Mary— and that bloodline was not cursed.

This means God got around His own curse by having Jesus be born of a virgin. Joseph's bloodline was cursed regarding its royal lineage, but so what? Joseph wasn't Jesus's blood father. Rather, He was conceived in the womb of Mary by the Holy Spirit. And Mary's pure, uncursed bloodline traces all the way back to King David. So Jesus has the legal right to reign through Joseph, and the pure bloodline on Mary's side.

This is why the virgin birth is essential to our salvation. It's not a secondary issue. It's not a fanciful tale, nor a Jewish version of ancient virgin birth myths from early cult religions. Everything depends on it. This was the firstfruits of God's crucial promise in Genesis 3:15 that the Seed of the woman would crush the head of the serpent. Biologically and theologically, women don't have seed; men do. But Mary carried in her child the seed not of a human man but of the Holy Spirit.

This is how serious God is about the scarlet thread of redemption: By working around a cursed bloodline, He ensured that we would be redeemed from the curse of the law and brought into the bloodline of His Son.[5]

Behold the Lamb

> *The next day John saw Jesus coming toward him, and said, "Behold! The Lamb of God who takes away the sin of the world!" (John 1:29)*

At the very beginning of Jesus's ministry, His cousin John the Baptist proclaimed these words. What did John mean by calling Jesus "the

Lamb"? From an animal perspective, a lamb isn't an impressive animal. No one uses sheep to protect property. People don't hang signs that say, "Beware of lamb." The idea of a lamb doesn't exude strength—but it's not meant to.

John was a PK—a priest's kid—and he knew what lambs were for: sacrifice. He was essentially saying, "Here's the one who's going to be sacrificed for the sin of the whole world." Maybe he was thinking back to Isaiah 53, which predicted that the Messiah would be "led as a lamb to the slaughter" (v. 7). Or perhaps he went back to the Passover, when a lamb was killed and its blood put on the doorposts of the Jewish homes in Egypt to save them from judgment.[6] That time it was one lamb per family; now, John was broadening it to include the whole world.

This concept of Jesus as the Lamb is critical to understanding His significance. People often say things like, "Well, I believe Jesus was just a good teacher." He was actually the best teacher, but He didn't come to earth just to teach. Others say, "I believe Jesus was a miracle worker. He made so many people happy through His miracles." Yes, He did, but that's not why He came. Still others say, "I like to think of Jesus as the ultimate example of love and acceptance." He certainly was that, but that wasn't His primary purpose in coming to earth. Jesus was first and foremost a sacrificial Lamb, and John nailed it: "Look! This is the Lamb who's going to take away the sin of the world." When John, this son of a Jewish priest, gave Jesus this title of a *lamb*, he was thinking blood!

> Jesus will come again as a Lion, but first He had to come as a sacrificial Lamb to pay for the sin of mankind.

The very name *Jesus* reveals this purpose for His birth, life, and death. Before He was even conceived in Mary's womb, an angel instructed Joseph, "You shall call His name JESUS, for He will save His people from their sins" (Matthew 1:21). In Hebrew, the name *Jesus* is *Yeshua*, which means "Yahweh/God is salvation." That's why He came: to save people from their sins.

The men in the Old Testament who shared Jesus's name pointed in limited ways to His purpose: Joshua was the defender of the faith who led Israel into the land of God's rest, and Jeshua, the high priest in Nehemiah's day, restored the essential practice of sacrifice in the second temple. And Jesus is the perfect fulfillment of the promise of their examples.

The Jews were looking for the Lion of Judah, a king to overthrow their oppressors; they didn't want a Lamb. But God knew what they needed, and that's what He gave them. Jesus will come again as a Lion, but first He had to come as a sacrificial Lamb to pay for the sins of mankind. And what motivated this sacrifice? Love.

The Gospel in a Nutshell

> *God so loved the world that He gave His only begotten Son,*
> *that whoever believes in Him should not perish but have*
> *everlasting life.* (John 3:16)

I don't have to tell you that John 3:16 is the most famous verse in the Bible. Gideons International, an association that puts Bibles in hotel rooms, prints this verse at the very front of their Bibles in different languages because they want to make sure no matter who you are or where you're from, it's the first thing you read when you open the book. In the greater tapestry of redemption, picture this verse doublestitched and framed with an ornate border.

John 3:16 is Jesus's summary of His rescue mission, spoken to Nicodemus during a late-night conversation. It's a verse so familiar to our ears that we have to be careful not to miss its impact—that it reveals the very heart of God: He loves people. He doesn't want to condemn us; He wants to save us.[7] That was the reason for the elaborate operation of sending Jesus—God become flesh—to the earth in fulfillment of Scripture as an atoning sacrifice—so that anyone who believes in Him would be saved. This verse is the core of redemption, the *ipso centro* of the biblical bloodline theme. In John 3:16, one can hear the blood dripping from the thread.

Then there's the other side of the coin: "He who does not believe is condemned already, because he has not believed in the name of the only begotten Son of God" (v. 18). In other words, you begin from a position of guilt, and only authentically trusting in Jesus can deliver you from a just condemnation. Why? Because every person is born into this world in sin, naturally estranged from God. Everyone needs a spiritual rebirth, and that can be found only in Jesus Christ. Let the tale woven in scarlet sink in: God loved *you* so much that He gave His only begotten Son *for you*—and He did so because He doesn't want you to waste your life or go to hell afterward. Everlasting life is His heart for you.

> The cross was paramount to Jesus; it was at the top of His to-do list.

Jesus already did the hard work. He did all the heavy lifting on the cross. All you have to do is admit that you have a need, look to Him, believe, and be saved. That's the gospel in a nutshell.

Jesus's Number One Priority

> *The Son of Man did not come to be served, but to serve, and to give His life a ransom for many.* (Mark 10:45)

When Jesus came to earth, He didn't travel first class as the King He is; He arrived in steerage, as a member of the peasant class.[8] He came to serve through teaching, preaching, and healing.[9] More than that, He came to give Himself as a ransom for many—not to be some revolutionary hero who would shed Roman blood, but to shed His own blood on the cross and serve the will of the Father in redemptive history. He came to serve humanity by saving humanity—by giving up His life so that we could truly live.

The height of Jesus's redeeming work on earth was accomplished on the cross. Thus the cross was paramount to Jesus; it was at the top of His to-do list. On one of the occasions Jesus foretold His own death, He said He "*must* go...and be killed, and be raised the third day" (Matthew 16:21). His crucifixion was His number one priority.

There's a growing tendency in the church to be ashamed of the cross and to cut out songs and sermons that deal with the blood of Christ.

After all, nobody wants to hear about a bloody religion, right? The idea is that if you want a popular ministry, you have to exclude the cross and include what makes people feel good about themselves, like positive social issues or personal fulfillment. But if redemption's thread isn't scarlet, it's not true redemption.

Jesus Himself focused on His death—the cross, the sacrifice, the bloodshed. Why? Because it was only through His blood-soaked death that He could save us from our sin. Jesus's focus changed the world, and no other religious tapestry boasts a God who sacrificed Himself to save His worshippers.

What Makes Jesus Cry?

> *As He drew near, He saw the city and wept over it, saying,*
> *"If you had known, even you, especially in this your day, the*
> *things that make for your peace! But…you did not know the*
> *time of your visitation."* (Luke 19:41-42, 44)

As Jesus marched toward Jerusalem for the grand finale of His life—His death on the cross—He drew near the city and wept over it. The construction of the original Greek text in this passage reveals that this was a loud, emotional lamentation—more of a sob than a sniffle. Why such a profound show of sadness? Jesus's heart broke because the Jews did not recognize "the time of [their] visitation," or the time of God visiting them.

I believe Jesus was referencing Daniel 9, the backbone of biblical prophecy. Verse 25 tells us that "from the going forth of the command to restore and build Jerusalem until Messiah the Prince, there shall be seven weeks and sixty-two weeks." I wrote about this back in chapter 8, but it's worth reviewing a bit here.

Most scholars believe that a "week" in this passage refers to a period of seven years. Back in the nineteenth century, a Scotland Yard official named Sir Robert Anderson decided to figure out when in history the edict came that Jerusalem should be rebuilt, and then count "seven weeks and sixty-two weeks"—483 years—from that point.

What he found was that the Persian king Artaxerxes Longimanus issued this particular edict on March 14, 445 BC. Counting 483 years from that date—using the Babylonian calendar and adjusting for leap years—he ended up on April 6, AD 32, the tenth of Nisan in the Jewish calendar.[10] It was on this very day that Jesus rode on a donkey into Jerusalem to present Himself to the nation—the day of the Jews' visitation from "Messiah the Prince." Daniel had given his people a timetable, and Jesus was right on time.

Again, this is staggering. The Old Testament predicted with perfect accuracy Jesus's arrival in Jerusalem, soon after which He would shed His blood on the cross for mankind. And Jesus wept over the fact that the Jews were blind to this. He held them personally responsible for knowing and understanding how the prophecies of the Old Testament pointed to Him—and He does the same for us too.

In total, Jesus uniquely fulfilled 330 prophecies. An astronomer and mathematician named Peter Stoner once calculated the odds of Jesus—or any person in history—fulfilling these messianic prophecies. He found that the odds of someone fulfilling just eight of them is one chance in 10^{17}. That's one chance out of 100,000,000,000,000,000.[11]

Stoner said that's like filling the state of Texas two feet deep with silver dollars, marking one of the silver dollars, mixing it in with all the others, and then blindfolding someone and giving that person one chance to find the marked coin. Those are steep odds—like, Everest steep! And for sixteen prophecies to be fulfilled, the numbers jump to one chance in 10^{45}; for forty-eight, it's one chance in 10^{157}. To illustrate the odds of that last probability, Stoner had to use electrons instead of silver dollars.[12]

When we take the time to dig into redemptive history, tracing the prophecies Jesus fulfilled reveals that He Himself is the grand theme of all Scripture, and the results are life-changing. It puts iron in our sin-anemic blood, building our trust in a God powerful enough to work out the details of our salvation long before it took place.

God Washes Feet

> Jesus...rose from supper and laid aside His garments, took a
> towel and girded Himself. After that, He poured water into a
> basin and began to wash the disciples' feet, and to wipe them
> with the towel with which He was girded. (John 13:3-5)

Some people think that God created the world, then went on to other things and left us spinning unattended in the cosmos. But Jesus tells us otherwise. God doesn't only superintend redemptive history, He wove Himself into the center of it.

That's essentially what God did in the incarnation—the Word becoming flesh, God becoming man in the person of Jesus.[13] The night before Jesus went to the cross, He spent a special evening with His closest friends, during which He washed their feet and basically acted out the incarnation—and His entire ministry—in parable form:

- Just as Jesus rose from supper to wash His disciples' feet, He had risen to leave His throne in heaven and do the Father's bidding on earth.

- Just as Jesus laid aside His garments, He laid aside His divine rights as God to pour Himself into a humble human body.[14]

- The towel He wrapped around Himself represented the cloak of His humanity—that He was God become flesh.

- The water He poured in the basin foreshadowed what would in a few hours be His blood, poured out to wash away the sins of all who believe in Him.

- When He dried the disciples' feet, He demonstrated that He finishes what He starts.[15]

Think of it—God washing your feet! One of redemption's most remarkable aspects is what God did to achieve it: He sent His Son to become one of us, to serve us and show us how to serve.

Passing Over the Passover

He took the cup, and gave thanks, and gave it to them, saying, "Drink from it, all of you. For this is My blood of the new covenant, which is shed for many for the remission of sins."
(Matthew 26:27-28)

When Jesus spoke these words to His disciples on that same night—hours before He was crucified and killed—He was essentially ending the relevance of the very Passover meal they were celebrating together by pointing to its ultimate fulfillment.

The Passover revealed two important truths: First, that there can be no redemption or aversion of divine wrath without death; blood has to be shed.[16] And second, there can be a substitute; another life can be substituted for your life. In the first Passover, for example, a lamb was slain and its blood applied to the doorposts of the Israelites' houses in Egypt, and in that way God's judgment passed over the people. The ritual shedding of blood would continue in Jewish religious practice, illustrating its ongoing significance.

These two great truths were about to be fulfilled in Jesus Christ, the Lamb of God, meaning this was the last Passover meal that would have any redemptive significance. For the 1,500-plus years since the exodus, the Jews had sacrificed millions of animals to atone for sin, but it was never enough—until now. The blood Jesus would soon shed on the cross would be enough to reconcile us to the Father forever.[17]

This is nothing less than monumental. If you look at Passover and all the sacrifices of the Old Testament as Sacrifice 1.0, then what Jesus did on the cross was Sacrifice 2.0—and it's the final version of the program. Through His blood, we're no longer under the old covenant but the new, just as He said.

Surrendered to the Cause

> *Jesus said to Peter, "Put your sword into the sheath. Shall I not drink the cup which My Father has given Me?"* (John 18:11)

As Jesus was about to be arrested in the garden of Gethsemane, Peter drew his sword and hacked off the ear of the high priest's servant. "Don't worry, Jesus," I can imagine Peter saying, "I've got this under control." But Jesus rebuked him.

Why? Well, from a human vantage point, the story looked like a disaster—Jesus was about to go to His death. Peter couldn't think of anything worse that could happen—and in one sense, he was right, but his actions showed a limited grasp of the greater scheme of redemptive history. Remember, the Holy Spirit hadn't yet been given to decode the big picture.[18] But Almighty God's sovereignty overshadowed the entire scene. Jesus secured a crucial juncture in the scarlet thread when He looked past this disastrous moment of betrayal and impending torture and essentially told Peter, "That's why I'm here: to drink this cup of suffering."

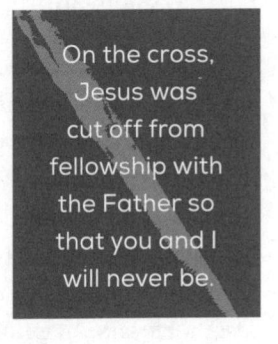

On the cross, Jesus was cut off from fellowship with the Father so that you and I will never be.

Jesus had already made the ultimate choice to surrender to the will of the Father and go to the cross, praying earlier that night, "My Father, if it is possible, let this cup pass from Me; nevertheless, not as I will, but as You will" (Matthew 26:39). In other words, "If there's any other way that mankind can have salvation, let it be so. But if not, I will do Your will Your way."

The next day, after being arrested and unfairly tried, Jesus drank the cup, taking the weight of the sins of the world and the penalty of God's wrath. In light of His words the night before, the very fact that He surrendered and went to the cross shows that there is no other way through which mankind can approach God and have a relationship with Him. On the cross, Jesus was cut off from fellowship with the Father so that you and I never would be. As the needle guiding the scarlet thread passed through His hands and feet, our sin separated Him from the Father, and He cried out in anguish, "My God, My God, why have You forsaken Me?" (Matthew 27:46).

That makes the whole negotiation in Gethsemane's garden that much more powerful. You would think Jesus would have thought of me, for example, and rightfully said, "Father, Skip is not worth it." But He said, "Nevertheless, not as I will, but as You will." Millennia earlier, God set up this moment in another garden, anticipating in Eden the day when His own Son would fully surrender to His desire to see mankind bought back from sin. That moment had finally arrived, and Jesus embraced it fully.

Mission Accomplished

> *When Jesus had received the sour wine, He said, "It is*
> *finished!" And bowing His head, He gave up His spirit.*
> (John 19:30)

When Jesus sacrificed Himself on the cross for our sins, it was once and for all. This is reflected in His last words: "It is finished!" In the original Greek text, that's the word *tetelestai*, which comes from another word that means "complete," "mature," or "perfect." Servants would use this word when they finished the work their master gave them to do. Remember what Jesus said as a twelve-year-old in the temple? "I must be about My Father's business" (Luke 2:49). Now on the cross, as a servant to His master, He said, "It is finished! I've done what You called Me to do."

Priests would also use the Hebrew or Aramaic equivalent of the term *tetelestai* when speaking to someone who had brought a lamb for sacrifice. They would look over the lamb to make sure it was without blemish or defect, and then they would say, "*Tetelestai*," or "It's acceptable." Peter would later make the point that Jesus Christ died for us as a lamb without spot or blemish, as a perfect sacrifice.[19]

Artists would use the term *tetelestai* when they had finished a painting or sculpture. On its own, the Old Testament didn't paint the full picture; it just pointed to the one who would finish it. Then Jesus came along and, like an artist, put all the finishing touches on what the Old Testament began. "Now the picture is completed—*tetelestai*."

And finally, merchants would use the term *tetelestai* to describe paying off a debt in full. You and I have a debt, don't we? "All have sinned and fall short of the glory of God" (Romans 3:23). That's a bill we could never pay. But when Jesus died on the cross, He said, "*Tetelestai*, Father—their debt is now paid in full because I've paid it."

Tetelestai is what we mean when we talk about the finished work of Christ: *The work is done.* You don't have to earn your salvation; it's a gift given to you based on the atoning sacrifice that Jesus, God in the flesh, made on the cross. And it's this sacrifice to which the entire Bible points. When Jesus died, the veil of the temple ripped in two from top to bottom,[20] and though the Jews sewed it up again, their stitchwork couldn't obscure what God had accomplished with His scarlet thread. The torn veil was Him saying, "Because of what My Son has done, there's no longer separation between mankind and Me. You can come close, and we can have intimate fellowship. All you have to do is receive Him."

The Best Kind of Heartburn

Beginning at Moses and all the Prophets, He expounded to them in all the Scriptures the things concerning Himself.
(Luke 24:27)

One of my favorite postresurrection stories is found in Luke 24, as I mentioned in the introduction of this book. Not long after the crucifixion of Jesus, a couple of disciples were walking along the road to Emmaus, and they were despondent. They didn't know Jesus had risen; they still thought their hopes and expectations about Him had been dashed. As they walked, along came Jesus, whom they were kept from recognizing. In fact, they thought He was a stranger from out of town. And do you know how Jesus revealed Himself to them? Through a Bible study.

After the two disciples explained to Jesus why they were so sad, Jesus said, "'O foolish ones, and slow of heart to believe in all that the prophets have spoken! Ought not the Christ to have suffered these things and to enter into His glory?' And beginning at Moses and all the Prophets, He expounded to them in all the Scriptures the things concerning Himself" (Luke 24:25-27).

Jesus rebuked their ignorance, then led them through Scripture. And it wasn't just any Bible study; it was a prophetic Bible study that was all about Him. He was showing them how the entire Bible has one subject: Jesus Himself! He was tracing for them the scarlet thread as it wound its way through the whole Old Testament. I don't often get goosebumps, but this account gives them to me.

By the time Jesus was finished, the two disciples begged Him to eat with them. So "it came to pass, as He sat at the table with them, that He took bread, blessed and broke it, and gave it to them. Then their eyes were opened and they knew Him; and He vanished from their sight.

And they said to one another, 'Did not our heart burn within us while He talked with us on the road, and while He opened the Scriptures to us?'" (Luke 24:30-32).

Notice they didn't say their hearts burned within them as they prayed to Him or as He gazed into their eyes. No, what really fired up their hearts was when they stopped talking and started listening to what He—and the Scriptures—had to say.

This heartburn was simply a new understanding of old things. It's like reading something in Scripture you've read before, but the light comes on and you finally get it. Jesus didn't tell these guys anything they didn't already know; they had heard the prophets and Moses all their lives—but not like this. And this is the kind of unveiling made possible for anyone who believes in Christ.

Every now and then I'll meet someone who says, "Yeah, I've heard all the stuff in the Bible before. I want something new." Listen, you don't need a new revelation; what you need is a new application of the old revelation. You need to read the same "old" Scriptures while praying that the Lord opens them up in a fresh or unexpected way. That's what caused these disciples' hearts to burn within them—and what I hope will cause your heart to burn, too, as we continue to follow the scarlet thread of redemption through the New Testament.

This holy bloodline is the overwhelming focus of the Gospels. So much leading up to this point in Scripture had prophesied and spoken of the Messiah and His atoning work on the cross, and everything in this fourfold account of His life zeroes in on the moment when He "[gave] His life a ransom for many" (Matthew 20:28). The entire Old Testament looked forward to the cross, and from this point on, the New Testament will look back to it as the touchstone of the Christian faith, the moment in history when God's main redeeming work in the world was accomplished.

THE WITNESS OF BLOOD AND SPIRIT

As Jesus's disciples, empowered by the Holy Spirit, began to spread the good news of His atoning death and resurrection throughout the known world, the newly birthed church grew by leaps and bounds. One of the big themes of Acts is that the church belongs to Jesus, not any leader or group of people. Why? Because Jesus didn't just found the church—He "purchased [it] with His own blood" (Acts 20:28). No leader or pastor ever died to redeem the church. No church board, deacon board, or denomination ever laid down their lives to pay the price of salvation for anyone. That's essentially what Paul later communicated when those in the Corinthian church were saying, "Well, I follow Paul." He said, "Hold on a minute. Did I get crucified for you? No way!"[21] Jesus bought us with His blood that He might own us. He's the head of the church; that's why we're called the body of Christ.

As the body of Christ, one of our main purposes is to spread the gospel—which provides an ongoing witness to the power of God in our lives. The church began with men and women who had personally witnessed Jesus's life, death, and resurrection, and over the centuries, it has at various times survived and at others thrived because individuals have experienced the life-changing power of Jesus's blood by faith, and shared with others the difference it has made. Acts is the story of the power of that redeeming witness.

The Original Jesus Movement

> *While they looked steadfastly toward heaven as He went up, behold, two men stood by them in white apparel, who also said, "Men of Galilee, why do you stand gazing up into heaven? This same Jesus, who was taken up from you into heaven, will so come in like manner as you saw Him go into heaven."* (Acts 1:10-11)

The book of Acts opens with the disciples standing on the Mount of Olives with their heads cranked back, staring into heaven after Jesus had ascended. Two angels appeared to them and said, "Hey, Jesus is coming back—but for now, don't just stand there. Get moving!"[22]

I came out of the Jesus movement of the '70s, and we expected Jesus to come back at any moment. I still hold to the doctrine of the imminent return of Christ, but the danger was evident when a lot of my friends quit their jobs and started getting lazy. "After all," they said, "Jesus is going to show up within the month."

Jesus could show up at any time, but we don't know when. He told us what we're supposed to do in the meantime: "You shall be witnesses to Me in Jerusalem, and in all Judea and Samaria, and to the end of the earth" (Acts 1:8). As the angels said, "Why are you standing around? There's work to do!"

It's good to look forward to Jesus's return, but not at the expense of what He wants you to do right now—namely, spreading the gospel and sharing God's grand plan of redemption with a lost world. Redemptive history pivoted at the cross and the empty grave; it didn't end there. Jesus is coming back, but that doesn't mean we should stand and stare at the sky. Jesus didn't expect His disciples to check out of life, sit on a hillside, strum a guitar, and wait for Him to show up again. Spreading the message of the finished work of Christ was the all-important task at hand. He wanted them to be busy about His business—so they got to it.

From this point on in the New Testament, the focus shifts as the disciples began to spread the good news, always looking back to what Jesus accomplished on the cross and acting as witnesses of what they had seen and heard, even when persecution followed.[23] The scarlet thread split at this point from the single bloodline of the Messiah into an arterial network, interconnected in Christ, growing constantly through a global mission with as many filaments as there are people who have received Him.

Just How Amazing Is Grace?

We believe that through the grace of the Lord Jesus Christ we shall be saved in the same manner as they. (Acts 15:11)

The early believers faced a crisis over the most important thing in the world: how a person is saved. Is salvation a work that's done by God or achieved by man? Unfortunately, this is still disputed in the church today because people have a hard time with the finished work of Christ and the free gift of grace: "Surely there's something I need to do to earn God's favor." That kind of pride or fear is a pair of pliers whose only purpose is to clamp off the power and freedom we get from God's bloodline.

The apostles—particularly Paul after his dramatic conversion in Acts 9—had been going around telling everyone, Jew and Gentile alike, that all they had to do was place their faith in Jesus Christ to be saved. But a group of people called the Judaizers were teaching that in order to be saved, Gentiles not only had to give their life to Christ but also keep the Law of Moses. The idea that a Gentile—without being circumcised or keeping any of the Old Testament law—could believe in Jesus and be admitted into the church and guaranteed heaven was an affront to them. After all, Jesus was a Jewish Messiah who fulfilled the Hebrew Scriptures, right?

The Judaizers were trying to mix the law and grace, which negates grace. They were trying to add to the finished work Jesus accomplished on the cross. That's legalism, and it's dangerous. God's grace through faith alone is what saves.[24] We do good works in response to and as a result of being saved by God's grace, not the other way around. Whenever we add *anything*—rituals, ceremonies, rules—to what the Bible requires as saving faith, it's the same as saying the blood of Jesus wasn't enough to secure our salvation.

The scriptural decision that came out of this threshold moment in the early church affirmed the source of our salvation: Faith in Jesus alone is enough to be saved. As Peter said, "Through the grace of the Lord Jesus Christ we shall be saved in the same manner as [Gentile believers]." He didn't say, "Gentiles can be saved like *we* Jews are"; he said, "We can be saved like *they* are—only by faith in Jesus."

James, the half brother of Jesus, said essentially the same thing, drawing from Scripture a prophecy about God's wide-flung salvation: "Simon [Peter] has declared how God at the first visited the Gentiles to take out of them a people for His name. And with this the words of the prophets agree, just as it is written: 'After this I will return and will rebuild the tabernacle of David, which has fallen down; I will rebuild its ruins, and I will set it up; so that the rest of mankind may seek the LORD, even all the Gentiles who are called by My name'" (Acts 15:14-17).

James was quoting the prophet Amos to explain that because David's tabernacle—his royal house—had been restored by Christ, the door of faith was now open for the Gentiles.[25] The house of David, as we've already seen, had been broken when his royal bloodline was cursed because of Coniah. The only way to fix that curse was through the virgin birth, which Jesus fulfilled as the Messiah, thus rebuilding the house and lineage of David—which, as prophesied, opened wide the doors of salvation.

This was done, as James noted, "so that the rest of mankind"—not just Jewish people—"may seek the LORD, even all the Gentiles who are called by My name, says the LORD who does all these things." Rooting his explanation in Scripture, James showed the early church that Amos said nothing about Gentiles becoming Jewish proselytes before being admitted into the kingdom. Rather, they could just come.

That's the gospel—that's the good news. The symbol of Christianity isn't scales, weighing our good and bad deeds or our adherence to the law, but a cross. And that cross speaks of forgiveness made available because Jesus shed His blood on it 2,000 years ago, wiping away every transgression and opening the floodgates of God's amazing grace to anyone who believes.

REDEMPTION'S NEW GROUND RULES

PAUL'S CHURCH LETTERS:
Romans, 1 and 2 Corinthians,
Galatians, 1 and 2 Thessalonians

The wondrous theme of all Scripture continues to thread its way throughout the apostle Paul's church letters: "Jesus Christ and Him crucified" (1 Corinthians 2:2). Redemption is the unifying message of the entire Bible. In the Old Testament, it is *anticipated*; in the Gospels, it is *accomplished*; in the New Testament letters, it is *applied*. Author Graham Scroggie noted,

> As running through all British Navy rope there is a thread of colour according to the dockyard in which it is made, so running through all the Scriptures is the saving purpose, so making the whole Bible an unfolding drama of redemption.[1]

Paul wrote these doctrine-focused letters to groups of believers scattered throughout the Roman Empire, from the central city of Rome to Galatia, which was located in what is now Turkey. Doctrine, which is simply good, healthy teaching, was number one on the early church's list of priorities,[2] and so it was for Paul in his letters. Because there's no narrative flow in Paul's church epistles (or any New Testament letters, for that matter), we'll simply highlight the places where the scarlet thread of redemption most clearly bleeds through, providing rich insight into what Jesus Christ's death and resurrection means to you and me. In fact, we will see the ground rules of redemption. As we finish in 1 and 2 Thessalonians, we'll see Paul look ahead to the end times, when God will tie off that blood-red cord and finish the good work of redemption He has begun in every believer's life.

GETTING RIGHT WITH GOD

The book of Romans is the most in-depth theological exploration of salvation in the New Testament. Martin Luther called it "the chief part of the New Testament."[3] In it, Paul made clear the difference between religion and the gospel. Religion puts up barriers and walls; the gospel bulldozes them down, saying, "Everyone falls short of God's standard, but anyone can be saved by calling on Jesus's name." The gospel says you don't have to be religious to be saved or work your way to heaven—you just have to trust in Jesus Christ and His finished work on the cross. Romans presents the clearest statement of mankind's biggest problem and God's solution to that problem. It showcases the depth of mankind's sin and the heights of God's mercy and love, revealing the strength of the scarlet thread and the length to which the Lord went to ensure we're justified and made right with Him.

Just-As-If-I'd (Never Sinned)

> *Being justified freely by His grace through the redemption that is in Christ Jesus...* (Romans 3:24)

Justification is an important biblical word that we need to bring back to the Christian vocabulary. It's essential in our understanding of redemption. It simply describes what happens at the moment of salvation: God takes you as you are, spiritually dead because of sin, and credits the righteousness of Jesus to you. From that point on, He declares you to be righteous and treats you that way.

Think of it like this: Billy Graham's classmate Roy Gustafson used to tell the story of an Englishman who had his Rolls-Royce shipped to mainland Europe for vacation. The Rolls-Royce broke down as the guy was driving it cross-country, so he called the factory in England, and they flew a mechanic over to fix it. The man wondered how much this was going to cost him, so when he returned to England, he wrote a letter inquiring about his bill. He received this reply in response: "Sorry, sir, but we don't know what you're talking about. Our records indicate that nothing has ever gone wrong with any Rolls-Royce."[4]

That's the concept of justification: We've messed up, but God keeps no record of our sin because of what Jesus did on the cross.

A good way to explain what it means to be justified is to break the word apart: God declares me righteous and then treats me *just-as-if-I'd* never sinned, all because of what Jesus did on the cross. Understanding the concept will spark within you an attitude of gratitude and devotion toward the Lord, for it demonstrates just how much God loves you and how far He was willing to go to weave you into the tapestry of redemption. Justification is the heart of Paul's letter to the Romans and of the Christian message.

What Kind of Love Is This?

> *God demonstrates His own love toward us, in that while we were still sinners, Christ died for us. Much more then, having now been justified by His blood, we shall be saved from wrath through Him.* (Romans 5:8-9)

God's love is foreign to the human experience because it operates on a totally different level than our love. Human love is object-oriented, whereas God's love is subject-oriented. It's not based on the worth or value of a person; it's based on God's personal character. It's His nature.[5] As amazing as you may be (or think you may be), there's nothing about you that makes God say, "Wow! I absolutely *have* to love this person!" God's love for you is not because of you. All the reasons that He loves you come from Him, pouring out of Him because of who He is.

That begs the question: When did God start loving you? When

you received Christ, did God say, "Now that you've received Me, I'm going to show My love to you"? No—Paul said that Jesus died for you while you were "still a sinner." Part of the wonder of the scarlet thread is that God loved you before the world was made—you were in His plans from before the beginning, an integral part of His desire to save mankind. And nothing you've done since coming on the scene—no matter how bad—can sever you from His love.

> It's impossible to appreciate the height of your salvation until you understand the depth of the sin from which you were saved.

God's love for you was fully demonstrated when He sent His Son to the earth to die on a cross. Almost every time the love of God is mentioned in the New Testament, it's in reference to the cross, the epicenter of redemptive history. The cross is a bridge to get people from earth to heaven, from their sinfulness to God's perfection.

Thus the cross shows the height of God's love as well as the depth of humanity's depravity, like a diamond set on pitch-black cloth. God has always had the same disposition toward sin. He's never winked at it or excused it—but He will forgive it. Because Jesus Christ died on the cross, God can justify and accept any sinner who believes in Him. As Paul said, once we've been justified by Jesus's blood, "we shall be saved from wrath through Him."

You can't separate God's wrath from God's grace. It's impossible to appreciate the height of your salvation until you understand the depth of the sin from which you were saved. The whole point of Romans is that nobody in this world escapes the wrath of God, except through Christ. God's judgment is real and certain, but His grace and matchless love are just as real. He paid the price to make sure that you would be in heaven with Him forever; that was the goal of the redemptive bloodline that began in the garden with Adam and Eve.

Adam Versus Jesus

Through one man's offense judgment came to all men, resulting in condemnation, even so through one Man's righteous act the free gift came to all men, resulting in justification of life. (Romans 5:18)

On one hand, comparing Adam to Jesus is like comparing a toddler beginning piano lessons to Paul McCartney playing "The Long and Winding Road." On the other hand, Adam was the first and best of us—physically perfect, no emotional baggage, a great relationship with his perfect partner—and he still blew it. We might think that in Adam's situation we would have done better, but we wouldn't have. Free will in an imperfect being means eventually choosing imperfectly. So when you read that Adam blew it for all of us, realize that none of us in our human imperfection could have done any better. Mankind's first and finest fell short, proving right off the bat that we needed a perfect man to save us.

In Romans 5, Paul drew a contrast between Adam and this perfect man, Jesus: Adam sinned; Jesus saves. When Adam did what he did, many died; because Jesus did what He did, many can live. What Adam did brought bondage; what Jesus has done can bring freedom. Adam disobeyed God his Creator; Jesus obeyed God His Father. When Adam sinned, people thereafter were declared unrighteous; because Jesus paid the price and gave the gift of His life, people thereafter can be declared righteous.

Because of what Adam did, the image of God in man was marred and sin was woven into the human bloodline, infecting every single person. But when Jesus came along, He said, "I'll take that infection Myself, because by taking the penalty for what Adam—and thus the entire human race—has done, I'll correct what's been messed up. I'll restore the image of God." Adam brought death; Jesus brought abundant life.[6] We were ruined by the one man's misdeed, but rescued by the other man's merit. That's what the scarlet thread of redemption is all about—not what we've done, but what Christ has done for us.

THE TWO STICKING POINTS

Corinth was a tough place to be a Christian, and Paul's first letter shows the struggle believers had with lax moral and social conditions.

In 1 Corinthians, Paul admonished the church at Corinth over a whole host of issues. "You were bought at a price," he told them, "therefore glorify God in your body and in your spirit, which are God's" (1 Corinthians 6:20). In other words, God purchased you with the blood of His Son on the cross, so you ought to live like it. But to do that, you must understand the significance of Jesus's crucifixion and resurrection. Paul explored these essential elements of God's rescue plan in this church epistle.

Cross Culture

> *The message of the cross is foolishness to those who are*
> *perishing, but to us who are being saved it is the power of God.*
> (1 Corinthians 1:18)

The Bible teaches—and the cross shows—that blood must be shed for sin to be cleansed. That concept bothers a lot of people. In fact, Paul said it is "foolishness to those who are perishing," or to those who are in the world. That's because they don't understand God's holiness and the seriousness of sin.

Jesus often spoke of His body and blood because that was the price of redemption.[7] This message is so plain and precious to the Christian church that for generations, the songs we've sung have largely been about the blood of Christ and the cross on which our salvation was procured. But this central truth isn't so plain to some so-called churches who want to drain Christianity of its very life source by removing all references to Christ's blood. They say things like, "We better not preach too much about the blood of Jesus because it's gory and might offend people."

Charles Spurgeon said, "There are some preachers who cannot or do not preach about the blood of Jesus Christ—I have one thing to say to you concerning those—Never go to hear them! Never listen to them! A ministry that has not the blood in it is lifeless, 'for the blood is the life thereof'—and a dead ministry is no good to anybody!"[8] Paul would have said, "Amen!" to that.

Without the cross, there is no Christianity. The center of our belief system is Christ and the cross—the shed blood, the sacrifice. Paul lived this out, saying, "I determined not to know anything among you except Jesus Christ and Him crucified" (1 Corinthians 2:2). Most people today see the cross as a mere religious symbol that may or may not have some power for their lives. Paul saw it as the focus of his entire life, front and center.

The way I see it, the church is to be a *cross culture*. The focal point of our distinctiveness as God's people is the sacrifice Jesus Christ made on the cross. After all, that's what Scripture shows us over and over again: Jesus's blood stains redemption's thread and cleanses every believer's heart. Where blood is flowing, life keeps going. Where blood is rejected, salvation is neglected. The cross isn't a crutch but a defibrillator.

Party Time at the Graveyard

> *If Christ is not risen, your faith is futile; you are still in your sins!* (1 Corinthians 15:17)

If Christianity ended at the cross, it would be a pretty morbid religion. Not only that, but it would never have gotten to us—it would've been stuck in the grave, so to speak. Why celebrate a dead man who stayed dead? What hope for change in your life could that possibly bring? But Jesus didn't stay dead, and that's the key to redemption.

As important as the sacrifice of the cross is to Christianity, as necessary as the blood of Christ is to pay sin's penalty, His resurrection is our cornerstone. To deny it happened is to deny the basis of the Christian faith—and some people were doing just that in Paul's day, which is why he addressed the futility of faith in an unrisen Christ: "If there's no resurrection, there's no living Christ. And face it—if there's no resurrection for Christ, everything we've told you is smoke and mirrors, and everything you've staked your life on is smoke and mirrors" (1 Corinthians 15:14-15 MSG).

In other words, the gospel must include the resurrection. It was

> When Jesus rose from the dead as the firstfruits of the new covenant, the winter of sin and death was over.

God's plan all along, and it's crucial to our faith. There's no good news in "Jesus died"; the good news comes in "Jesus rose and conquered death." That's because the resurrection of Christ started a chain reaction of events that includes our resurrection—He was "the firstfruits of those who have fallen asleep" (v. 20).[9]

Every year the Jews had a feast of firstfruits, during which they would bring the Lord an offering of their early crop and express gratitude for the fact that God had seen them through another winter and for the harvest that would soon follow.[10] The feast was celebrated the Sunday after Passover—what the church now celebrates as Resurrection Sunday, or Easter. So when Jesus rose from the dead as the firstfruits of the new covenant, the winter of sin and death was over. God brought new life out of the dead ground, and the harvest—the permanent resurrection of all God's children—would follow.

When Jesus left the tomb on Easter morning, it wasn't only to prove that He was the Messiah and God in human flesh. Even more powerfully for us, He rose to show that just as He bodily rose from the dead, we also will bodily rise from the dead. How incredible is that? Our future resurrection is as much a part of our salvation as justification or any other aspect of it, inextricably woven together by the scarlet thread of Jesus.

THE GREAT EXCHANGE

In Paul's highly personal second letter to the Corinthian church, he gave us one of the most important verses in the Bible, 2 Corinthians 5:21. This is the clearest single-verse explanation of what's been called "the great exchange"—Jesus taking the penalty for our sinful nature so that we can take on His divine nature. Jesus Christ, in His perfection, paid the price for all of our sin-stained imperfection. This substitution allows us, by faith, to be reconciled with God.

The Deal of a Lifetime

All things are of God, who has reconciled us to Himself through Jesus Christ, and has given us the ministry of reconciliation, that is, that God was in Christ reconciling the

*world to Himself, not imputing their trespasses to them, and
has committed to us the word of reconciliation…He made
Him who knew no sin to be sin for us, that we might become
the righteousness of God in Him.* (2 Corinthians 5:18-19, 21)

When you were younger, did you ever have to deal with another kid
who, for whatever reason, you didn't get along with? How did you usu-
ally approach him or her? Maybe you pushed his buttons, or maybe
you just ignored her and hoped she would go away. What do you think
would have happened if you had gone out, bought a nice toy, and given
it to him? It's possible that you could have won a friend.

That's the key thought of reconciliation. In these verses, the
Greek word translated "reconciliation" is *katallassó*, which means "to
exchange," or "to turn hostility into friendship." God is in the business
of taking the hostility that exists between man and God and turning
it into friendship.

How does He do that? By "not imputing their trespasses to them."
God doesn't put your sins on your account; He puts your sins on Jesus's
account and puts Jesus's righteous life on your account. How can He
do that? Because of the effect of the sacrifice Jesus Christ made on
the cross: "You, who once were alienated and enemies in your mind
by wicked works, yet now He has reconciled in the body of His flesh
through death."[11] We're not reconciled to God by our acts, but by
Jesus's singular act in history.

This is what 2 Corinthians 5:21 so beautifully summarizes: Jesus
bore our sins so that we could bear His righteousness. This is the clearest declaration in all Scripture of what theologians call the vicarious,
or substitutionary, atonement. *Atonement* means you've made peace
with God. *Vicarious* means it had to happen through someone else—
namely, Jesus Christ. Even though you should have received the punishment for your sin, Jesus took it instead; He became your substitute
when He went to the cross. In the Old Testament the Day of Atonement foreshadowed this truth: After a priest transferred the sins of the
nation to a scapegoat, it was released into the wilderness, signifying that
the sins of the people had been taken away.[12]

Trust me, we want that goat to run away. Sin is offensive to God because He is holy, and our sin creates a gap between us and Him. We sin by nature and by choice, and the cost of that is death. When Jesus went to the cross, He became our sin so that our penalty would be paid in full. He felt the wrath of God toward sin in His own body. He fully drank the cup of suffering, becoming the substitute for you and me. On the cross, Jesus was treated as if He were guilty of every sin committed by everyone. Put another way, God the Father treated Jesus like you deserve to be treated so that God could treat you like Jesus deserves to be treated. This is the grand truth that's woven into every fiber of the tapestry of redemption. His atonement makes reconciliation possible, and all we have to do is say yes to it.

This concept first struck me the night I received Christ. As Billy Graham was preaching on TV, he described what Jesus did on the cross and what He was offering me. I thought, *Wow, this doesn't make sense, God. You're getting a really bad deal here.* It blew my mind that God would take my sinful, filthy life and in exchange give me a pure, holy, righteous life. That night I told Him, "You're getting the raw end of the deal." But then I thought, *That means I'm getting the deal of a lifetime, and I would be an idiot to pass it up.* That's when I received Christ. That's what Jesus's sacrifice was all about. That's vicarious atonement in a nutshell.

(RESCUED FROM) THE LONG ARM OF THE LAW

Paul's epistle to the Galatians is the Magna Carta of spiritual emancipation. He wrote to the churches in the region of Galatia in response to the Judaizers, a group of people who were tampering with the very heart of the gospel, mixing legalism with salvation and the law with grace, annulling Christian liberty and leading believers astray.[13] He had harsh words for anyone who changed or added to the work of the blood of Jesus: "Even if we, or an angel from heaven, preach any other gospel to you than what we have preached to you, let him be accursed" (Galatians 1:8). In the rest of Galatians, Paul explained how we've been redeemed and set free from the law, for "a man is not justified by the works of the law but by faith in Jesus Christ" (2:16). The accomplishment of the rescue is so great because the reach of the law was so widespread, so thoroughly condemning—and that makes the freedom it bought worth fighting for.

The Curse Breaker

> *Christ has redeemed us from the curse of the law, having become a curse for us (for it is written, "Cursed is everyone who hangs on a tree"), that the blessing of Abraham might come upon the Gentiles in Christ Jesus, that we might receive the promise of the Spirit through faith.* (Galatians 3:13-14)

The law is not a blessing; it's a curse. Why? Because the law demands a strict and complete obedience, and we all fall short, no exceptions. What's the solution? *Jesus.* He took the curse for us by "hanging on a tree"—getting nailed to the cross—as Paul explained in these verses.

Now, under Jewish law, capital punishment was death by stoning. Jesus suffered capital punishment, but it was by crucifixion—a Persian invention later adapted by the Romans. The Jews didn't crucify because, according to Scripture, anyone who was crucified was cursed.[14] But that was God's solution: The full penalty of the law fell upon Jesus Christ as all of our sins were placed on Him, and He died on the very implement that the Jewish law said cursed a victim.

When God gave Israel the law, He was telling the people to live in a way that reflected their relationship with their holy God. The law set a standard we could never live up to, spelled out in hundreds of rules, regulations, and requirements that even when followed to a tee couldn't bring us into a complete, lasting, intimate relationship with our Maker.

The law didn't remove the curse; it just amplified it. The law itself became a curse because it couldn't cleanse; it could only point out what was wrong. So Jesus took the curse of our sins upon Himself. Only then could we be redeemed from the curse of the law and adopted as sons and daughters of God.

The Adoption Process

> *When the fullness of the time had come, God sent forth His*
> *Son, born of a woman, born under the law, to redeem those*
> *who were under the law, that we might receive the adoption*
> *as sons.* (Galatians 4:4-5)

We've read repeatedly in this book about the scarlet thread woven all through the Old Testament and leading to the arrival of the Messiah. But why did God send His Son Jesus Christ into the world at the time that He did? Why 2,000 years ago? According to Paul, it was the *fullness of the time*. The season was right; the perfect time had come, like ripe fruit hanging on a tree, ready to be plucked.

Up until that point, Paul wrote, the Jews were tethered to their religious system of Judaism just as a child is tied to his teachers and guardians until he comes of age.[15] But this tethering shackled the Jews to their sin. Because they could never keep the law God gave them, He included in the law a system of animal sacrifices so that innocent blood would cover their failures and sins. But those sacrifices weren't enough. The endless, tedious rituals and ceremonies didn't bring them any closer to God, and they caused within the Jewish people a longing and anticipation for the Messiah, their Deliverer.

> Because of the cross, you are a child of God, adopted into the bloodline of God.

Then, finally, Jesus came at the perfect time, as predicted, conceived by the Holy Spirit and born of a woman, Mary. He was born fully human because He had to be able to represent humanity on the cross, yet He remained fully God, meaning His sacrifice was able to pay sin's cost. Jesus was also born under the law. He was a Jewish man who followed the law, but unlike other Jews, He was able to keep the law because He was perfect and sinless.

So He was God, human, and Jewish, and He came at a time when messianic expectation was at an all-time high—but to what end? For what reason?

Paul told us: "To redeem those who were under the law, that we might receive the adoption as sons," or children of God. *Redeem* is a slavery-related term; to *redeem* means "to buy back from another's ownership." God went to the slave market of sin, bought you with the blood of Jesus, adopted you as His child, and is in the process of taking you home to Him. That means you're not under bondage any longer. You don't have to grit your teeth and try to perform to make God like you. Yes, He wants you to be obedient to Him, but lifelong obedience doesn't determine salvation. Because of the cross, you are a child of God, adopted into the bloodline of the Son of God.

END GAME

The church at Thessalonica was only a few months old when Paul wrote to them, and though the believers were growing by leaps and bounds, they were also going through the fire of intense persecution. Satan hadn't managed to prevent the Messiah's atoning sacrifice, but he continued to work through various means, including the Roman government and even certain Jewish authorities (such as Paul before his conversion), to destroy the rapidly expanding bloodline of God. So Paul wrote 1 Thessalonians to encourage Christians to hold fast to their salvation. More specifically, he highlighted for them how God would weave the scarlet thread of redemption all the way through to the end-time events of the rapture and the second coming of Christ. The Thessalonian letters look forward to heaven, our ultimate destination and final home.

Survival Gear for Last-Days Believers

> *Let us who are of the day be sober, putting on the breastplate of faith and love, and as a helmet the hope of salvation. For God did not appoint us to wrath, but to obtain salvation through our Lord Jesus Christ, who died for us, that whether we wake or sleep, we should live together with Him.* (1 Thessalonians 5:8-10)

In a book about the scarlet thread of redemption, it's imperative that we not only consider the cross, but also the end to which all redemptive history is moving: the last days, including the day of the Lord.

The day of the Lord is a concept that's mentioned throughout the Bible, particularly in 1 and 2 Thessalonians, and it refers to a future time of great difficulty for the earth—the tribulation period. It is during the end times that God will intervene and pour out His judgment and wrath on the earth. But Paul didn't conceive of the church remaining on the earth during this time. That's why he told the Thessalonians that "God did not appoint us to wrath, but to obtain salvation through our Lord Jesus Christ."

The wrath Paul spoke of could refer to God's eternal wrath, which makes sense: As believers, we're no longer appointed to face judgment in hell for our sin. But in context, Paul was primarily referring to God's temporal wrath—the tribulation period. God will deliver believers from the wrath that He's going to pour out on earth in the day of the Lord; we're going to be removed from the earth altogether in an event we know as the rapture.[16]

So how are we supposed to live in light of that fact? Paul made it clear: Those of us "who are of the day [must] be sober." The idea of being sober isn't just to not get drunk or high, but to avoid being intoxicated by worldly ideas and goals. We ought to be spiritually self-controlled and disciplined. That's not our natural inclination; we must deliberately protect ourselves from being captivated and led astray by the amusements and distractions of this world.

Paul told us to put on the appropriate survival gear for the last days, including "the breastplate of love and faith" and the helmet of "the hope of salvation." A breastplate protects the chest, while a helmet protects the head. So protect your heart with faith, trusting in God and loving other believers; and protect your mind with a helmet of hope, thinking of what God has in store for you in the future. Finally, meditate on His promises, knowing that because of what Christ did on the cross, you're on your way to heaven.

JUSTICE IS COMING

Continuing the theme of his first letter to the church at Thessalonica, in 2 Thessalonians Paul explained that before the tribulation period begins, the rapture has to take place, along with the revealing of the "man of sin" (2 Thessalonians 2:3), or Antichrist. He encouraged the spiritually young believers that though they lived in a society that was flat-out antagonistic toward their belief system, the day would come when God would take vengeance on His enemies and bring eternal rest to His kids. The assurance of God's impending justice should afford us some comfort.

Giving Rest to the Troubled

> *It is a righteous thing with God to repay with tribulation*
> *those who trouble you, and to give you who are troubled rest*
> *with us when the Lord Jesus is revealed from heaven with His*
> *mighty angels, in flaming fire taking vengeance on those who*
> *do not know God, and on those who do not obey the gospel of*
> *our Lord Jesus Christ.* (2 Thessalonians 1:6-8)

At a future point in world history, God is going to stand and vindicate His children. In the end times, the Lord will judge the earth, eradicate sin, wipe out Satan, and exalt Jesus Christ. After a time of unprecedented trouble on earth, there will be an unprecedented time of rest for God's people—the fulfillment of a promise that goes all the way back to Joshua crossing the Jordan River into the land of promise. This land was a place where God's people were meant to live securely, free from their enemies, and where salvation was foreshadowed—the ultimate rest we have only in Christ.[17]

According to Revelation 8:3-5, the cries and prayers of all God's people that have gone up before Him will be answered during this time. Believers have been praying since Paul's day, "How long, O Lord?" and in the end times, He will answer that prayer. Though God is patient and longsuffering, 2 Thessalonians tells us that one day He will intervene, bringing justice to His children and redeeming all our suffering along the way.

Paul's letters to the early church demonstrate a new development in redemption's path. In the Old Testament, the scarlet thread wound its way through Israel's history like a rabbit trail, over hill and dale, at the forefront of the law and behind the scenes of the exile, weaving strands of history with streams of prophecy to point toward the Messiah's arrival and atonement. But in the New Testament, the thread is a binding cord, uniting all who receive Jesus as Lord and Savior, casting a much broader net and retrieving a much broader catch while winding down toward the return of Christ and the final redemption of all creation.

This is the great hope we can look forward to, all made possible because of Jesus's atoning death and glorious resurrection. May that hope carry us through to the time when God will tie off the scarlet thread once and for all, finishing the tapestry He began back in the Garden of Eden.

GOD'S UNSTOPPABLE PLAN

PAUL'S PRISON LETTERS:
Ephesians, Philippians,
Colossians, and Philemon

Thematically, the four letters Paul the apostle wrote from jail are diverse, but the thread running through them all points to the work of one person: Jesus Christ. He is the sum and the substance of all biblical revelation, dominating the biblical landscape from start to finish. Paul knew that even from the dark depths of a prison cell, the blood of Jesus still reigned supreme and the gospel was still being preached—including by Paul himself—and because of that, he could rejoice. As "an ambassador in chains" (Ephesians 6:20) for the gospel, Paul had a one-track mind focused solely on Jesus Christ. Ruminating on the rich life he had in Christ, he looked past his circumstances and saw the great beauty and meaning of the cross and the redemptive plan into which he had been woven. The blood of Jesus gave him every reason to face his uncertain future with a certain hope, whether he lived or died. Though Paul was imprisoned, God's continuing plan for the scarlet thread of redemption never could and never would be shackled.

YOU'RE RICH!

In Ephesians, Paul opened up the Christian's bankbook. He described the riches we have in and through Christ: "In Him we have redemption through His blood, the forgiveness of sins, according to the riches of His grace" (Ephesians 1:7). Because of what Jesus did on the cross, you have access to the vault! You can come directly to God the Father. Under the old covenant, the people had to worship from afar.[1] "But now," as Paul wrote, "in Christ Jesus you who once were far off have been brought near by the blood of Christ" (Ephesians 2:13). Jesus bridged the gap between you and God, and He invites you to come to Him, to experience His presence in your life and know Him personally. The same God who turned on the lights in the universe, who created everything from atoms to eyeballs, says to you, "Follow Me. Let's walk through life together. I'll give you everything you need!"

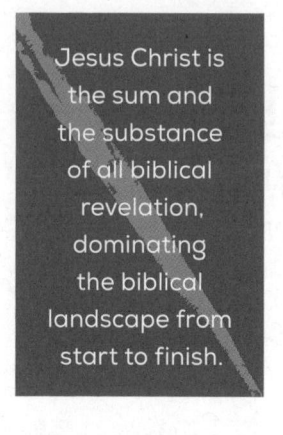

Jesus Christ is the sum and the substance of all biblical revelation, dominating the biblical landscape from start to finish.

A Bottomless River of Blessing

Blessed be the God and Father of our Lord Jesus Christ, who has blessed us with every spiritual blessing in the heavenly places in Christ. (Ephesians 1:3)

If you're reading this book, you're probably a saved person. You're going to spend eternity in heaven, not hell, and that's cause for celebration. But God wants you to enjoy this life too. Because of what Jesus did, He has given you access to His immeasurable resources. But are you drawing on them? Charles Spurgeon said, "Most Christians, as to the river of experience, are only up to the ankles; some others have waded till the stream is up to the knees; a few find it breast-high; and but a few—oh! how few!—find it a river to swim in, the bottom of which they cannot touch."[2]

What would you do if you won the lottery? On one hand, after hearing all the stories of people's lives being ruined by all that money, and all the taxes they had to pay, you would probably have a few concerns. On the other hand, would you tear up the check? Probably not.

Look at your salvation this way: You've won the ultimate lottery, and you didn't have to gamble to do it. You simply had to say yes to Jesus. After that, though, you still have to cooperate with God to get the most out of what He has for you in this life. It's like the children of Israel inhabiting the Promised Land: The land was a free gift, like salvation, but they had to actually enter in and occupy it. Similarly, it's great if you've crossed over into the land—if you've received Christ as Savior—but don't stop there. Keep walking and see all that God has for you.

Imagine your spiritual life as a balance sheet. Before Christ, your account was in the red—a debt with so many zeroes on the end that you would never be able to get back in the black. But in Christ, not only has that impossible debt been paid in full, you have unlimited resources. What resources? "Every spiritual blessing...in Christ." Do you regularly apply those blessings? I sometimes hear people pray, "O God, give me more power or more influence or more this or more that," and I think, *Lord, You don't need to give them more—just help them understand what they have already in Jesus, our true wealth and source of blessing.*

Possess what Jesus has given you. Read the ledger—God's Word—and find out how rich you are in Christ. Ephesians 1 is just a taste of what you'll find: In Christ, you've been chosen, you're holy and blameless, you've been adopted as God's son or daughter, redeemed by His unmerited love, forgiven and accepted. You've been let in on "the mystery of His will" (v. 9), which is the good news of Christ and the solution He provides to all the world's troubles. The same authority that has kept the scarlet thread going since Eden, the power that raised Christ from the dead, is part of your life *right now.*

Christ's blood has given you access to all those wonderful gifts and more. Sadly, too few Christians embrace their connection to Jesus and live in a way that reflects the resources available to them. Paul walked in the confidence of his faith and impacted the world on levels that were both personal and hugely global. This is the power of the bloodline—to know what you're plugged into in Christ and then to step out into your life and trust Him to give your prayers, words, and deeds maximum impact.

No Paybacks

> *By grace you have been saved through faith, and that not of yourselves; it is the gift of God, not of works, lest anyone should boast.* (Ephesians 2:8-9)

How is it that God can bless you with every spiritual blessing? Because of what Jesus did. Spiritually, you were born DOA, dead in your sins.[3] But God's great love, displayed for you on the cross, has "made [you] alive together with Christ" (v. 5). Because Jesus rose from the grave, you have too, spiritually—and after you die, you'll have life eternally, together with Him.

Salvation is a free gift. God gave it to you by grace—by undeserved favor. Nothing you have done or could ever do would earn it. You trust God, and He just gives it to you. That's why grace is called amazing—because it is. Human nature is to take credit for ourselves, but we can't do that with salvation. We can only respond to what God has done—Jesus's blood gives us nothing to brag on ourselves about. You can brag on God and how great He is, and you should respond to what He's done for you by doing good works once you're saved,[4] but you can't earn God's favor by doing good. There's no way you could ever pay the price God paid to save you—but in Christ, you don't need to pay Him back. Instead, you receive His gift and respond with humility and obedience.

If you gave your friend a gift out of the goodness of your heart—you saw something in a store and thought, *I know he'd love that; I'm going to get it for him*—what would you do if he pulled out his wallet and said, "Here, I'll pay you back"? You'd refuse, right? In fact, you'd probably be offended, even insulted.

Don't you think God is offended when you try to earn His favor, when you try to remind Him, "Well, God, I've done this and that this week. Here are the reasons You should bless me"? Isaiah 64 says that "all our righteousnesses are like filthy rags" (v. 6). Next time you think you can boast about anything you've done, remember that verse. If you try to wear your own righteousness, you will be standing naked before God.

The highest insult to God is human goodness used as a substitute for true righteousness. God loved you even when you were at your worst. When you try to gain God's affection or somehow secure your salvation, you're in effect telling Him, "Your Son didn't do enough. He died and He said, 'It is finished,' but I think He needs a little help to complete the job." Listen, you don't add to God's scarlet thread—you grab it like the lifeline it is and hold on tightly. Anything else is an insult to His whole redemptive plan.

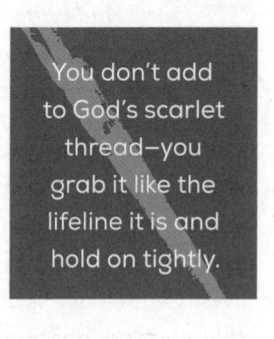

You don't add to God's scarlet thread—you grab it like the lifeline it is and hold on tightly.

Have you been trying to earn God's favor? Instead, graciously take the gift He's given you and let it motivate you to serve Him—and others—out of love,[5] knowing that you've been grafted and woven into the tapestry of redemption by His grace alone.

ONE-TRACK JOY

Every time I read Paul's words in the book of Philippians, I step away thinking, *Who is this guy?* Rich or poor, free or jailed, the soundtrack in his mind played one song: glory to God in Jesus Christ. Paul mentioned other people here and there, but only in that one greater context. Jesus was all Paul talked about. Paul knew that whether he lived or died, whether he stayed in prison or was released, there was life on either side of the equation because of what Jesus did. That was his life's motto: "For to me, to live is Christ, and to die is gain" (Philippians 1:21). In other words, "As long as I live, one thing sums it up: Jesus Christ. And if I die? That will be better yet—I'll be with Him. Either way, I win. Either way, I'm going to rejoice." The blood-red cord of redemption, Paul knew, had enough keeping power to take him from earth all the way to heaven. How could he *not* be joyful?

Poured Out

Let this mind be in you which was also in Christ Jesus, who, being in the form of God, did not consider it robbery to be

*equal with God, but made Himself of no reputation, taking
the form of a bondservant, and coming in the likeness of
men. And being found in appearance as a man, He humbled
Himself and became obedient to the point of death, even the
death of the cross.* (Philippians 2:5-8)

Paul wanted us to understand that though salvation is a freely
offered gift, it was costly to God. In order to save us, Jesus became
human, and in becoming a man, He gave up some of His divine priv-
ileges. This is called His *kenosis*, the emptying process. Jesus didn't
divest Himself of His divine nature, because that's impossible. He was
still fully God, but becoming fully human was a sacrifice in itself. He
denied Himself the prerogatives of deity.

To what extent did Jesus empty Himself? The Creator of the heavens and the earth, the one who owns "the cattle on a thousand hills"
(Psalm 50:10), was born into a poor family of low status among the
tribes of Israel. Before then, as the Lord of glory, the King of heaven,
He was in the presence of angels, receiving their praise. He was in constant, harmonious community with the Father and the Holy Spirit.
But He gave all of that up, humbly entering time and space in a human
body, making Himself subject to sin's repercussions in the physical
world—growth and decay, pain, longing, and hunger. He left heav-
en's magnificence for earth's mess, fully aware that His mission would
end in a painful death. Second Corinthians 8:9 says, "Though He was
rich, yet for our sakes He became poor, that you through His poverty
might become rich."

Jesus's poverty and humility were painful but purposeful. He
accomplished His rescue operation, and God richly rewarded His service and humility. Because Jesus humbled Himself and obeyed the
Father, the Father gave Jesus "the name which is above every name"
(Philippians 2:9)—the supreme, divine title as the Lord of all.[6] Not
only that, but it was through His humiliating, gruesome death that
the greatest thing in history happened: He redeemed us from sin and
death, crushing the serpent's head and thus fulfilling Genesis 3:15, the
first messianic promise in all of Scripture.

In securing our salvation, Jesus also modeled for us how we're to live as redeemed people. We live in the age of self—self-realization, self-determination, self-esteem, selfies—but He showed us the way of humility and selflessness. Any selfishness in your life opposes Christ in you. You are never more like Satan than when you are selfish, and you are never more like Jesus than when you humbly serve and practice lowliness of mind—that is, when you have the same attitude toward people that He demonstrated, that blend of unvarnished truth and compassionate love. When you think like Jesus thought, the right attitudes will translate into the right actions.

The *kenosis* of Jesus should become the motivation for your demonstration of humble, loving service. Jesus didn't just *think* about coming to the earth to serve and to save—He actually came, served, and saved. The Father had it in His mind from eternity past to weave His Son into the tapestry of redemption, and Jesus came and accomplished what the Father called Him to do, humbling Himself and ensuring that we could be with Him in heaven forever. But, as Paul found out, we have to forsake our own righteousness and embrace Jesus's righteousness to recognize our real need and allow true salvation to take place.

Flush It!

> *I also count all things loss for the excellence of the knowledge of Christ Jesus my Lord, for whom I have suffered the loss of all things, and count them as rubbish, that I may gain Christ and be found in Him, not having my own righteousness, which is from the law, but that which is through faith in Christ, the righteousness which is from God by faith.*
> (Philippians 3:8-9)

Before Saul of Tarsus became Paul the apostle, he was so confident in his religiosity and self-righteousness that he said, "I'm going to keep God's law to the max, every part of it." To show just how far his self-righteousness had once stretched, he wrote at length about his religious pedigree: "If anyone else thinks he may have confidence in the flesh, I more so: circumcised the eighth day, of the stock of Israel, of the tribe

of Benjamin, a Hebrew of the Hebrews; concerning the law, a Pharisee; concerning zeal, persecuting the church; concerning the righteousness which is in the law, blameless" (Philippians 3:4-6).

Looking back, Paul was saying, "This isn't my testimony but my
brag-imony. I thought I was something—the crème de la crème of
God's chosen people. I had kept every bit of the law." As a Pharisee, he
kept not only the written Torah but also the oral law, all the hundreds
of personal interpretations rabbis had added to the law. But like anyone else who uses religion as an end in itself, he lost sight of God and
saw only his service, his accomplishments, his version of holiness. He
had self-righteousness when salvation required God's righteousness.

Saul of Tarsus had enough morality to keep himself out of trouble
but not enough righteousness to get into heaven. That's the danger of
religion: It can use smugness and self-assurance as a substitute for hard
but simple truth. This is why it's especially difficult for religious people
to accept salvation, because they often don't see their need for a Savior.
They get busy weaving their own redemptive history and fail to recognize God's scarlet thread, His lifeline, as it stretches throughout Scripture: We're fallen people, unredeemable by our own merits. We need a
Savior beyond ourselves.

After Paul's run-in with the living God, he came to count all his self-
made accomplishments as "rubbish." Everything he had done—keeping the law, being a Pharisee, trying his hardest to serve God—was a
good thing. So why did Paul kick it all to the curb? Because a good
thing becomes a bad thing if it keeps you from the best thing. A background in religion can be a good thing, but not if it keeps you from a
genuine relationship with Christ through His work alone.

That's why Paul referred to his religious righteousness as rubbish. And the literal translation of the original Greek word used here
wouldn't be suitable for our study. Put simply, it refers to the excre-
ment of animals. Paul was saying, "My life apart from Christ—even
the best, most religious part of my life that I was so proud of—stinks.
It's all dung next to His righteousness." Paul had an impressive religious
resume, yet he shoveled it into the trash can because he realized it was
keeping him from a relationship with God.

If being raised in a religious home or following your own spirituality actually worked to get you right with God, why would Jesus need to come and die? We've seen over and over again, particularly in the Old Testament, the answer to that. Our Creator is holy, and our sin, which has broken the world and killed us spiritually, offends His holy nature. Because sin brought death into the world, only life— in the form of blood—can cleanse it. And just as each of us in our God-given free will chooses our own way over His, we have to make it right with Him on an individual basis. Only Jesus can help us do that. Oth- 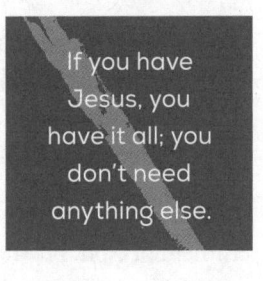 ers can point us to Him, but ultimately, each of us has to do business with Him on our own. If we try to get saved by anything other than His blood, we're using manure to try to clean ourselves.

The happiest day of Paul's life was when he stopped trying to be righteous and believed that he was righteous because he was in Christ. He had spent far too long trying to manufacture a right standing with God before he realized, "True righteousness can't be produced by determination; it must be provided by God through faith in Christ." His human bloodline couldn't do the job; only God's can. This is the thread that connects the Old and New Testament, revealing the purpose of the law and the reason Jesus came: The law highlighted our need for a Savior, and Jesus was that Savior.

THE CENTER OF THE UNIVERSE

It's impossible to overstate how central Jesus Christ is to the Bible. We've seen it throughout this book—Jesus is the grand theme of Scripture, after all. This is particularly true for the book of Colossians. Paul's driving point here is that nothing and no one should usurp Jesus's position at the center of your life, because if you have Jesus, you have it all; you don't need anything else. So often in spiritual matters we think we need to add something to Jesus in order to be saved—Jesus plus fasting, Jesus plus social justice, or Jesus plus attendance at a certain church.

But because God once and for all "made peace through the blood of His cross" (Colossians 1:20) and wove us into His tapestry of redemption, we have everything we need in Him.

Choose Your Kingdom

> *He has delivered us from the power of darkness and conveyed us into the kingdom of the Son of His love, in whom we have redemption through His blood, the forgiveness of sins.*
> (Colossians 1:13-14)

Before the creation of the world, there was one kingdom: the government of God. He ruled in perfect harmony and righteousness. Then at some point, Lucifer introduced a rebellious splinter. He said, "I will exalt my throne above the stars of God…I will be like the Most High" (Isaiah 14:13-14), and led an uprising of a third of the angels. Because of their rebellion, they were pushed out of heaven, out of God's presence, and they established another kingdom—the kingdom of darkness. Ever since then, Satan has been seeking to entice man, God's pinnacle creation on the earth, into that kingdom. He is attempting to weave a counterfeit tapestry, snipping God's threads where he can but unable to break any of the core strands of redemption.

Man was created to serve God in a perfect environment. But given the power of choice, man—beginning with Adam—chose to follow the usurper Satan's advice. Thus, because of the fall, every human being enters this world with a sin nature, destined for the kingdom of darkness.

That Satan is a master tactician compounds the problem. He knows how to steer people away from God. One tactic he uses is to make the kingdom of darkness look good and glittery and satisfying to unbelievers. He gets people to use their freedom to choose what is fun or expedient or feels urgent and necessary in a bad moment, and their sin mounts up to the point where going to hell doesn't seem so bad because, as they say, "All my friends will be there, and we're gonna party!"

Another tactic Satan uses is to disguise himself as an angel of light, making human attempts to save ourselves seem enlightened and noble, or neutralizing potentially effective Christians into following the world's lead instead of God's Word. Satan makes sin look as enticing as he can, but the wages of sin will always be death. The free gift of God, by contrast, is eternal life. The good news of the gospel is that you don't have to go on living on the substitutes of the kingdom of darkness. Rather, you can be "conveyed"—transported, free of charge—into the kingdom of God's Son and find real satisfaction and purpose.

The closer you draw to Christ, the more centered you'll become, and the better you'll be able to distinguish the enemy's fake tapestry, like an archeologist knowing the difference between an ancient potsherd and a chunk of clay from the local garden supplier. Whereas Disneyland calls itself the magic kingdom, this is the Master's kingdom; it's both free of charge and forever!

How to Get Out of Debt

> *You, being dead in your trespasses and the uncircumcision of your flesh, He has made alive together with Him, having forgiven you all trespasses, having wiped out the handwriting of requirements that was against us, which was contrary to us. And He has taken it out of the way, having nailed it to the cross.* (Colossians 2:13-14)

The cross is known around the world as a symbol of the Christian faith. But who is responsible for it? Who did this to Jesus? We could blame the Romans, the Jewish leaders, the crowd who chanted for Jesus to be crucified, or even Judas Iscariot. But we have to look in the mirror to get the full picture. Who's responsible for the cross? We are. First Corinthians 15 plainly says that "Christ died for our sins" (v. 3). We put Him on that cross.

Yet on the cross, Jesus did what religion and rituals could never do: He took the burden of guilt that comes from our failure to keep God's law and got rid of it when He died. When Paul wrote that Christ wiped out the "handwriting of requirements that was against us," I believe he had in mind a certain practice that took place in the ancient Greek world: When someone owed a debt, he signed a legal handwritten charge of debt. This note served as a public declaration to remind the lender and the borrower that life wasn't quite right between the two of them until the debt was paid off. But once that obligation was paid, a public notice was made to announce that the debt was removed—paid in full.

Paul was saying that we owed a huge debt because of our sin—a debt we could never pay. And Jesus Christ came and paid that bill in full and even left a tip. He died on the cross, was buried, and rose from the dead, conquering death and promising new life to anyone who believes that what He did was enough. That's what the cross is all about.

C.S. Lewis wisely wrote, "It costs God nothing, so far as we know, to create nice things: but to convert rebellious wills cost His crucifixion."[7] Because Jesus poured out His blood on our behalf, our debt is paid in full, written off and nailed to the cross. As the hymn says, "Jesus paid it all. All to Him I owe; sin had left a crimson stain, He washed it white as snow."[8] All to Him we owe, indeed. The one who is at the center of Scripture deserves our deepest devotion and highest praise.

REDEMPTION FOR A SLAVE

The book of Philemon is the shortest and most personal letter in the New Testament, and though in it Paul deals with the controversial subject of slavery, it's by no means devoid of the scarlet thread that's stitched through every page of Scripture. In fact, its subject matter makes it prime material for exploring the themes of redemption and restoration and how they play out in the Christian's everyday life.

Turning a Profit

> *I appeal to you for my son Onesimus, whom I have begotten while in my chains, who once was unprofitable to you, but now is profitable to you and to me.* (Philemon 10-11)

Reading between the lines of this epistle, it's generally believed that Onesimus, a slave of the Christian leader Philemon, stole money from his master and ran away to Rome, thinking, *I'll just blend in and get lost in this big city.* Instead of getting lost, however, Jesus found him: Somehow

Onesimus met Paul, who was still in prison, and Paul led him to Christ and found out his story. In this letter, Paul appealed for Philemon to receive Onesimus back to him not just as his slave, but as his new brother in Christ.

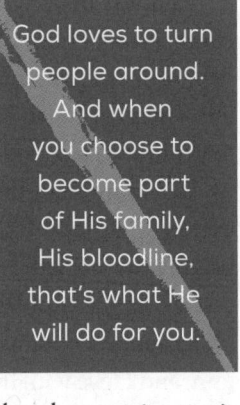

God loves to turn people around. And when you choose to become part of His family, His bloodline, that's what He will do for you.

What's interesting about Paul's wording in the verses above is that the name *Onesimus* means "useful" or "profitable." Paul was using a play on words: "Mr. Profitable was once useless, but now he's living up to his name and his potential because of what Jesus has done in his life. Now that he's a Christian, he has the capacity—spiritually—to really be profitable to you as a brother, as he's been to me."

This is what happens when God gets a hold of you and me. We started out on the run from God, but Jesus found us and gave our lives meaning and purpose. Before Christ, we were dead in our sins and useless in any long-term, lasting sense. But now that we're connected to the true source of life, we are useful; we've been redeemed to walk in good works.[9] That's the great story of the gospel.

My dad once gave me an older car that I restored to its original condition. In fact, it was better than factory specs—it was a new and improved *classic*. Everywhere I went, people admired the attention to detail and the commitment I had made to refurbishing what some would've considered junk.

That's how it is with God: He loves to restore people. He looks for hearts that are broken, for people who have made bad choices, who are beat up and scarred. He loves to turn people around. And when you choose to become part of His family, His bloodline, that's what He will do for you. If you bring your broken heart to Him, the master mechanic, He will rebuild it. He's in the business of restoration and redemption.

Picking Up the Bill

> *If he has wronged you or owes anything, put that on my account...I will repay—not to mention to you that you owe me even your own self besides.* (Philemon 18-19)

Paul was making a powerful statement in these verses. He was in effect saying, "Hey, Philemon, I know Onesimus owes you a material debt, but you owe me a spiritual debt you can't repay—your eternal life—because I won you to Christ." He leveraged Philemon's gratitude to get him to respond to the situation with brotherly love.

But more than that, Paul asked Philemon to do with Onesimus exactly what Jesus Christ has done with us. Here Paul was loving two brothers in the faith and calling them to love each other, but love alone doesn't fix the problem; love has to pay the bill. So Paul said, "Look, Philemon, if Onesimus owes you anything at all, I will pay for it. I love him, and I love you. If he owes you any material debt, put it on my tab."

That's what God has done for us. God so loved the world, but love alone isn't enough to do anything; it's a decision that must result in action. So He gave His only begotten Son. And now Jesus can say to the Father, on behalf of you and me, "I know this sinner owes you a debt, but You can put it on My account because I paid for his sins on the cross."

Jesus is our great debt-payer, and Paul proclaimed this truth as clearly and consistently as he could. In each one of his prison letters—Ephesians, Philippians, Colossians, and Philemon—he pointed us again and again to the great redemptive work Jesus Christ accomplished on the cross and how we can live our lives in right standing before the Lord because of it, even from a jail cell. Paul never ceased to be thankful for God's debt-relief program. Even though Paul's time on earth eventually came to an end, his words have echoed through the centuries and continue to highlight how God has woven the scarlet thread of redemption deeply into the lives of those who recognize its meaning and act accordingly in faith.

PUTTING UP A BLOODY FIGHT

PAUL'S PASTORAL LETTERS:
1 and 2 Timothy, Titus

P art of living as redeemed people whose sinful past has been washed by the blood of Jesus is putting up a fight for the truth. By that I don't mean toting guns into battle or hitting people over the head with your Bible. But according to Scripture, every believer has a solemn duty to fight for and resist attacks on the truth.[1] And what exactly is that truth? It's the belief that, according to the scarlet thread that runs all the way through the Old Testament and New, the God-man Jesus Christ shed His blood on a cross to atone for the sins of humanity and bring as many people as possible into His spiritual bloodline.

Pastors in particular are held to a higher standard than others when it comes to teaching and defending this truth.[2] We see this play out in Paul's letters to Timothy and Titus, who were young pastors in the early church. Error was on the move, waging war against the truth that had been taught in the fledgling Christian assemblies. It was time for the leaders to engage the enemy. Paul's exhortations to them underscore that critical truth, which serves all who follow Jesus as a banner, a vanguard, and an arsenal. The scarlet thread binds us to the truth, making it clear what we're fighting for and how to do it.

WAGING THE GOOD WARFARE

In 1 Timothy, Paul specifically charged Timothy, the young protégé he left to pastor the church in Ephesus, to wage the good warfare of fighting for the truth.[3] *Fighting for the truth* has become such a foreign concept in our postmodern culture, where the prevailing belief is that nothing can be known absolutely and thus tolerance is the noblest virtue. Even some who claim to be Christians hesitate to say, "I know the truth, and it's the gospel."

There's been a battle for the truth in every single generation since Paul wrote 1 Timothy. Why? Because Satan, the god of this world, has blinded the minds of those who do not believe.[4] To see the truth of the gospel and grasp the scarlet thread of redemption, people must do two things: realize who they are before a holy God, and trust in the one Mediator who can bridge the gap between them and that holy God—Jesus Christ. Paul clearly communicated that truth to Timothy in this letter.

Our Greatest Need Is Jesus's Greatest Accomplishment

> *This is a faithful saying and worthy of all acceptance, that Christ Jesus came into the world to save sinners, of whom I am chief.* (1 Timothy 1:15)

When you bring up the subject of salvation in this day and age, some say humanity needs saving from political instability or economic woes. Others say we need saving from prejudice or negative thinking. Still others think the human race needs to be saved from poverty or disease or cultural baggage. But God sent His Son on a rescue mission to save us from the single greatest and most fatal infection we face: the sin virus. Without exception, everyone is *S-I-N positive*.

Jesus's very name—which means "God is salvation"—denoted His mission. Consider the first words out of His mouth when He was on the cross: "Father, forgive them, for they do not know what they do" (Luke 23:34). Why was that His first prayer while He hung on that instrument of torture, making that holy transaction? Because forgiveness is our greatest need, and our greatest need became His greatest mission and accomplishment. God has saving sinners at the top of His list.

Paul knew this truth deeply. He called it "a faithful saying...worthy of all acceptance," and even nicknamed himself the chief of sinners. But sin is the very reason not many people are interested in Jesus Christ. They don't see their need for a Savior because they don't see or admit the reality of sin in their lives. When a person can't or won't admit they've fallen short of the glory of God, they won't be looking for someone to save them, and that's when they reject Jesus as merely a good teacher or a countercultural rebel instead of the only one who can give them what they need most.

> Forgiveness is our greatest need, and our greatest need became His greatest mission and accomplishment.

Yet everyone I've ever met senses that they need forgiveness from someone for something. When I was a kid and I offended my mom or my dad (which was often), I always sensed the need to make things right. I wanted to seek reconciliation and hear them say, "I forgive you." I often wanted forgiveness more than anything else, and I still find that to be true in the other relationships in my life.

That's because humanity's greatest need isn't information, technology, money, pleasure, or even peace—it's forgiveness. The scarlet thread speaks to this need, and it's why God sent us a Savior. As we've seen, this was God's plan from the beginning: to send a Messiah to save us from our sin, acting as the Mediator between us and Him.

Don't Cut Out This Middleman

> *There is one God and one Mediator between God and men,*
> *the Man Christ Jesus, who gave Himself a ransom for all.*
> (1 Timothy 2:5-6)

As we read the Old Testament story of Job's suffering, we see that his pain drove him to a point of isolation so desperate that he cried out to God, "If only there was a mediator between You and me who could lay his hand on both of us."[5] A mediator is a middleman or go-between. In ancient times, his role was to bring together two parties that were distinctly different, even opposite from each other—in Job's case, God and man. Job held firm to the belief that not only would he one day have a mediator with God, but that mediator would be God-sent and would stand on the earth.[6] Without knowing the name of his redeemer, Job anticipated Jesus Christ.

I had a mediator growing up; I called her *Mom*. Whenever I got in trouble with my dad, my main relief was to have my mom step in, say a few words on my behalf, and bring my father and me together. She had a special way of mitigating whatever judicial action my father wanted to levy on me.

Going back to 1 Timothy 2:5-6, Jesus is the perfect Mediator between us and God. He is fully man and fully God—a unique nature theologians call *theanthropic*—and thus He alone is able to bring holy God and sinful mankind together. As God incarnate, Jesus can represent God to us perfectly, and as God in human flesh—as a man—He can represent us before God perfectly. He is the perfect representative to bring us together, the only middleman we could ever have or need.

And Jesus was the perfect representative because He was the perfect ransom. A ransom refers to the price someone pays for something held captive. But the Greek word Paul used in verse 6 for ransom—*antilutron*, which is found nowhere else in the Bible—indicates that Jesus didn't just come to pay the ransom for you; He actually *became* the ransom through His death on the cross. He died in your place, then He rose again and now lives to represent you before the Father. That's why we preach the cross and emphasize the necessity of the blood of Christ.

Because Jesus is the perfect Mediator, you shouldn't let anyone take you back to Old Testament times and try to mediate between you and God, whether as a priest, pope, pastor, or rabbi. Under the old covenant, a priest represented the people before God and brought the words of God to the people. But there's only one Mediator in the new covenant, and it's Jesus Christ. You don't have to go through Mary or the saints—you can't, in fact. You can come directly to God through His Son, and only through His Son.

In the Old Testament, priests stood between God and men, offering sacrifice after sacrifice to maintain the peace. But under the new covenant, we have only one High Priest, Jesus Christ, who offered His blood once, and once was enough. The Bible says we ourselves as the church have become a nation of priests,[7] meaning we don't need a human being to represent us before God anymore. Based on the high priesthood of Jesus, every believer has the authority to come boldly before God.

Any religious system that adds to this reality insults God. Because of what Jesus did on the cross, He is the only Mediator between God and man. You and I can go directly to the throne of the Lord because of the work of the one who said, "I am the way, the truth, and the life. No one comes to the Father except through Me" (John 14:6). Think of Jesus's mediating work like this: On the cross, with His arms stretched out, Jesus laid one hand on God and one hand on humanity, and by His death He brought us together in Himself.

THE ONE AND ONLY
SOURCE OF SALVATION

Second Timothy reveals the last written thoughts of one of the most influential Christians who ever lived. The backdrop, in part, of this second letter Paul wrote to Timothy was apostasy—a falling away or departure from the truth. It had been only three decades since Jesus ascended to heaven—thirty years since the gospel first began to spread throughout the ancient world—and yet people were dropping like flies, casualties on the battlefield of truth even within the church. Paul, knowing his own death was imminent, called Timothy to hold fast to the Word of God, which alone points to the one and only source of salvation: Jesus Christ.

Holding Out for the Hero

> *From childhood you have known the Holy Scriptures, which are able to make you wise for salvation through faith which is in Christ Jesus.* (2 Timothy 3:15)

As a pastor, Timothy had a solid background in the Word of God; he had been brought up in the Scriptures by his mom and grandma, Eunice and Lois. But what we sometimes forget is that 2,000 years ago, the Scriptures consisted only of the books of the Old Testament. In time, as the New Testament was written, it came to include more than 300 direct quotations and another 1,000 inferences from the Old Testament. Early believers—as well as Jesus Himself[8]—clearly believed the Old Testament was inspired and authoritative. It's what Timothy as a young Jewish man was weaned on spiritually and what Paul was referring to when he mentioned "the Holy Scriptures" in this verse. When Jesus sent the Holy Spirit to the church, the Spirit decoded God's plan of redemption so that those Scriptures were clearly seen by the church as a key part of redemption's bigger picture.

> It takes the whole text of Scripture to complete our understanding of God's plan of redemption—to see the entire tapestry through which the scarlet thread is woven.

According to Paul, it was these Holy Scriptures—the Old Testament—that made Timothy wise for salvation. Can you name any other book in history that can do that? If you read the Qur'an, the Book of Mormon, the Upanishads, or any other sacred book—much less a medical or law book—you won't uncover the truth you need in order to become saved. Furthermore, none of those works can cause true spiritual transformation; only the Bible makes you wise for salvation. Why? Because it's the living Word of God. God inspired it directly; it holds His power.[9] Yet it tells you how bad off you are. If you read it, you'll discover you're like everyone else who has ever lived, a sinner. You're in a dire situation with no means of returning to God.

But then you meet the hero of the story, Jesus Christ, who came to fix the problem of sin. And He is unlike any other hero in any other story, ever. At the key moment of the story, the hero was defeated and died—but that death turned out to be the ultimate victory when He battled back hell and death and rose from the grave. Paul was essentially reminding Timothy of the unique wonder of the story, stating that the clues to

Christ's death-conquering victory were woven throughout the Scriptures Timothy grew up learning.

The Old Testament anticipated the New. The two testaments are like pieces of a puzzle that fit together perfectly. As I've shared, the New is in the Old contained, and the Old is in the New explained; the Old predicts and anticipates the New, and the New reveals the mystery and wonder of the Old. It takes the whole text of Scripture to complete our understanding of God's plan of redemption—to see the entire tapestry through which the scarlet thread is woven.

And Jesus is not a last-minute hero but the entire focus of the Bible. In the Sermon on the Mount, He said, "Do not think that I came to destroy the Law or the Prophets. I did not come to destroy but to fulfill" (Matthew 5:17). To the Pharisees, the Bible readers of His day, He said, "You search the Scriptures, for in them you think you have eternal life; and these are they which testify of Me" (John 5:39). In other words, "I'm the very theme of the whole book, of the Bible itself." When it comes down to it, studying the Bible won't get you to heaven; only Jesus will. And if you study the Bible, it will always point you to Him. It will make you wise for salvation through Christ alone, and it will cause you to anticipate and look forward to another major redemptive event: His second coming.

Joy to the World, the Lord Is Coming

> *Finally, there is laid up for me the crown of righteousness, which the Lord, the righteous Judge, will give to me on that Day, and not to me only but also to all who have loved His appearing.* (2 Timothy 4:8)

It goes without saying that we as Christians should long for the return of Jesus Christ. The thought of the second coming should stir our hearts—it's when Jesus will return and make everything right. So many songs written by believers throughout the centuries have anticipated that glorious time. Julia Ward Howe wrote the "Battle Hymn of the Republic" during the Civil War as a way of looking forward to when Jesus would come and end all wars. And Isaac Watts's famous song "Joy to the World," far from being about Christmas, was written in anticipation of when earth will receive her King, who will rule and reign in righteousness.

Facing his final days on earth, Paul had a similar focus, defining in verse 8 what a Christian is: someone who loves and longs for Jesus's appearing. There are essentially two attitudes you can have toward the second coming: You can either look at it, or you can look for it. You can be an observer full of knowledge about prophecy and astute to the chronology of the last days but without a personal connection to Jesus. Or you can be someone who doesn't necessarily know everything there is to know about end-times theology, but you're so in love with Jesus that you can't wait for Him to come back, and you live your life in light of His promised return.

It's the difference between being a wedding guest and being the bride. The guests come and observe the wedding, but the bride has been eagerly looking forward to this day—she has longed for it. In the same way, the church should ache for Jesus's return.

Jesus promised that He will come back again,[10] and one day we'll see that promise come to fruition. He also pledged to avenge His elect, bringing wrath and judgment on the earth—and He will do that too.[11] Some people don't like the promises of judgment, wrath, and vengeance in the Bible, so they just avoid or disregard them. But Jesus is just as faithful to keep those promises as He is to keep the ones about salvation and comfort and rest. What He said will come to pass. One day He will come as the warrior King to set up His everlasting kingdom as the Lord of all lords.

When you look at the news these days, it's easy to be disgusted, nervous, and angry. But to long for His return means you move past those immediate reactions and say, "I can't wait until You set up Your kingdom, Lord Jesus." It will be a day of justice, righteousness, and peace—a day worth hoping for and setting your mind on. When you get a handle on the scarlet thread of redemption and understand not just your personal salvation but God's ultimate plan for humanity as it will play out in the end times, you can't help but look forward to and long for Jesus's second coming.

PUTTING THINGS IN ORDER

When the young pastor Titus received a letter from Paul, he knew he was getting his marching orders: to provide solid teaching and strong leadership to the church he was in charge of on Crete. The island of Crete was a difficult place for ministry—geographically, politically, culturally, and spiritually—thus Paul called him to take on the role of a spiritual orthopedist and set straight the out-of-joint spiritual lives of the people there. How was he to do that? By giving them sound Bible teaching that focused, as any good Bible teaching does, on God's redemptive plan. As we've seen, part of understanding that scarlet cord means looking ahead to Jesus's second coming.

Looking Forward to the Blessed Hope

> *The grace of God that brings salvation has appeared to all men, teaching us that, denying ungodliness and worldly lusts, we should live soberly, righteously, and godly in the present age, looking for the blessed hope and glorious appearing of our great God and Savior Jesus Christ, who gave Himself for us, that He might redeem us from every lawless deed and purify for Himself His own special people, zealous for good works.* (Titus 2:11-14)

"Are you sure God is up there?" a little boy once asked his mom.

"Yep," she said, "I'm sure He is up there."

"Don't you wish He would poke His head out every now and then and show Himself?"

We can all relate to that little boy's feeling, wishing that God would show Himself or that Christ would return. Back in the New Testament era, however, every church lived in the expectation that Jesus could come back at any moment. They didn't have a long, drawn-out, sophisticated eschatology; they just knew He was coming. Paul instructed believers to live in that kind of expectancy—what he called in Titus the "glorious appearing" of Jesus, our "blessed hope."

Notice Paul didn't call it the irresponsible hope or the escape-route hope. I've heard people say, "It's so careless of you Christians to wait for God to zap you out of here." No, it's not. It's called the blessed hope because believing Jesus could come back at any time keeps you on your toes—it keeps you living a pure lifestyle. As John wrote, "We know that when He is revealed, we shall be like Him, for we shall see Him as He is. And everyone who has this hope in Him purifies himself, just as He is pure" (1 John 3:2-3).

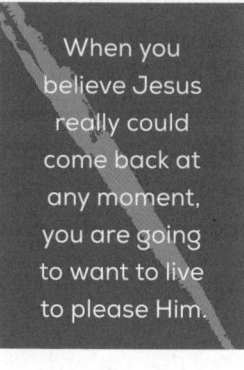

When you believe Jesus really could come back at any moment, you are going to want to live to please Him.

Our hope is that one day we'll no longer have to live by faith, believing in what we can't see, because we'll see Jesus face to face and be totally changed. But until then, we walk by faith and not by sight as we live soberly, righteously, and godly. This is why Jesus redeemed us "from every lawless deed" (Titus 2:14)—so that He could purify us for Himself as His special chosen people. There's a close relationship between end-times prophecy and holiness: When you believe Jesus really could come back at any moment, you are going to want to live to please Him. You are not going to treat your beliefs as a two-hours-on-Sunday obligation but a lifelong action plan. You are going to start thinking, *If I do this and Jesus comes back right now, what will that be like? Will I say, "Uh-oh, He caught me," or "I'm glad You're here; I was waiting for You"?*

When I was little, one simple sentence from my mom could keep me from acting like a total goon in the house: "Your father will be home soon." Now, I honored and loved my father, and I couldn't wait to hang out with him when he got home, but those words put a holy fear in me. I knew what they meant, and it was all my mother had to say to get me back in line. That's the effect this blessed hope should have on us. The early church anticipated it, and we ought to follow their example.

We're to be spiritually alert to the second coming of Christ, not cavalier, apathetic, or uncertain. A deeper knowledge of the scarlet thread of redemption provides the perfect remedy for apathy. At His first coming, Jesus came in peace as a sacrificial Lamb to take away the sin of the world. When He returns, He will come as a Lion to execute wrath and judgment, make war on His enemies, and rule and reign forever. Living with the awareness of God's ultimate plan of redemption for the world, we can see, looking around us, that the Lion of the tribe of Judah is on the move.

And because Scripture shows us the ultimate end to which the whole world is moving, there's no better time than now to step forward, speak up, and tell everyone you know that Jesus Christ is the way, the truth, and the life, and through Him, you can go to heaven. Paul's exhortation to Timothy and Titus to fight for and stand up for the truth of the scarlet thread still rings out loud and clear to us today.

THE CONTINUED WEAVING OF A REDEEMED LIFE

GENERAL LETTERS:
Hebrews; James; 1 and 2 Peter;
1, 2, and 3 John; Jude

From the theologically rich book of Hebrews to the short, pull-no-punches epistle of Jude, the general letters of the New Testament—written by a number of people to Jews and Gentiles alike—are as rich and varied as their authors and intended audiences. Their overarching theme, however, is the same as the rest of the New Testament: Here's what Jesus has done for us, and here's how we're to live because of that. Redemption's red cord features heavily in these special letters addressed to the early church, in which Jesus is presented as our Great High Priest and Advocate who bought us with His precious blood and calls us to live out our belief in Him, contending against false teachers and standing up for the faith. These letters make it clear that the blood-red thread of God's redemptive tale continues to be woven in and through the lives of those He came to save, the proof of which we see in transformed lives.

THAT NEW COVENANT SMELL

Hebrews is essentially the New Testament response to the Old Testament law. Whereas in the law the children of Israel had to keep up the continuous sacrifice of animals to atone for sin, under the new covenant—as explained by the author of Hebrews—Jesus Christ was offered as the perfect sacrifice once and for all, and we no longer have to trust in the blood of bulls and goats. Because Jesus poured out His own blood for us, we live under a far superior promise than the covenant of the law: the covenant of grace. This new arrangement was in God's mind from the beginning, predicted and foreshadowed in the Old Testament and fulfilled in the New. All the sacrifices of the Old Testament cast their shadow toward the cross,[1] toward the way God would take care of the problem we could never solve by sending His perfect, sinless Son to sacrifice Himself for us once and for all. What's more, unlike the law covenant with its continual requirements, this grace covenant is timeless and eternal.

Take a Seat

> *This Man, after He had offered one sacrifice for sins forever,*
> *sat down at the right hand of God.* (Hebrews 10:12)

Under the old covenant, priests were constantly busy. They would get up in the morning, put on their holy uniforms, and get to work. They were always on their feet, standing to minister. That's why, of all the articles of furniture that were in the tabernacle, one was noticeably absent: a chair. A priest wouldn't sit until his work was done for the day and he went home. But the work of an Old Testament priest was never really done. He would get back up and do the same thing over again the next day—and the next month, and the next year, and the next decade, generation after generation.[2]

Enter Jesus Christ. After He sacrificed Himself on the cross, rose from the grave, and ascended back to heaven, He sat down at God's right hand. There was no more work to do. His sacrifice was once and for all; He doesn't have to do it again and again. Redemption was similar to creation. On the seventh day, God rested from all His work.[3] He rested not because He was drowsy but because He was done. Likewise, Jesus sat down because the work of redemption was finished.[4]

Because of Christ's death and resurrection, God's main work of redemption is complete. We can now step back, look at the tapestry of redemption in full, and understand the purpose of the scarlet thread that winds its way through all of redemptive history. Jesus's sitting down symbolized that the old method of sacrifice—which existed solely to point to His coming sacrifice—was over.

I was raised in a religious system that believes in the continual sacrifice of Jesus Christ via a ritual called the Mass, and that each time this ceremony is performed, Christ's sacrifice is renewed, thus adding a tad bit more merit toward one's salvation. I remember when I read Hebrews 10 and realized, *That ritual is an Old Testament concept, not New. It's old covenant; it's obsolete.*

When Jesus died, He acted as the High Priest offering the sacrifice, and He also acted as the sacrifice, offering Himself for the sin of the world. We can stop queueing up the lambs and oxen and doves to stand in for us. Jesus's perfect, sinless blood paid sin's bill in full. He was killed, He was raised, He ascended into heaven, and He sat down, which means only one thing: The work He did on the cross was enough. Jesus's shed blood is sufficient to cleanse anyone. Our High Priest finished the task once and for all.

When Jesus was offering up His own life on the cross and He shouted, "It is finished!" the word He used was *tetelestai*, which comes from a word that means "complete," "mature," or "perfect." Jesus was saying, "Father, the price is paid in full. They couldn't pay it, so I did. *Tetelestai.*" His payment for us was so complete that He could sit down at the right hand of His Father—mission accomplished.

This means you can't add anything to what Jesus has done for you. To attempt to do so would be insulting to God. You can't earn God's love or righteousness by doing good works. Instead, because Jesus sat down, you too can sit down and relax. The work of salvation is done, once and for all. We don't look to the future hoping to do better tomorrow or next week so that God will accept and receive us. Rather, we look back to the cross as ground zero of redemption and say, "If Jesus sat down and rested in His finished work, then I can too."

REDEMPTION'S PROOF
IS IN THE PUDDING

The practical theology of the book of James is unsurpassed among the general letters of the New Testament. Under the new rules of redemption, we as new covenant Christians can sometimes get sloppy when it comes to obeying God's Word. Our reasoning looks like this: Because obedience was required by the law, and we're not under the law anymore, we don't have to live any certain way. "After all," some say, "if I can't add anything to this finished work by good behavior, why not live it up a little?"

But does being under the covenant of grace really mean we can do whatever we want? "God forbid," said Paul in Romans 6:15 (KJV)—and James agrees. In fact, once you're saved, your part in the redemptive tapestry is to weave yourself into God's work— to cooperate with Him so you can become more like Jesus, open to whatever divine appointments He has specially planned for you. For the watching world, that's part of the evidence that sets you apart as His.

> Once you're saved, your part in the redemptive tapestry is to weave yourself into God's work— to cooperate with Him so you can become more like Jesus, open to whatever divine appointments He has specially planned for you.

Will Your Faith Have a Funeral?

> *Faith by itself, if it does not have works, is dead. But someone will say, "You have faith, and I have works." Show me your faith without your works, and I will show you my faith by my works.* (James 2:17-18)

Though we're now part of God's bloodline, woven into the tapestry of redemption, that doesn't mean we can do whatever we want. The issue of being obedient to God is trans-testamental—it spans the old and new covenants. Jesus said, "If you love Me, keep My commandments" (John 14:15). He didn't say, "If you love Me, you'll have warm fuzzies and feel sentimental," or "If you love Me, just buy a nice Christian bumper sticker and feel free to do whatever you want." No—if you love Jesus, you'll attest to and authenticate that love by your obedience. James stated this key fact in simple, up-front terms: Faith without works is dead. True faith is accompanied by obedience; profession and practice go hand in hand.

Think about it like this: What makes a tennis player? Is it somebody who buys a tennis book, looks at the pictures, uses a highlighter pen at all the key points, and says, "I love tennis. Look at what I've highlighted in this book. Listen to what I've memorized. Sometimes I get together with other people who have this book and we talk about it"? No way! If you were to meet someone like that, you would ask, "So how long have you *played* tennis? How's your serve? How's your return, your backhand?" And if the person replied along the lines of, "Well, I've never really actually gotten on the court," you would know right then and there that he or she is not really a tennis player.

In the same way, a Christian is more than someone who buys the Book, looks at the maps, and underlines the promises. It's someone who gets out on the court of life and obeys Christ.[5] God's Word must be acted on, responded to, put into practice. Hearing must lead to heeding. That's not optional. When you hear the truth, you've got to put shoes on it. If you don't, God's Word won't have any impact on your life, and that's not only bad for your spiritual health, it makes you dangerous to others. No wonder James admonished us with these tough words.

Faith without works is dead, but it's also true that works without faith is dead.[6] You need faith, and true faith will produce works. You can talk about what you believe all day long, but if there's no corresponding life change, it's dead faith. Put another way, saving faith is a faith that works. It provides real evidence that you've been redeemed by the blood of Jesus Christ. He didn't get off the cross so you could sit on the couch. To be connected to His bloodline is to draw on His strength and purpose, to do everything He has set aside for you to do for your good and His glory. Active faith is real; anything less, and you're just attending a funeral for what you wrongly call your faith.

HOW THE VERY WORST
BECAME THE VERY BEST

The fisherman-turned-apostle Peter wrote his first letter to a group of suffering new Christians, encouraging them by showing how purposeful Jesus's own experience with pain was: "Christ also suffered once for sins, the just for the unjust, that He might bring us to God" (1 Peter 3:18). The very worst thing that happened—the death of God incarnate—became the very best thing that could happen to us. By purchasing us with His Son's precious blood, God brought us into His family line, conferring on us a value unmatched by any other created thing.

How Much Do You Think You're Worth?

> *You were not redeemed with corruptible things, like silver or gold, from your aimless conduct received by tradition from your fathers, but with the precious blood of Christ, as of a lamb without blemish and without spot.* (1 Peter 1:18-19)

The world can be ruthless when it comes to the value it places on a human being. We've all experienced it: A person's worth is gauged by outward beauty, personal wealth, accomplishment, or status. That's why we so often play the comparison game and assign value to ourselves based on the perceived value of other people. The result either shortchanges us or the person we're comparing ourselves to.

> God didn't lowball the worth of your soul; He paid the ultimate price. You cost everything to Him, and He was willing to pay it.

But how does God value us? He looks at us through a totally different lens. For one, He sees you as priceless—like a fine treasure. The key word of this short passage from 1 Peter is *redeem*, which means "to set free by paying a price." In the first century, this term typically referred to buying a slave in the marketplace. It also sometimes meant paying money to set free a prisoner of war. In both cases, the fact that a price was paid showed that the particular slave or prisoner being ransomed was highly valued.

Thus redemption infers value. Beauty is in the eye of the beholder, and your Beholder sees you as beautiful!

Your value as a human being comes from the fact that God loves you. He was willing to pay the highest price possible to buy you out of your bondage, your POW status as a slave of sin. In God's eyes, you are worth the very lifeblood of His Son. He didn't lowball the worth of your soul; He paid the ultimate price. You cost everything to Him, and He was willing to pay it. Many Christians have a hard time believing that. I pray that learning the fact that God's plan to redeem you stretches from Genesis to Revelation has opened your eyes to the greatness of your value to God.

> No matter what you think about yourself or what other people say about you, you are valuable to God.

What makes the blood of Jesus Christ so precious? First, He is the only person who ever lived a perfect life; He was "without blemish and without spot." A blemish is an inherent defect, while a spot is an acquired defect. Christ was not born in sin, nor did He commit a sin. The second reason His blood is so precious is because it's the only antidote to the sin virus we're all infected with. As 1 John 1:7 says, "The blood of Jesus Christ His Son cleanses us from *all* sin." Bleach may remove everyday stains on your clothing, but the only way to get rid of sin stains is with the blood of God's Lamb, Jesus Christ.

Do you remember what lambs were used for in the Old Testament? Substitution—a lamb died so that you wouldn't have to. This goes all the way back to when Adam and Eve blew it in Genesis 3: God took the skin of an animal—many scholars believe it was a lamb—and covered them with it. In that case, it was one lamb for one person. At the first Passover in Egypt, the children of Israel took the blood of a lamb and put it on the lintels and doorpost of their homes. In that case, it was one lamb for one family.

Later, when the Day of Atonement was established, the high priest would sprinkle the blood of a lamb on the mercy seat in the tabernacle, and all twelve tribes were atoned for—one lamb for one nation. When Jesus came along in the New Testament, John the Baptist said, "Check

it out—it's the Lamb of God who takes away the sin of the world!"[7]
Now it had become one Lamb for one world—including you and me.

No matter what you think about yourself or what other people say about you, you are valuable to God. Through the Son's death on the cross, the Father was saying, "You are worth everything, and I gave everything to purchase you for Myself." No one is too evil, and no one is too good. We all need redemption—and only His precious blood can make it possible.

TWISTED SCRIPTURES

As wonderful as the precious blood of Jesus is and its metaphorical counterpart the scarlet thread, we must constantly keep an eye out for anyone who would twist that thread into an indistinguishable knot, teaching things that are contrary to Scripture. These false prophets are the very reason Peter wrote his scathing second letter. Think about it this way: If a blind man was walking on a path that led to a cliff and he asked you for directions, what would you say? Would you tell him, "All directions are valid. Just walk as your heart tells you"? If you did, you could be sending him to his death. In the same way, we must be careful when we're giving eternal directions—and learn to recognize the tactics of those whose directions are deadly.

How to Spot a Fake

> *There were also false prophets among the people, even as there will be false teachers among you, who will secretly bring in destructive heresies, even denying the Lord who bought them, and bring on themselves swift destruction.* (2 Peter 2:1)

Several years ago I was in the port city of Kuşadasi, Turkey, when I saw a sign that caught my attention: "Fake Watches." I went and bought one. I was with a guy who had the real version of what I bought, and even he couldn't tell the difference between the two. Another friend of mine who knows watches well looked at it and concluded, "You can tell it's fake by opening it and looking inside." The same goes for detecting false prophets.

One of the telltale signs of a false prophet is that he denies the person and work of Christ—as Peter said, "Even denying the Lord who bought them." The next time you encounter someone from a group that claims to be Christian but his teaching doesn't seem quite right, ask him a simple question: Who is Jesus? Is He God, or is He just a highly advanced human? Did He actually die on the cross, or merely come close? Was His resurrection real, or imagined? You'll discover within moments whether the person affirms or denies Christ. The telltale sign is when he says things about Jesus that Jesus never said about Himself. To contradict Jesus and His redemptive work on the cross is to deny Him. In a nutshell: Christianity is Jesus Christ, and anyone who denies that or any of His claims is a false teacher.

God takes false teachers seriously because there's nothing more offensive to Him than deception. Those who falsify facts about Him are like my fake watch—counterfeits. Peter made it clear that false prophets who enter the true church will face severe, certain judgment. That's because it really does matter what you eat, spiritually speaking. My mom often said, "You are what you eat," and I was always afraid I would turn orange if I ate too many carrots. What you take into your life, listen to, and meditate on—especially when it comes to your view of Jesus Christ—is important because it can bring you life or it can destroy you. Remember, Satan is constantly seeking to counter God's work with his own destructive endeavors. If he can get you thinking that there are other ways to redeem what you sense is wrong with your life, he's got you like a fly in a web.

That's why God gave this warning and posted a "Fake Watches" sign, so to speak. He loves you enough to tell you the truth about false prophets. He cares for you enough to say, "Being able to tell the truth of Scripture is all-important to your spiritual well-being—and your salvation."

SURE SALVATION

Growing up, I was taught that you couldn't be sure of your salvation until you died. The best you could do was to try hard to please

God, but you wouldn't know your eternal destiny until judgment day. *Umm, by that time, isn't it a little too late to find out you were wrong?* The apostle John wrote the letter of 1 John with a different view of the matter: "These things I have written to you who believe in the name of the Son of God, that you may *know* that you have eternal life, and that you may continue to believe in the name of the Son of God" (1 John 5:13). According to John, the Christian life is not built on empty wishes or flimsy hopes, but on a strong, confident assurance that you're saved by Jesus's sacrifice and on your way to heaven. The scarlet cord is a secure lifeline! How can you be so sure of that? One reason is because of the Advocate you have before God the Father.

The Best Defense Attorney in the World

> *My little children, these things I write to you, so that you may not sin. And if anyone sins, we have an Advocate with the Father, Jesus Christ the righteous.* (1 John 2:1)

We're redeemed people. Hooray! But we all still struggle with sin. And Satan still accuses and condemns us before the throne of God day and night.[8] He's got the dirt on you. He doesn't have to manufacture things about your life before God. All he has to do is read the record and state the facts: "Hey God, listen to what these kids of yours said today. That woman nags her husband. This guy yells at his kids and looks at porn." Satan's accusations about you are true, and he has enough evidence as a prosecuting attorney to incriminate you.

But here's the good news: While we certainly have an accuser, we also have an Advocate in the court of heaven right now—Jesus Christ. An advocate is someone who stands on our behalf, like a lawyer or attorney, and we have the best defense attorney in the world. As Paul wrote in Romans 8, "Who shall bring a charge against God's elect? It is God who justifies. Who is he who condemns? It is Christ who died, and furthermore is also risen, who is even at the right hand of God, who also makes intercession for us" (vv. 33-34).[9]

You can't lose with a lawyer like that. Any incriminating evidence that Satan might bring before the Father won't be news to Him. When it comes to your sin stains, it's not possible to shock God. And Jesus stands ready to say, "Hey, Dad, do You remember when I shed My blood on the cross for this person? Forgive him—My finished work covers his blunders."

When Satan accuses and condemns you, don't retort with an excuse like, "I didn't mean to do that. I'm not a bad person at heart." Instead, say, "You're right. But the blood of my defense attorney, my Advocate Jesus Christ, has cleansed me from all sin. It's not because of anything I've done. It's all about His blood, His good name, and that's enough." That's why you can stand before God and defeat Satan and his accusations.[10] One of the most remarkable and humbling aspects of being included in Jesus's bloodline is that you get the family lawyer to stand up for you in court. As a great old hymn puts it, "I hear the accuser roar, of ills that I have done; I know them well, and thousands more; Jehovah findeth none."[11]

TRUTH IN LOVE

In the little letter of 2 John, the apostle John focused on the relationship between truth and love. Christian love has been greatly misunderstood—even redefined—by the unbelieving world. It's been reduced to the idea that we're to give a tolerating little smile and wink to everyone and anything—including sin and false doctrine. But if that's the standard the Bible holds up as true love, even Jesus Himself didn't measure up![12]

Humbly telling or confronting someone with the truth is one of the most loving things you can do. This is certainly true when it comes to graciously pointing out to others their own sinful condition so that you can direct them to the glory of God's redemption.

The Interconnected Beauty of Truth and Love

This is love, that we walk according to His commandments.
(2 John 6)

When John wrote about Christian love, he didn't command his audience to love one another indiscriminately or without boundaries.

To truly walk in love means to walk according to God's commandments—according to the truths of Scripture. Truth and love are married in the Christian life. As Paul wrote in
1 Corinthians 13, love "does not rejoice in
iniquity, but rejoices in the truth" (v. 6).

> True love seeks the highest good of someone else, especially when it involves a person's relationship with God.

I have a friend who claimed to have been
treated cruelly by a family doctor. The doctor
ran some tests and then said the meanest thing
imaginable: "You have cancer." Isn't it horrible
for a doctor to say something like that? That
would make anyone feel awful, right?

You're probably thinking, *Skip, that's
what doctors do. They give truthful diagnoses.*
That's my point. One of the most loving things you can do is tell people the truth, not hide it from them. It wouldn't do any good if the doctor had told my friend, "You have nothing to worry about. Go home
and take some aspirin; you'll feel better in the morning." No, a credible
doctor would say, "You have a life-threatening disease; we need to treat
this right away." The Bible uses a special term for that kind of love: *agape.*
It's love that is completely sold out for the highest good of the one being
loved. It's how God loved us in sending Jesus to die for us, and it's how
Christians are to love God and others.

True love doesn't mean you are tolerant, indulgent, lenient, or relaxed
toward sin or false doctrine. That's *sloppy agape.* Love and truth should be
inseparable. You don't increase love by decreasing truth; in fact, whenever
you compromise the truth, you end up devaluing love. True love seeks
the highest good of someone else, especially when it involves a person's
relationship with God. Anytime you sense a disconnection from Christ,
in yourself or someone else, act on it—as gently and humbly as possible, but with the serious intention of a doctor seeking to get rid of cancer.

A HEALTHY DISSATISFACTION

John's third epistle is essentially an appeal to the church to grow in
the grace and knowledge of Jesus Christ by following the good examples

set by other believers. We all reach plateaus in our spiritual lives, but we should never say, "I've grown as much as I need to." A healthy dissatisfaction can be a good thing—it can spur you toward pursuing the Lord with all your heart and growing in the good works He's planned for you.[13] The reason? Doing good is an indicator that you belong to the Lord—that you're truly part of the bloodline of Jesus Christ.

Imitating the Good

> *Beloved, do not imitate what is evil, but what is good. He who does good is of God, but he who does evil has not seen God.* (3 John 11)

In 3 John, the apostle used a praiseworthy Christian named Demetrius as an example of the goodness we are to imitate as redeemed people of God.[14] We need role models in the church, people who will stand up for the truth and say, "Follow me as I follow the Lord." That doesn't mean you put another believer between you and God as some kind of perfect model—no believer is flawless. But you should be looking for examples of behavior and practice to use as models of how to know and imitate Jesus better.

There's nothing wrong with following someone if that someone is following Christ. In fact, the apostle Paul called the early church to do that. Multiple times, he instructed his fellow believers to imitate him as he imitated Christ.[15] This was not arrogance. Even though Paul was no doubt a model citizen of heaven, he was not putting himself on a pedestal; he was placing himself on a platform next to other believers and saying, "As I pursue Christ and His goodness with all of my being, I invite you to do the same." Blood-bought believers need other blood-bought believers to show them how to walk.

Here's the principle: We are all foreigners making our way on a pilgrimage toward heaven, and we all need examples to follow because the journey is hard. We need people who have walked before us or will walk beside us and show us, in real time, how it's done. It's essential to have people around who will encourage us as we live a redeemed life based on the work Jesus accomplished.

KICKING IT INTO GEAR

Jude's letter makes a crucial point: The redeemed life can't be lived in neutral. Yes, Jesus did all the heavy lifting on the cross, but that doesn't mean you can veg out or start cruising; you need to stay engaged. Otherwise it's like pedaling a bicycle uphill: If you're not making progress, you'll go backward. Jude made it clear that we ought to be in the business of reinforcing our faith, especially against false teachers—so that we aren't vulnerable to being torn down by them.

Put Away That Umbrella

> You, beloved, building yourselves up on your most holy faith, praying in the Holy Spirit, keep yourselves in the love of God, looking for the mercy of our Lord Jesus Christ unto eternal life. (Jude 20-21)

How exactly do you build up your faith? You start by establishing it on the most holy faith itself—the truth of God's Word. You

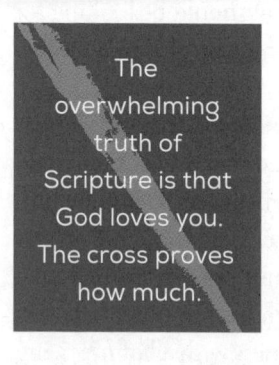

The overwhelming truth of Scripture is that God loves you. The cross proves how much.

strengthen it by praying in the Holy Spirit— God's way of sustaining you by His grace as you go through life's ups and downs and look ahead to the promise of eternal life. But notice what else Jude instructed his audience to do: "Keep yourselves in the love of God." He didn't say, "Keep yourself lovable before God"—you can't do that, for God's love is unconditional, unmerited, and undeserved. But keep yourself in a place where God's love can reach and bless you.

Imagine that God's love is like the sun. When the sun is shining, you can keep its warmth from reaching you by holding an umbrella over you. In the same way, the light of God's love is always shining, but our perceptions may get in the way of that love. You don't always feel or experience His love, do you? This could be because you are holding up an umbrella of sin or disbelief that keeps you from feeling the effects of God's love. When that happens, what can you do? Get rid of anything that will keep God's love from getting to you. Don't allow anything to prohibit your enjoyment of His love. Keep yourself in it.

The overwhelming truth of Scripture is that God loves you. The cross proves how much. But have you experienced that love? Or is it just an ethereal, abstract concept? God put flesh and bones to His love by becoming flesh and bones and dying on a cross for you. Living your life tied to His great tale of redemption means living in light of the fact that He planned your salvation from the beginning of time, foretold it throughout the Scriptures, and then executed it perfectly. You didn't do anything to deserve it, but He gave everything to make it happen.

As Jude said, you can live that out by extending mercy to others, just as God gave it to you at the cross. You can make decisions based on loving others because God's love drove Him to make the hardest decision possible: sending His Son to die for you. You can share the amazing story of the scarlet thread—that God's good plans go back to the beginning of the world, they wind through history to a hope-filled future, and they include both you and the person you're talking to.

THE LAMB BECOMES A LION

THE LAST LETTER:
Revelation

ere we are: the end. We've explored the biblical panorama of redemptive history and watched its thread woven through the pages of both the Old and New Testaments, marking out a trail by which God has provided a single way out of the mess we've made of His creation.

We've seen God make heaven and earth, sun, moon, and man, and call them all good. We've witnessed a serpent uncoil a venomous agenda, deceiving the first man and woman and infecting all creation with sin and death, setting God's beloved mankind on the path to hell. We've watched a war in heaven spill into our world, and a cursed general summon his satanic forces against God's promise to buy us back and bring about his end.

We've seen God identify and call out a special group of people for Himself, promise them a home, deliver them from slavery, and give them His holy law—and we've scratched our heads as they spurned Him again and again over the centuries.

We have beheld the warnings and prophecies of God's messengers as they heralded the keeping of His promises through His Messiah—and

> Boiled down to its irreducible minimum, the Bible is about one person and two events: Jesus Christ and His first and second comings.

we have seen that Messiah arrive on earth in humility, bent on accomplishing His Father's rescue mission. Our hearts have been pierced as we bore witness to the brutality of His success, been reminded of the cost of sin and our great need for forgiveness—even as it all demonstrated that no love can compare to His.

We have looked across the millennia-long valley we ourselves now occupy as we await His second coming, the final fulfillment of our redemptive arc, when He will come and conquer evil and establish His kingdom on earth for 1,000 years. We have yearned for His return as we learned how all of it is connected—this scarlet thread that winds both through history and our hearts, connecting us to God's very bloodline through Jesus Christ. We cannot wait to see Him face to face, to see Him revealed at last as we shout "Hosannah!" and bow in total surrender to the praise brimming in our hearts.

And here at the end, we get a glimpse of Him, Jesus Christ, Lord of all, King of kings, revealed, unveiled, both Lamb and Lion, the Lover of our souls and the Champion of God's justice. That is the revelation of the book of Revelation: Jesus Christ Himself.

All through this journey we have seen very clearly that at the center of all Scripture is a single person: the Lord Jesus Christ. He is the megatheme, the protagonist from Genesis to Revelation. In the Old Testament, Christ is promised by the prophets. In the Gospels, Christ is presented. In the book of Acts, Christ is proclaimed. In the epistles, Christ is pondered. And in the book of Revelation, Christ's return is predicted. It's all about Jesus. Boiled down to its irreducible minimum, the Bible is about one person and two events: Jesus Christ and His first and second comings. Jesus dealt with sin the first time He came, and the second time, He will rule and reign with those who are cleansed from sin.

The grand finale of Scripture, the book of Revelation, portrays Jesus Christ as the King of kings and Lord of lords, the Lamb slain from the foundation of the world who is worthy of the kingdom that He will one day set up on earth. Here, the Lamb of God becomes a fierce Lion who roars from heaven and takes full and final control of earth. At the end of our mortal world, when God creates a new heaven and new earth and the eternal state begins, the scarlet thread of redemption will be tied off once and for all, signifying that God's redemptive plan has been completely and totally accomplished and those who have trusted in Christ can now enter their eternal rest.

Get Ready

Blessed is he who reads and those who hear the words of this prophecy, and keep those things which are written in it; for the time is near. (Revelation 1:3)

The prophecies of Revelation are focused on a future that God controls. It's not a series of spiritual allegories or symbols that anyone can apply as they please. John's vision is specific because God knows how everything began and how it all ends.[1] We live in a high-anxiety age. People are worried about the future, grasping at straws to unearth a clue through horoscopes or psychics or tabloids or religion, and all too often, they ignore the Bible. They miss the truth that could give them peace: God has the future under control, and He gives us enough details in Scripture to know what's coming during earth's last days.

Redemption doesn't end with a past-tense experience of forgiveness. It goes far past the cross of Christ into a home prepared for the redeemed.

It's less about getting caught up in all the imagery and symbolism than it is getting connected to God. He has had all the specifics of redemptive history sorted out from the start, and the end will be no different. He will take care of the details, and we can find peace in knowing that. Redemption doesn't end with a past-tense experience of forgiveness. It goes far past the cross of Christ into a home prepared for the redeemed. The blessing of reading Revelation is getting to know Jesus better, living in light of eternity, knowing that He wins, and that when you're His, you win with Him.

Meeting Your Maker

> *When I saw Him, I fell at His feet as dead. But He laid His right hand on me, saying to me, "Do not be afraid; I am the First and the Last. I am He who lives, and was dead, and behold, I am alive forevermore. Amen. And I have the keys of Hades and of Death."* (Revelation 1:17-18)

When John saw Jesus for the first time since Jesus ascended, he didn't recognize Him. He had seen Jesus as a man, as the Lamb of God, there to take away the world's sin, a spotless sacrifice, mild and meek. But in this vision, as Jesus reintroduced Himself to John, He made it abundantly clear that John was seeing the Lion of Judah, God Himself. Gone was the voice of the Galilean carpenter whom John had heard for three years; in its place was a resounding trumpet, a roaring waterfall, a voice that splinters cedars, shakes the earth, and strikes like lightning.[2]

Jesus is God. In calling Himself the "First and the Last," Jesus was calling to mind Isaiah's description of God's sovereignty and might.[3] The Jews reading John's letter would recognize that Jesus was calling Himself by a title reserved for God alone, just as the Gentile audience would have understood the same meaning in the terms *Alpha* and *Omega*. Furthermore, Jesus evoked the name by which God introduced Himself to Moses: "I AM WHO I AM" (Exodus 3:14), the one "who is and who was and who is to come, the Almighty" (Revelation 1:8). Part of Jesus's reintroduction to John was as "He who lives, and was dead, and behold, I am alive forevermore" (v. 18). Here the tapestry of Christ's identity unmistakably reveals the scarlet thread represented by His death on the cross. In a single verse, the death, resurrection, and eternality of Jesus becomes the banner for His everlasting reign.

John also gave us the Bible's only physical description of Jesus's appearance—and it's certainly not what He has been pictured as over the centuries. Every culture has appropriated the image of Jesus for themselves; it's fascinating, but irrelevant. God saw fit to give us only this picture of Jesus, and we can easily see why He had to tell John not to be afraid: Though in the form of a man, Jesus is armed for war, "hair a blizzard of white, eyes pouring fire-blaze, both feet furnace-fired bronze, his voice a cataract, right hand holding the Seven Stars, his mouth a sharp-biting sword, his face a perigee sun" (vv. 14-17 MSG). This is Jesus in His glory. Isaiah told us there was nothing extraordinary about Jesus's appearance when He came the first time,[4] but upon His return, there will be no mistaking Him.

John saw the face of an all-conquering King, the one true God. Even though redemption's thread has been regularly endangered, frayed to the point of breaking over the course of history, when we see Jesus this way, we understand that the thread was forged with the unbreakable strength of its maker, and that there was no way that God was not going to save us, and there is no way He is not going to come back and finish what He started.

The Title-Holder

Behold, the Lion of the tribe of Judah, the Root of David, has prevailed to open the scroll and to loose its seven seals. (Revelation 5:5)

John witnessed a tense scene in heaven's court: An angel asked if anyone was worthy of taking the title deed to the earth (pictured here as a scroll) back from Satan's possession, where it has been since Adam handed it over back in Eden. And John saw what he—and all of us—already knew: "No one in heaven or on the earth or under the earth was able to open the scroll, or to look at it" (Revelation 5:3). What else could John do but weep at that point? Would things never be made right? Would justice never be served, redemption never fulfilled throughout God's sin-marred creation?

But then Jesus stepped up. Only John didn't call Him Jesus in this passage. Instead, we see Him described by a number of what should be familiar phrases by now, titles we've seen previously conferred by prophets throughout the Bible: "the Lion of the tribe of Judah, the Root of David [and]…a Lamb as though it had been slain" (vv. 5-6).

Way back in Genesis 49, Jacob had prophesied that Judah, whom he called a "lion's whelp" (v. 9), would hold the scepter of power in Israel,[5] and Isaiah had foretold a day when the "Root of Jesse [David's dad]... shall stand as a banner to the people" (Isaiah 11:10). This is the culmination of the prophecies of the Branch, the one who would come from David's line to save mankind and restore the earth to God's justice as His Servant, a man who is both our King and Lord.[6] Here the Lion steps forward to roar His dominion as king of earth's jungle.

So much of what we've seen foreshadowed and predicted is being completed here. This is Jesus as the Lamb of God, recognized by John the Baptist at the Jordan's banks,[7] presaged by Abraham and Isaac on Mount Moriah and the blood-smeared doorposts of the Passover,[8] the "Lamb slain from the foundation of the world" (Revelation 13:8). Here is the kinsman-redeemer we saw in Ruth. Jesus met all the requirements of the law to buy back that which was lost—in this case, creation, which had been forfeited to sin. Because He became a man, Jesus is our kinsman. Because He is creator and owner of all that is, He can afford the transaction. And because of His work at the cross, He is clearly willing to complete the redemptive work.

What relief and joy John must have felt when he saw heaven's response to this worthy title-holder: "They sang a new song, saying: 'You are worthy to take the scroll, and to open its seals; for You were slain, and have redeemed us to God by Your blood out of every tribe and tongue and people and nation'" (Revelation 5:9). This celebration had been a long time coming.

Signed, Sealed, Delivered

> *Then I saw another angel ascending from the east, having the seal of the living God...saying, "Do not harm the earth, the sea, or the trees till we have sealed the servants of our God on their foreheads." And I heard the number of those who were sealed. One hundred and forty-four thousand of all the tribes of the children of Israel were sealed...After these things I looked, and behold, a great multitude which no one could number, of all nations, tribes, peoples, and tongues, standing*

before the throne and before the Lamb, clothed with white
robes, with palm branches in their hands, and crying out with
a loud voice, saying, "Salvation belongs to our God, who sits
on the throne, and to the Lamb!" (Revelation 7:2-4, 9-10)

I've mentioned the prophecies regarding the 144,000 Jews, a group
comprised of 12,000 members from each of Israel's twelve tribes, called
out and sealed by God to be witnesses to God and His Messiah Jesus
Christ during the tribulation. God's angels will withhold judgment on
the earth temporarily until these select servants have been sealed on the
foreheads, a fulfillment of God's requirement in the law that His people should bind His Word on their foreheads as a reminder of the one
to whom they belong.[9]

Jesus carried God's seal of approval[10] and extends it to those who
trust in Him, in the form of the Holy Spirit: "Having believed, you
were sealed with the Holy Spirit of promise, who is the guarantee of our
inheritance until the redemption of the purchased possession" (Ephesians 1:13-14). During the church age, it's His guarantee that we belong
to Him. After the church has been raptured, anyone who comes to
faith will still receive the Holy Spirit, but there will also be this special
gift of God's sealing to these 144,000 Jews. It makes sense that these
144,000 Jewish believers will be the result of two witnesses, introduced
in Revelation 11, sent by God to Israel during this time of international
tribulation. Then the eager witness of almost 150,000 Jewish evange-
lists will in turn influence millions of people around the world, making
the tribulation period the setting for perhaps the greatest revival in history. As Isaiah said, Israel being a light to the world was part of God's
original design for the nation.[11]

This is God keeping His promises to the Jews and thereby blessing
the Gentiles. And He will do it right on time, according to the timetable He set up in Daniel 9—the seventy-weeks prophecy. Sixty-nine of
those weeks have passed, completed in the return of Israel to their land
after the exile and the coming of the Messiah to purchase mankind's
redemption on the cross. When the last soul has been saved into the
church—whenever and whoever that is—God will remove the church

from the earth, initiating the seventieth week of Daniel, the tribulation. This last week hasn't happened yet, but it will, and one of its hallmarks will be the sealing of the 144,000.

Paul spoke of this moment when he described how the Jews' failure to recognize Jesus the first time He came resulted in the gospel spreading to the Gentiles—and he affirmed that God would still keep His promise to Israel: "Now if their fall is riches for the world, and their failure riches for the Gentiles, how much more their fullness!" (Romans 11:12). We're all the beneficiaries of that blessing, to God's glory, and His redemptive plan includes bringing His chosen people, the Jews, into the work of spreading the good news of Christ in the last days. Ezekiel saw a type of this moment when, as God prepared to judge Jerusalem for its habitual, unrepentant sin, He told His angels to "put a mark on the foreheads of the men who sigh and cry over all the abominations that are done within it" (Ezekiel 9:4). Furthermore, when judgment came, He said He would spare anyone who had that soft heart, that desire to repent.[12]

Interestingly, the Hebrew word translated "mark" is *tav*. In the ancient Greek translations of the Hebrew text, *tav* looks like a cross. Perhaps it's indicative of the witness this group will have in those last days, a time when Jesus said, "This gospel of the kingdom will be preached in all the world as a witness to all the nations, and then the end will come," referring to His second coming (Matthew 24:14). The 144,000 will carry out one final evangelical mission, one last chance for repentance before the King returns and knots off the scarlet thread, making all choices permanent.

The Light at the End of the Tunnel

> We give You thanks, O Lord God Almighty, the One who is
> and who was and who is to come, because You have taken
> Your great power and reigned. The nations were angry, and
> Your wrath has come, and the time of the dead, that they
> should be judged, and that You should reward Your servants
> the prophets and the saints, and those who fear Your name,
> small and great, and should destroy those who destroy the
> earth. (Revelation 11:17-18)

The tribulation will be the worst period in earth's history. Given all the wars and natural disasters and genocide so many have already endured, that's saying something—but at the same time, it's an understatement. We can scarcely imagine the magnitude of God's wrath being poured out on earth as world leaders and millions upon millions of people give themselves over to the Antichrist. The church will be gone, raptured, and then the seven scroll judgments will begin by bringing false peace, followed by world war and its devastating, famine- and inflation-stricken aftermath, all contributing to the death of a quarter of the world's population. It might seem that the scarlet thread will be all but absent or unavailable to people. But God gives mercy even in judgment.[13]

The Antichrist will become the leader of a global government and institute a religious system the Bible calls "Mystery Babylon,"[14] deceiving millions who don't have the church on earth as a counterbalance and martyring everyone who doesn't fall into line. The scroll judgments will be topped off by a massive earthquake, the likes of which has never been seen, and the start of the trumpet judgments.[15]

Picture the crippling level of destruction worldwide, the decimated infrastructure and inability to restore services, the panic and inevitable rioting and violence. Imagine the demoralized (and yet defiantly immoral) populace waiting to see if things can possibly get worse. They do. The seven trumpet judgments commence the day of the Lord, a period of God's unrelenting wrath marked by a third of everything left green and growing being burned by fiery, bloody hail. Then a burning, mountain-sized mass will ruin the seas and a meteor will poison a third of all fresh water. The light of the sun, moon, and stars will be reduced by a third. In the dim terror, hordes of demons will be released upon the earth, tormenting but not killing, soon to be joined by four angels whose only job, preordained for this exact moment, is to kill a third of whoever's left.

Even with half the world's population destroyed by these judgments and up to another quarter martyred by the Antichrist's forces after receiving Christ through the witness of the 144,000, many people still won't repent.[16] God will send His two witnesses (thought by many to be Moses and Elijah), who will prophesy, be killed and resurrected, and then taken back up to heaven, after which another huge earthquake will strike.[17] It's at this point that John's view breaks away to heaven's throne room, where we see a shout of prophetic praise go up. This is a victory chant: "The kingdoms of this world have become the kingdoms of our Lord and of His Christ, and He shall reign forever and ever!" (Revelation 11:15). The great tribulation will lead to a greater triumph: The Promised One, the Messiah, the Serpent-Crusher and Sin Bearer, will take ownership of the fallen world He came to die for—but not just yet.

> Monarchs and rulers, presidents and tyrants have strutted across history's stage, but in the end only one kingdom will stand: that of the King of kings and Lord of lords.

Keep in mind this brings us only halfway through the tribulation, and the worst is yet to come. But these are the words that all creation has longed to hear since Eden's lament began. All the times mankind has wondered, *Where is God? Why is He not doing something about this screwed-up world?* are about to be answered. But for God, what we call history and the future are all *now*—all as evident as if they were happening in the present. He is always right on time. The kingdom of Christ will come, as predicted—the giant boulder out of heaven that Daniel saw, crushing the failed governments of the world and standing alone forever.[18] Monarchs and rulers, presidents and tyrants have strutted across history's stage, but in the end only one kingdom will stand: that of the King of kings and Lord of lords. Even in the midst of the tribulation, heaven will rejoice because His reign is as good as established. His kingdom is coming.

Framing the Battle

The dragon stood before the woman who was ready to give birth, to devour her Child as soon as it was born. She bore a male Child who was to rule all nations with a rod of

iron. And her Child was caught up to God and His throne.
(Revelation 12:4-5)

We have followed the behind-the-scenes battle between Satan and God's people since it began back in Genesis 3. We have seen how, since his fall from heaven, our adversary has made it the goal of his cursed existence to wreak havoc on earth. We know that he doesn't make appearances himself as much as he operates behind the scenes in an obscene imitation of God's providence, making every attempt through schemes and manipulation to neutralize Christians and destroy lives. We know much of this because of this symbolic glimpse God provided here in Revelation 12: "A great sign appeared in heaven: a woman clothed with the sun, with the moon under her feet, and on her head a garland of twelve stars" (v. 1). As she cried out in labor pains, another sign appeared, a huge, red dragon who "drew a third of the stars of heaven and threw them to the earth" (v. 4).

At this point, the players in this celestial scene are familiar: The dragon is Satan, the woman is Israel, and the Child is the Messiah. Their identities are revealed, respectively, in Revelation 12:9 (that "serpent of old," Satan), Genesis 37:9-10 (Joseph's dream of his parents and brothers as the sun, moon, and stars that would form Israel), and Isaiah 9:6 (the hope of every Jewish mother, to give birth to the Child who would be Messiah, who will one day rule with a rod of iron, the government upon His capable shoulders).

John saw these massive images, this "great sign," and knew they represented the most important actors on history's stage. Satan has wanted to crush God's plans for his destruction ever since God announced them back in Genesis 3:15, and though he managed to bruise the woman's Seed at the cross, the Child beat death and hell to rise again and end the devil's hopes of ever winning any kind of eternal victory. There have been many close calls over the years, but, considering he was up against God, Satan never really had a chance. The collateral damage has been significant, but because of what this Child has done, anyone can have lasting hope that the scars of this world can be redeemed in this life and will fade in eternity's light. This passage frames the ongoing cosmic battle for us. We know our enemy, his strategies and tricks, but we also know he loses. And we know our Savior, His strategies of prayer and knowing God's Word, and that He wins.

The Struggle Is Real, but So Is the Victory

They overcame him by the blood of the Lamb and by the word of their testimony, and they did not love their lives to the death. (Revelation 12:11)

We've seen that Satan is our constant accuser, that even though hell awaits him, he still has some access to God, and he uses it to air our dirty laundry before our Maker. We've also seen that we have the best possible defense attorney in Jesus. Every time Satan breaks out any kind of evidence in an attempt to condemn you—and he's got plenty on all of us—Jesus responds according to the one fact that can acquit us: His blood. If Christ is not standing in for you, you'll stand in for yourself. As A.W. Tozer put it, "Whoever defends himself will have himself for his defense, and he will have no other."[19] If you are covered by the blood of Christ, however, you have nothing to fear from the devil's accusations. By Christ's blood, we are overcomers. Who can be against us?

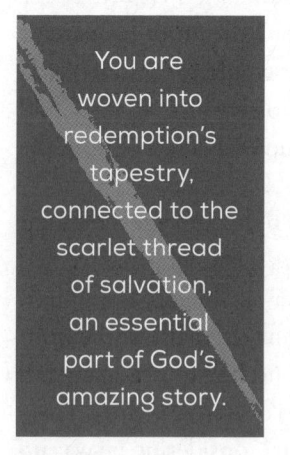

You are woven into redemption's tapestry, connected to the scarlet thread of salvation, an essential part of God's amazing story.

Another part of overcoming the accuser is "the word of [our] testimony." When we share who Jesus is and all that He has done for us, we not only open the door of redemption for others, we intimidate the enemy because we are demonstrating the evidence of God's work in changing our hearts. "The testimony of Jesus is the spirit of prophecy" (Revelation 19:10). Prophecy authenticates Christ. Our testimony connects us to His story, part of all the predictions and signs and wonders that have pointed throughout Scripture to the Messiah and His rescue mission.

And finally, we overcome Satan by not clinging to our lives. To receive Jesus as Lord and Savior is to surrender our rights to our own lives, trusting that He is the better way. To follow His example and be willing to give up our lives for His sake is even more powerful. As Jesus said, "Whoever desires to save his life will lose it, but whoever loses his life for My sake will find it" (Matthew 16:25).

Your life is incredibly valuable to God; He showed that on the cross. But your life is just one part of a much bigger picture made up of billions of lives that Jesus loved enough to die for. That's both humbling and affirming. You are woven into redemption's tapestry, connected to the scarlet thread of salvation, an essential part of God's amazing story. Against all odds, you are an overcomer.

Posse in the Sky

I saw heaven opened, and behold, a white horse. And He who sat on him was called Faithful and True, and in righteousness He judges and makes war...And the armies in heaven, clothed in fine linen, white and clean, followed Him on white horses. (Revelation 19:11, 14)

Jesus's second coming is the ultimate revelation: Not only will He return, but everyone will see Him. This is the culmination of earth's history; all accounts will be settled—the righteous rewarded and the wicked judged. Jesus will establish His kingdom on earth at this time. His disciples had expected His kingdom to appear immediately at His first coming; instead, He told them the parable about the nobleman who went to a far country and told his servants to invest wisely while he was away. When he returned, he would reward them according to their dividends.[20] They couldn't have imagined it at the time, but He was preparing them for His second coming. And there would be no mistaking His purpose this time: At His first coming he had ridden into Jerusalem on a donkey, a symbol of peace. This time, He will sit astride a white horse, the King riding to war.

In his vision, John saw Jesus depicted in ways that spoke of His power and authority: fiery eyes, representing His penetrating, soul-deep gaze; multiple crowns, showing His singular authority over every nation; a robe stained with blood—not *His own* blood, which had been depicted and predicted throughout Scripture, but the blood of His *enemies*, in haunting fulfillment of Isaiah's prophecy of this moment:

> I have trodden the winepress alone, and from the peoples no one was with Me. For I have trodden them in My anger, and trampled them in My fury; their blood is sprinkled upon My garments, and I have stained all My robes. For the day of vengeance is in My heart, and the year of My redeemed has come (Isaiah 63:3-4).

Jesus's appearance brings the battle of Armageddon to a close. And though Isaiah called Him the "Prince of Peace" (Isaiah 9:6), Jesus will wage war to make peace. The first time He came, wicked men judged Him unjustly, but upon His return, He will judge all men in righteousness. Jesus has always been about saving as many as would come to Him, but at this point, those who spurned Him as Savior will now face Him as Judge. And His judgment and rule will be ironclad in His absolute, unyielding control. That's great news for all who belong to Him and terrifying for all who have rejected Him.

Though Jesus doesn't need an army to accomplish His victory, He will be accompanied by one. Heaven's armies, His posse clothed in pristine white linen, will consist of all the saints—the church and those martyred during the tribulation—and all His angels. The saints are mentioned in Revelation 19:8 as being dressed in clean, white linen, too close a parallel with the description of this army in verse 14 not to be one and the same. Jude foretold that the Messiah will come "with ten thousands of His saints, to execute judgment on all" (vv. 14-15), also fulfilling the prophecy of Zechariah 14:5: "Thus the LORD my God will come, and all the saints with You." And Jesus Himself said in Matthew 25:31 that He would return with "all the holy angels." This will be quite the

> Even at history's final bow Jesus will seek and save the lost, connecting as many as possible to His bloodline.

entourage (the Lion and saints and angels—oh my!). And even though the true war to end all wars is at hand, all they'll have to do is sit back and watch Jesus conquer all the gathered armies of the world. He will do this by using only one weapon: His sword—that is, the word of His mouth.

Even as Jesus brings righteous judgment against all those who have hated God and rejected His kingdom, and even as He brings the hammer down on the Antichrist, reminding Satan that there is only one God (and he isn't Him), an enormous multitude of people—both Jews and Gentiles across the planet—will be saved during this worst episode of world history. Even at history's final bow Jesus will seek and save the lost, connecting as many as possible to His bloodline.

Judgment: The Final Frontier

Then Death and Hades were cast into the lake of fire. This is the second death. And anyone not found written in the Book of Life was cast into the lake of fire. (Revelation 20:14-15)

No one likes to think about judgment. If you are saved, your joy is tempered by the thought of those who aren't, who will be separated from God forever, tormented in flames that never stop. If you don't believe in Jesus, God, or heaven and hell, this will be the most horrifying moment of your life, and its impact will literally last forever.

But God must judge. Not only is He the only one qualified to do so as the perfect, just Creator of all that is, but if He doesn't, He would be untrue to Himself. If God does not judge, then He isn't just. If He isn't just, then He is not perfect. And if He's not perfect, then He is not God. If there's one thing this look at redemptive history has taught us, it's that God maintains a consistent character no matter what is going on in the world He made. Jesus came to take our eternal judgment by His vicarious death on the cross. If we refuse His remedy, then we're left to feel the full brunt of God's judgment forever.

The Bible makes it clear that each of us follows a pattern: We all live, we all die, and we all will be resurrected. But not everyone lives the same way, dies the same way, or gets resurrected the same way. The

Bible speaks of life in three different ways: physical life, psychological life, and eternal life. That last one is what Jesus came to give us. It's not only life that never ends, it's life that has a high quality, an ongoing sense of purpose and satisfaction that begins when you receive Christ in this life and then continues throughout eternity. The Bible says two things live forever: The Word of God and the souls of men. Even after you die, you will live on. The real question, then, is not "Do I have eternal life?" but "Where will I spend my eternal life?" The answer to that question is why it's essential to get connected to Christ's bloodline.

Physical death ends physical life, but it's also the gateway to eternity. If you are a believer, when your soul is separated from your body at death, you will go to be with the Lord.[21] Then you will await the first resurrection, which will happen at the rapture, fulfilling Jesus's promise to raise us on the last day.[22] And just as Jesus rose in the glorified version of His body, He will raise us in ours, transforming "our lowly body that it may be conformed to His glorious body" (Philippians 3:21). That's great news—if you belong to Him. Otherwise, you'll find there's a fate worse than death: dying a second time.

After your physical death, if your name is written in the Lamb's Book of Life—if you received Jesus as Savior during your physical life—you won't have to worry about the second death. As Jesus said, "The hour is coming in which all who are in the graves will hear His voice and come forth—those who have done good, to the resurrection of life, and those who have done evil, to the resurrection of condemnation" (John 5:28-29). Daniel foresaw as much: "Many of those who sleep in the dust of the earth shall awake, some to everlasting life, some to shame and everlasting contempt" (Daniel 12:2). That's the second death—the condemnation of the dead who rejected Jesus.

We will all be resurrected, but Jesus said some will be raised to life, and others to condemnation. If you're born once, you'll die twice; but if you're born twice, you'll die only once. "Blessed and holy is he who has part in the first resurrection. Over such the second death has no power, but they shall be priests of God and of Christ, and shall reign with Him a thousand years" (Revelation 20:6).

All New, for All Time

> *I saw a new heaven and a new earth, for the first heaven and the first earth had passed away...Behold, I make all things new.* (Revelation 21:1, 5)

We love new things, whether it's a car, a pair of shoes, or a fresh start. At the end of the millennium, God is going to give everyone who belongs to Him a whole new world, fresh off the presses. Isaiah saw it coming:

> For behold, I create new heavens and a new earth; and the former shall not be remembered or come to mind. But be glad and rejoice forever in what I create; for behold, I create Jerusalem as a rejoicing, and her people a joy. I will rejoice in Jerusalem, and joy in My people; the voice of weeping shall no longer be heard in her, nor the voice of crying (Isaiah 65:17-19).

When the millennial reign is over, redemptive history will be completed. Satan will be allowed to rebel one last time, then he will be locked away in hell forever, along with everyone whose name isn't found in the Book of Life.[23] Then Jesus will press *stop* on this world, and it will pass away. He will create a new heaven and earth, with a new Jerusalem as its capital, fulfilling His promise to make all things new. Even though John gave a glorious description of this city made of gold and precious stones, it's safe to say he couldn't do it justice. It will offer a brand new climate and terrain suited for our glorified bodies. The Bible doesn't give many details; suffice it to say our new habitation will be different and better than we could ever imagine. Paul's quotation of Isaiah is enough for me: "Eye has not seen, nor ear heard, nor have entered into the heart of man the things which God has prepared for those who love Him" (1 Corinthians 2:9).[24] Paul did add, "But God has revealed them to us through His Spirit" (v. 10). In other words, we may not know all the details, but we have some clues in Scripture, and we know that because of Jesus Christ, we will find out what awaits us.

Best of all, we will be with Jesus, and He will be the center of our lives. John said, "I saw no temple in it, for the Lord God Almighty and the Lamb are its temple. The city had no need of the sun or of the moon to shine in it, for the glory of God illuminated it. The Lamb is its light" (Revelation 21:22-23). In the Old Testament, people were separated from God's presence by the veil that blocked the entrance to the Holy of Holies. In the New Testament, and now, during the church age, we are connected to God in Christ, but there is a veil of sorts, our flesh, that keeps us from knowing God fully. All of that will be gone in the new heaven and earth. The scarlet thread will be tied off for good because there will no longer be a need for it. John reiterated Isaiah's forecast, revealing there will be "no more death, nor sorrow, nor crying. There shall be no more pain, for the former things have passed away" (v. 4). Best of all, "there shall be no more curse" (Revelation 22:3).

God will fully heal all that has been broken and heal it so completely that it will be as if sin and death and evil never happened. We will dwell in God's presence, with nothing holding us back from knowing Him fully. As David said, "I will see Your face in righteousness; I shall be satisfied when I awake in Your likeness" (Psalm 17:15). It's a truly marvelous thought, driven by a defining characteristic of God: grace.

"The grace of our Lord Jesus Christ be with you all. Amen" (Revelation 22:21). John's parting words are much more than a standard sign-off. They reflect the journey of redemption's thread, through all the ups and downs, the human foibles and cosmic conflict, and God's superintendence of all of it, guaranteeing a happy ending for those who trust in Him. The story that began with a curse ends in grace.

EPILOGUE

And so, God's tale is complete, and in the fabric of His story is the unmistakable blood-red cord of Jesus's sacrificial death. Revelation shows us both the beginning and the end of God's plan to rescue us, summed up perfectly in Jesus, "the Lamb slain from the foundation of the world" (Revelation 13:8). That which was anticipated is now completed; that which was foretold is now finished. The once-predicted one is now the all-powerful one.

The history of the world hangs on three trees: the tree of the knowledge of good and evil, the tree of life (both found in the Garden of Eden), and the tree Jesus died on, the cross at Calvary. The first tree took away man's spiritual life when Adam and Eve disobeyed God, for He promised, "In the day that you eat of it you shall surely die" (Genesis 2:17). The second tree, the tree of life, threatened to keep humankind alive forever in that fallen and separated state (which is why God banished Adam and Eve from Eden—to protect them from eternal condemnation).[1] But that third tree, the cross of Christ—the theme we have followed throughout this book—made it possible to have spiritual life restored. What was lost in Eden will be reinstated in eternity. And heaven will forever remember and point back to that third tree, for there Jesus is referred to by His sacrificial title "the Lamb."

The Scottish expositor William Barclay noted,

> The Cross is the proof that there is no length to which the love of God will refuse to go, in order to win men's hearts. The Cross is the final proof of the love of God; and a love like that demands an answering love. If the Cross will not waken love and wonder in men's hearts, nothing will.[2]

My earnest hope is that this book has helped to awaken your heart to the immense love of God for you. From the beginning of creation to the burden of the cross, God had you in mind. Even now, He longs to be as close to you as you will allow Him to be. Has He won over your heart yet? In Jesus Christ, God was saying, "I love you enough to see My Son suffer and die for you." Answer that love by your own loving surrender. The forgiveness you need, the peace you crave, and the purpose you lack are all right there for you. You are a prayer away from connecting to His bloodline.

ENDNOTES

Introduction: Redemption's Scarlet Thread
1. William Evans, *Great Doctrines of the Bible* (Chicago: Moody Press, 1974), 70.
2. Exodus 26 and 28.

Chapter 1—Our Rescue Operation Begins
1. See Isaiah 14:12-15.
2. Genesis 2:17.
3. Isaiah 14:12.
4. Romans 5:12.
5. Genesis 15:6.
6. 2 Corinthians 1:19-22.
7. Genesis 15:13-16.
8. Hebrews 9:22.
9. Galatians 3:24.
10. Philippians 2:5-8.
11. John 14:9.
12. Exodus 40:34.

Chapter 2—There Must Be Blood
1. Hebrews 9:22.
2. Romans 3:23.
3. John 1:29.
4. See Romans 9:4-5.
5. Numbers 9:1-5.
6. John 19:36, fulfilling Exodus 12:46; Numbers 9:10-12; Psalm 34:20.
7. John 3:14-15.
8. Numbers 35:6-34.
9. Deuteronomy 6:5, quoted in Matthew 22:37; Mark 12:29-33; Luke 10:27.
10. Deuteronomy 24:1-3, quoted in Matthew 5:31; 19:7; Mark 10:4.
11. Deuteronomy 19:15, quoted in Matthew 18:16.
12. Deuteronomy 6:13, 16; 8:3, quoted in Matthew 4:4, 7, 10; Luke 4:4, 8, 12.
13. Acts 7:37-38.

Chapter 3—A Strong Cord in Thin Fabric
1. Joshua 1:2-4.
2. Hebrews 4:8-10 says, "For if Joshua had given them rest, then He would not afterward have spoken of another day. There remains therefore a rest for the people of God. For he who has entered His rest has himself also ceased from his works as God did from His." Because of Israel's widespread unbelief, God allowed only Joshua and Caleb to enter Canaan, out of the entire generation He delivered from Egypt.
3. Numbers 13:26-33.
4. Joshua 2:12-14.
5. Hebrews 11:31.
6. Joshua 7:2-9.
7. Joshua 6:18-19.
8. Judges 17:6; 21:25.

9. Ephesians 4:17-24.

10. Revelation 12:10.

11. Ronald Reagan said these words while speaking at the Phoenix Chamber of Commerce on March 30, 1961.

12. Judges 1:21, 27-33.

13. Acts 10:42.

14. See Ephesians 5:25 and 1 Corinthians 11:2.

15. See Matthew 1:5. Note that Boaz's mother was Rahab—the same woman from Joshua whose saving faith was rewarded by becoming part of Christ's bloodline.

16. Revelation 19:6-9.

17. Deuteronomy 25.

18. Matthew 13:44-46.

19. Ruth 4:21-22.

20. 1 John 5:19.

21. Romans 5:12-21.

Chapter 4—The King Is Coming

1. 1 Samuel 13:14.

2. John 10:11-18.

3. 2 Samuel 7:10-16: (1) "I will appoint a place for My people Israel"; (2) "The LORD tells you that He will make you a house"; (3) "I will set up your seed after you"; (4) "I will establish his kingdom"; (5) "I will establish the throne of his kingdom forever"; (6) "I will be his Father"; (7) "If he commits iniquity, I will chasten him."

4. Acts 2:29-31.

5. Philippians 2:9.

6. Isaiah 2:2-3.

7. Isaiah 2:2-3; 35.

8. Revelation 21:22-23.

9. 1 Peter 3:14-16.

10. 1 Corinthians 3:16.

11. 2 Kings 11.

12. Donald Grey Barnhouse, *The Invisible War* (Grand Rapids, MI: Zondervan, 1965), 27.

13. Galatians 5:16-26.

Chapter 5—Beyond Fate and Nature

1. Alexander Pope Quotes, BrainyQuote.com, Xplore Inc, 2018, https://www.brainyquote.com/quotes/alexander_pope_118537 (accessed February 13, 2018).

2. Jeremiah 29:10.

3. Jeremiah 29:10-12.

4. Matthew 1:12-13; Luke 3:27.

5. 1 Corinthians 6:19-20.

6. Daniel 9:26-27; Revelation 11:1-2.

7. 2 Thessalonians 2:4.

8. Leviticus 17:11.

9. Matthew 7:29.

10. Ezra 10:1.

11. Luke 19:41-44.

12. John 2 and Matthew 21, respectively.

13. John 11:41-42.

14. Hebrews 4:16.

15. Romans 3:24-26.

Chapter 6—Heart, Mind, Body, and Soul

1. Norman L. Geisler, *A Popular Survey of the Old Testament* (Grand Rapids, MI: Baker, 1977), 181.
2. Geisler, *A Popular Survey of the Old Testament*.
3. 1 John 2:1.
4. Romans 8:34.
5. Psalms 2; 8; 16; 22; 23; 24; 40; 41; 45; 68; 69; 72; 89; 102; 110; 116; 118.
6. This is corroborated by its being quoted in Acts 4:25 and 13:33, Hebrews 1:5 and 5:5, and Revelation 2:26-27, which mention the Messiah as God's only begotten Son, the one who will rule with a rod of iron, overcoming the defiance of earthly minded rulers.
7. Psalms 15:1 and 24:3.
8. Paul noted that Jesus, upon His death, "descended into the lower parts of the earth" (Ephesians 4:9). Some have translated this as "hell" but the Hebrew word for a similar phrase used in the Old Testament is *sheol*, which refers to the grave, the place where souls go after death—as opposed to the hell which is the final place of punishment for Satan, his angels, and all who have rejected Christ. And remember, Jesus told the thief on the cross that he would join Him in paradise that very day (see Luke 23:43). In other words, Jesus and the thief went into the Father's presence after they died, where Jesus then awaited the resurrection by the Holy Spirit on the third day—which is why David prophesied that Messiah's body would not see decay (see Psalm 16:10). Randy Alcorn's *Heaven* is an excellent resource for further information on this subject.
9. Matthew 27:46.
10. There are almost forty references in Scripture to Jesus praying, from His baptism to His ministry to after His ascension. He prayed with His friends and disciples and in the midst of crowds, but also in solitude, praising God and seeking fellowship with Him. Currently, He intercedes and advocates for us before the Father in heaven.
11. Proverbs 30:18-33 describes wonders in nature and how their design and function are meant to humble us: "If you have been foolish in exalting yourself, or if you have devised evil, put your hand on your mouth" (v. 32). The wisdom behind God's creation is embodied in Jesus Christ, a point Paul drives home in Colossians 1: "He is the image of the invisible God, the firstborn over all creation. For by Him all things were created that are in heaven and that are on earth, visible and invisible…All things were created through Him and for Him" (vv. 15-16).
12. For example, John the Baptist referred to Jesus as the "bridegroom" in establishing His unique identity (John 3:29). In 2 Corinthians 11:2, Paul said, "I have betrothed you to one husband, that I may present you as a chaste virgin to Christ." He made the point again in Romans 7:4: "Therefore, my brethren, you also have become dead to the law through the body of Christ, that you may be married to another—to Him who was raised from the dead, that we should bear fruit to God." Finally, Paul connected marriage to the mystery of Jesus's relationship with the church in Ephesians 5:25-32, particularly when he said, "Husbands, love your wives, just as Christ also loved the church and gave Himself for her, that He might sanctify and cleanse her with the washing of water by the word, that He might present her to Himself a glorious church, not having spot or wrinkle or any such thing, but that she should be holy and without blemish" (vv. 25-27).
13. E.J. Young, *An Introduction to the Old Testament* (London: Tyndale, 1949), 327.
14. Ephesians 5:25-27.
15. Iain Provan, *The NIV Application Commentary: Ecclesiastes, Song of Songs* (Grand Rapids, MI: Zondervan, 2001), 254.
16. Luke 19:41-44; Matthew 23:37-39.

Chapter 7—Near and Far, Deep and Wide

1. Paul wrote about the "mystery" of the work of Jesus Christ and the church in Romans 16:25 and Ephesians 3:3-10, the idea being that God did not reveal the fullness of His plan to save all of mankind, Jew and Gentile alike, until the church age. This is the wonder of the body of Christ,

that anyone who wants to, by faith in God's grace in Christ, can become part of God's family, adopted on equal footing as a co-heir with Jesus.

2. Jeremiah 23:5-6; 33:14-17.
3. Bringing to completion Isaiah 7:16-17: "For before the Child shall know to refuse the evil and choose the good"—that is, before he comes of age in his ability to reason—"the land that you dread will be forsaken by both her kings. The LORD will bring the king of Assyria upon you and your people and your father's house."
4. Matthew 1:18-25.
5. Matthew 12:18-21.
6. In Revelation 7:4-8, God will seal—set aside for His purposes—144,000 Jews, who will serve Him as prophets during the tribulation, testifying to the lordship of Jesus Christ as Savior and King of kings.
7. Isaiah 49:7.
8. Isaiah 50:8-11.
9. Matthew 7:13-14.
10. John 14:6.
11. Isaiah 52:14-15 says, "Just as many were astonished at you, so His visage was marred more than any man, and His form more than the sons of men; so shall He sprinkle many nations. Kings shall shut their mouths at Him; for what had not been told them they shall see, and what they had not heard they shall consider." This is reflected in the Gospels, in Matthew 27:54, Mark 15:39, and Luke 23:47.

Chapter 8—One King to Rule Them All
1. Babylonian Talmud 4.37.
2. John 3:3-8.
3. Jeremiah 29:10-14.
4. Ezekiel 37:1-14.
5. Revelation 7:1-8.
6. In Daniel 10:2, the same Hebrew term is used to describe a week of seven days.
7. Daniel 9:2.
8. In Leviticus 25:1-20, God told Israel to take every seventh year off from farming to let the land rest, trusting in Him to supply enough in the sixth year to last them through the Sabbath year and the year afterward, till the new crops came in. In Jeremiah 25:11-12 and 2 Chronicles 36:21, God made it clear that they had not done so, and there would be consequences.
9. Based on historians' assessment of Nehemiah 2:1, which gives the date of the month of Nisan in the twentieth year of Artaxerxes' reign.
10. Ezekiel laid out the dimensions of this final temple to which the glory of the Lord would return (Ezekiel 40–43). He had also foreseen the destruction of the first temple, detailed in Ezekiel 7–12. See chapter 5 for more.

Chapter 9—Going the Distance
1. Amos 7–9.
2. Matthew 23.
3. Matthew 12:41.
4. Micah 5:2.
5. John 5:22.
6. Romans 1:17; Galatians 3:11; Hebrews 10:38.

Chapter 10—Message Sent
1. Galatians 6:8.

2. Deuteronomy 4:29.
3. Revelation 20:6.
4. Zechariah 3:1-8.
5. Zechariah 10:4.
6. Ephesians 2:19-22.
7. Matthew 21:44.
8. Luke 19:28-34.
9. Luke 19:41-44.
10. Luke 7:27.
11. Mark 1:7.
12. Ezekiel 43:1-4; Zechariah 14:4; Isaiah 2:1-4.

Chapter 11—Rescue Operation: Complete

1. William Evans, *Great Doctrines of the Bible* (Chicago: Moody Press, 1974), 70.
2. Guinness World Records, "Heaviest Birth," 2018, http://www.guinnessworldrecords.com/world-records/heaviest-birth (accessed February 12, 2018).
3. Isaiah 7:14.
4. Jeremiah 22:26-30.
5. Galatians 3:13; John 1:12.
6. Exodus 12.
7. John 3:17.
8. Philippians 2:5-8.
9. Matthew 9:35.
10. Sir Robert Anderson, *The Coming Prince* (Grand Rapids, MI: Kregel Classics, 2008), xiii.
11. Peter W. Stoner and Robert C. Newman, *Science Speaks: Scientific Proof of the Accuracy of Prophecy and the Bible*, "Chapter 3: The Christ of Prophecy," 2002, http://sciencespeaks.dstoner.net/Christ_of_Prophecy.html#c9.
12. Stoner and Newman, *Science Speaks*.
13. John 1:14.
14. Philippians 2:5-7.
15. Philippians 1:6.
16. Hebrews 9:22.
17. Hebrews 10:11-14.
18. John 16:13.
19. 1 Peter 1:19.
20. Matthew 27:50-51.
21. 1 Corinthians 1:12-13.
22. Jesus will return first for His church in what we call the rapture (1 Thessalonians 4:16-17), and then at the second coming (Revelation 19).
23. Acts 4:19-20; 8:1.
24. Ephesians 2:8-9.
25. Amos 9:11-12.

Chapter 12—Redemption's New Ground Rules

1. Graham Scroggie, *The Unfolding Drama of Redemption* (Grand Rapids MI: Zondervan, 1981), 32.
2. Acts 2:42
3. Martin Luther, *Commentary on Romans*, trans. J. Theodore Mueller (Grand Rapids, MI: Kregel Classics, 1976), xiii.
4. Warren W. Wiersbe, *Key Words of the Christian Life* (Grand Rapids, MI: Baker, 2002), 16.
5. 1 John 4:8.

6. John 10:10.

7. John 6:51.

8. Charles Spurgeon, "Freedom Through Christ's Blood," The Charles Spurgeon Sermon Collection, http://thekingdomcollective.com/spurgeon/sermon/3106 (accessed March 12, 2018).

9. See also Acts 26:22-23.

10. Leviticus 23:10-11.

11. Colossians 1:21-22.

12. Leviticus 16.

13. See Acts 15.

14. Deuteronomy 21:22-23.

15. Galatians 3:23-25; 4:1-3.

16. 1 Thessalonians 4:16-17.

17. Deuteronomy 12:8-10.

Chapter 13—God's Unstoppable Plan

1. Exodus 24:1.

2. Charles H. Spurgeon, *Spurgeon's Sermons on Prayer* (Peabody, MA: Hendrickson, 2007), 13.

3. Ephesians 2:1.

4. Ephesians 2:10.

5. Ephesians 5:2.

6. Philippians 2:9-11.

7. C.S. Lewis, *Mere Christianity* (New York: HarperCollins, 2001), 212.

8. "Jesus Paid It All," by Elvina M. Hall, 1865.

9. Ephesians 2:10.

Chapter 14—Putting Up a Bloody Fight

1. Jude 3.

2. James 3:1.

3. 1 Timothy 1:18.

4. 2 Corinthians 4:4.

5. See Job 9:32-33.

6. Job 19:25.

7. 1 Peter 2:9.

8. John 10:35.

9. Hebrews 4:12.

10. John 14:3.

11. Revelation 19:11.

Chapter 15—The Continued Weaving of a Redeemed Life

1. Hebrews 9:11-15.

2. Hebrews 10:11.

3. Genesis 2:2.

4. John 19:30.

5. Luke 6:46-49.

6. Romans 3:28.

7. John 1:29.

8. Revelation 12:10.

9. See also Hebrews 7:25.

10. Revelation 12:11.

11. "I Hear the Accuser Roar," by Samuel Grandy, date unknown.

12. See Matthew 23:13-36; Luke 13:31-32.
13. Ephesians 2:10.
14. 3 John 12.
15. 1 Corinthians 4:16; 11:1; Philippians 3:17.

Chapter 16—The Lamb Becomes a Lion
1. Isaiah 46:10.
2. See Psalm 29.
3. Isaiah 41:1-4.
4. Isaiah 53:2-4.
5. Genesis 49:10.
6. See Zechariah 3:8 and 6:12; Jeremiah 23:5-6; and Isaiah 4:2.
7. John 1:29.
8. Genesis 22:1-18; Exodus 12:1-30.
9. Deuteronomy 6:8.
10. John 6:27.
11. Isaiah 49:6; 60:1-5; 66:13-19.
12. Ezekiel 9:5-6.
13. Habakkuk 3:2.
14. Revelation 17:5.
15. Revelation 6:1-17.
16. Revelation 8-9.
17. Revelation 11:1-13.
18. Daniel 2:44-45.
19. A.W. Tozer, *The Pursuit of God* (Camp Hill, PA: Christian Publications, 1982), 29.
20. Luke 19:11-27.
21. 2 Corinthians 5:1-8.
22. 1 Thessalonians 4:13-18, fulfilling John 6:40.
23. Revelation 20:7-15 describes Satan's final rebellion and the subsequent Great White Throne Judgment.
24. Quoting Isaiah 64:4.

Epilogue
1. Genesis 3:23-24.
2. William Barclay, *The Letters to the Philippians, Colossians, and Thessalonians* (Louisville, KY: Westminster Press, 1975), 123.

You Can Understand the Book of Genesis

Genesis is chock-full of some of the Bible's most exciting stories, from Adam and Eve in the Garden of Eden to Joseph's reunion with his family. Do you ever wonder if God really *did* create the world in seven days? What's the deal with Cain and Abel anyway? And just how *big* was that boat Noah built?

Start at the beginning with pastor Skip Heitzig and the accounts on which the rest of Scripture is built: the creation of the world, the fall of mankind, and God's establishment of the history of the nation of Israel. Follow along and learn not just the origins of man, but also the origins of God's plan for redemption.

Understanding the book of Genesis is crucial to understanding the rest of the Bible. It all starts in the beginning.

You Can Understand the Book of Revelation

Some shy away from the book of Revelation because of its mysteries. Others get uncomfortable with what it says about the end times. And still others are skeptical that any of it will come true.

Yet God promises *blessing* to those who read Revelation. He *wants* us to read it—for within it are vitally important truths that will help you...

- gain a deeper appreciation for the majesty and power of Christ
- know exactly what God says about the last days
- discover how God's plans for the future apply to you right now
- learn how to be ready for Christ's return

God's promises have never failed. The end *will* come. Are you prepared? This book will help you know.

To learn more about Harvest House books and
to read sample chapters, visit our website:

www.harvesthousepublishers.com

HARVEST HOUSE PUBLISHERS
EUGENE, OREGON